Weathering and Durability
in Landscape Architecture

Weathering and Durability in Landscape Architecture

Fundamentals, Practices, and Case Studies

NIALL KIRKWOOD

WILEY

JOHN WILEY & SONS, INC.

Copyright © 2004 by John Wiley & Sons, Inc. All rights reserved

Published by John Wiley & Sons, Inc., Hoboken, New Jersey
Published simultaneously in Canada

For general information on our other products and services or for technical support, please contact our Customer Care Department within the United States at 800-762-2974, outside the United States at (317) 572-3993 or fax (317) 572-4002.

Wiley also publishes its books in a variety of electronic formats. Some content that appears in print may not be available in electronic books.

Library of Congress Cataloging-in-Publication Data:

Kirkwood, Niall.
    Weathering and durability in landscape architecture: fundamentals,
practices, and case studies / Niall Kirkwood.
        p. cm.
Includes index.
    ISBN 0-471-39266-9 (Cloth)
    1. Landscape architecture. 2. Landscape design. I. Title.
        SB472.K58 2004
        729—dc22

                                    2003017376

Printed in the United States of America

10 9 8 7 6 5 4 3 2 1

CONTENTS

PREFACE

Weathering marks the passage of time.
Mohsen Mostafavi and David Leatherbarrow, On Weathering

Time is a dimension of all workmanship.
It all fails, to be sure: but it fails either sooner or later.
Durability is thus a preoccupation of every workman.
David Pye, The Nature and Art of Workmanship

Weathering and Durability in Landscape Architecture concerns the weathering and durability of constructed landscapes over time and its relationship to landscape architecture design. This book focuses on four areas of significance in contemporary landscape design and in the conception, development, implementation, and evolution of built landscape work. First, it introduces the range of ideas related to permanence in the built landscape. Second, it describes the range of pragmatic and sometimes not immediately evident factors and issues that acts upon landscape design elements in the broader landscape environment. Third, it illustrates and discusses design approaches to what is considered temporary and what is to be considered timeless in landscape work. In these design approaches aspects of both continuity and change in the built landscape are described and the flexibility of common landscape elements and technological systems are examined as they evolve over the life of a project. This involves an analysis of their materiality, physical form, program, and construction as they change, are enhanced, or degrade over time. Finally, the relationship between the designer's intent and the resulting altered landscape materials and forms is closely examined as a record of creative and responsive design attitudes currently at work in practice, including approaches to stewardship of the landscape. Together these four areas cover the topics of weathering and durability as core issues within professional landscape education and practice.

Purpose of the Book

That being said, the question of why a book on this topic is undertaken at this particular time needs to be raised particularly as the making of built landscapes remains a central activity of the profession. The concerns of continuity and change have been ever present in landscape architecture education, and it is accepted that the materials of landscape architecture, in particular plants, alter, grow, and in some cases die in ways not predicted or desirable. Recently, however, built landscape design works have been deteriorating at an alarming rate. Many projects built over the last twenty years now require intensive redesign, reconstruction, or indeed removal, and it is clear that the landscape work under construction today will fail even faster. Do designers want the results of their work to last? Based on the repetitive nature of these failures, it suggests that they do not. While this is good news for the engineers, project managers, and builders who will profit from this circumstance, it is troublesome for the landscape profession—a profession that has difficulty demonstrating to clients its value as a field of design grounded in the practical realities of climate and the construction site. *Weathering and Durability in Landscape Architecture* is therefore conceived as a textbook to be used in design schools and a reference for young design professionals in offices. It also is envisioned as contributing to the start of a discussion in the field about the way designers conceive and construct built landscape work over time.

Origins

My teaching and landscape research interests are concerned with the making and remaking of landscapes and are focused on landscape technology and the application of technological theories and methods as a core of landscape practice. This overarching subject is interpreted here through a focus on not only how landscapes are initially conceived and implemented but how built landscapes are to be considered over time. This book has been planned as a sequel to a previous examination by the author of built landscape work, *The Art of Landscape Detail: Fundamentals, Practices and Case Studies* (New York: John Wiley & Sons, 1999). It extends the groundwork established in that book on the relationship between landscape design, technological thinking and the making of built landscape architecture by advancing the technological nature of the site and its context through the issues of time, change and longevity.

The opening chapters of *The Art of Landscape Detail* focused on a few fundamental things in the physical world—gravity, the structure and economy of materials we have, or make, and the way these materials are put together spatially. Chapter 5 of that book, Detail Durability, for example, concentrated on the relationship between landscapes and durability and "the viability of landscape detail as built elements over time." It focused broadly on the topics of landscape detail and design practices and processes, illustrating the relationships between conceptual landscape ideas and their evolution and development through construction at the detail scale. The subject matter presented there was narrow in scope. This material is a broader consideration of the viability of entire built landscapes over time and in particular to the responsibilities and role of landscape architects in this regard.

It is worth noting that the subject matter and design responses to the transitory nature of so many designed landscapes hides a vast untapped field of endeavor for design students, practitioners, and academics in landscape architecture. Through case studies of contemporary built design projects and in particular discussions with their designers, this book documents a range of landscape design approaches and site strategies taken from current professional practice. The case studies illustrate the specific challenges brought about by weathering and durability within the landscape architectural design process as well as offering a reconsideration of the landscape architect's role in the stewardship (or otherwise) of past and current landscape projects.

Main Themes

The study of weathering and durability has been long neglected, and this text fills the gap in the current literature on landscape design, technology, and construction implementation. The premise of this book is to link together the way landscape ideas are conceived and implemented with the predictable as well as the unpredictable nature of how they may exist over time. *Weathering and Durability in Landscape Architecture* focuses on the exchanges between the material nature of landscape elements and design construction brought about by the actions of climate and the site processes and patterns of use over time. These exchanges range from instantaneous and drastic large-scale transformations to site installations and built landscape elements, to the more minor and sometimes little noticed daily alterations to landscape materials, forms and surfaces incrementally over long periods of time through the wearing actions of natural processes. No aspect of landscape architecture has such a significant influence on the current physical condition and visual appearance of the built landscape environment or on the success or failure of individual landscape architectural projects.

Weathering and Durability in Landscape Architecture focuses on how current designers must not only be aware of these exchanges during the life of a project but must address the inevitable modifications to landscape materials, forms, and details as part of the design, development, and future life of the project. The book is therefore grounded in daily practical design concerns while pointing the way to future research and study by landscape practitioners, students, and critics alike.

In short, the subject of weathering and durability in landscape architecture is presented as a design concern and activity that landscape architects can embrace with enthusiasm or ignore at their peril.

Niall Kirkwood
Cambridge, Massachusetts

ACKNOWLEDGMENTS

The profession and discipline of landscape architecture has not been served particularly well by research and publications on the subject of change in the built landscape. Documentation in the usual sense is almost nonexistent and sporadic when it has appeared over the years in journals or as part of books on other design subjects. These resources, limited though they are, are noted in the bibliography at the end of the book. Acknowledgment, therefore, has to be given to those whose thoughts on the subject took on greater significance in the planning and execution of this book. Individuals who should be acknowledged for their critique and help include landscape architects Alistair McIntosh, ASLA, RIBA; Richard Burck, ASLA; and Daniel Winterbottom, ASLA. Early discussions on this subject were started with my graduate teaching assistants Tim Mackey, Matthew Gaber, Sally Coyle, and Terrall Budge who all have gone on to accomplished professional design careers in landscape architecture. A special acknowledgment is given to Allison Towne who, as a graduate student in 1995 in the Department of Landscape Architecture at the Harvard Graduate School of Design, carried out an independent study on weathering and durability under my supervision. Entitled "Weathering in the Post-Modern Landscape," it was one of the first pieces of work I had seen in any landscape graduate or professional setting that had carried out a serious and focused investigation into the phenomena of weathering and durability.

In addition, the following landscape architects were invited to participate in the case studies for this book, and I wish to thank them for agreeing to do so and taking the time away from their own busy daily schedules and the work of their respective offices. They are, in alphabetical order, Julie Bargmann, Cheryl Barton, Edward Blake, Michael Blier, Eric Fulford, Mary Margaret Jones, Mikyoung Kim, Elizabeth Mossop, Margie Ruddick, Peter Lindsay Schaudt, Ken Smith, and H. Keith Wagner.

The graphic material of this book originates from three quite different sources: First, my own personal collection of photographs, drawings, documentation, and analysis carried out over the course of twenty-five years in the design field; second, the content of academic design studios and courses in landscape technology that I taught at the Harvard Design School; and finally, the results of design case studies in Part Two on the conception, development, and implementation of built design work in daily professional landscape practice in North America and Australia.

A great deal of credit should be given to individual faculty and generations of landscape architecture graduate students as well as particular representative classes of landscape students who participated in course assignments, field trips, and discussion on the subject of weathering and durability over the last eight years.

Thanks are due at John Wiley & Sons in New Jersey, to Margaret Cummins, Senior Editor, who has again guided the complex process of manuscript proposal to publication with her usual steady professional hand, as well as Rosanne Koneval and Donna Conte.

I also want to thank Grace Kulegian of the Office of the Department of Landscape Architecture, Harvard Design School, for her administrative assistance and Joelle Pelletier, formerly of the same office, for administrative help in the transcription of the interviews.

The preparation of this book was assisted by a generous grant from the Graham Foundation for Advanced Studies in the Fine Arts, which I wish to thank for its continued support.

Finally, I want to thank my wife Louise and daughter Chloe for their continued support throughout the period of manuscript preparation.

Introduction

> The city, however, does not tell its past, but contains it like the
> lines of a hand, written in the corners of the streets, the gratings
> of the windows, the banisters of the steps, the antennae of the
> lightning rods, the poles of the flags, every segment marked in turn
> with scratches, indentations, scrolls.
>
> *(Calvino, 1974)*

1. ORIGINS

I had the great fortune to be raised in an ancient place. Not the fictional
realms described above by Calvino but in a physically hard and practical
northern European city. The soil there is thin and sharp—a skin over stone,
and it has never lost any mark or line it has acquired. In the worn pave-

ments and steps, in paved stone streets and public promenades, by ancient trees and battered walls exists a remarkable legacy of constructed and weathered landscapes, both old and new, existing side by side. There is a sense of timelessness here, operating at a range of material scales and traditional and progressive forms and elements, coupled with a matter-of-fact attitude by the resident population to living in an inhospitable climate (cold, damp, and windy). Actions of this unforgiving weather have led, not surprisingly, to a cycle of landscape replacement and reconstruction. In those earlier days, I had little interest in the conception, design, and formation of these cobbled alleyways, courtyards, and craggy hillside parks, always, it seemed, in various states of upheaval, destruction, repair, and rejuvenation. And let alone had any understanding of how they may have evolved over time; they were simply there—to be used, to pass through, or to be inhabited for a short period of time. A number of the city's residents over the centuries were aware, however, that a large part of this familiar landscape could and did endure. The writers Sir Walter Scott and Robert Louis Stevenson and a range of civic planners and engineers immortalized the city's built landscape character in novels, literary sketches, and through built public works—monuments, parks, sculpture, gardens, streets, and bridges that were intended, like the publications, to withstand the test of time. From these endeavors, the city's residents gained a sense of the continuity of the built landscape—remembering what had been lost from previous generations, recognizing and recording what continued and endured in the now worn and familiar landscapes, as well as supporting the need to continue to make their mark on the city by building in and for their own generations.

The fundamental idea in this book is that landscapes endure through weathering. Making a built landscape occurs in sequence, is derived from site and context, and to gain significance over time must be durable. In short, weathering is central to the making of place and is a design activity.

A broader view of weathering and durability of built landscapes in time is introduced and focuses, in particular, on the significance of material landscape change to the conception and development of designed landscapes. It is also concerned with how and when landscapes weather, the permanence or otherwise of built landscape elements, as well as the design goals that are a result of the processes of weathering and durability. It explores and illustrates the nature of simple change in landscape materials, forms, and elements as they evolve, alter, or degrade over time, and it demonstrates this primarily through discussion with individual landscape architects over a range of design issues and approaches to weathering and durability taken from their own professional landscape design work.

The subject of this book addresses the following three questions: Why are weathering and durability in a designed landscape important? What lessons from the study of weathering and durability are important for landscape architects to know in the design of built landscape space? How can the landscape field integrate this knowledge into its daily design practices as well as in landscape architecture education?

After my early experiences in weathering and durability from that aged northern city, the topic of landscape weathering was pursued more intensely through research projects to observe and record the durability of contemporary built landscape projects. While I was traveling on foot around the environs of Boston and Cambridge, Massachusetts, with landscape architecture students, it became clear with each passing year that the constructed fabric of designed landscapes we observed together was weathering badly, and as a consequence, breaking down extremely fast. It also appeared that there was a great danger of repeating the same pattern of weathering as before as the landscape projects were repaired or rebuilt in a similar manner to the originals. This was in contrast to many of the public spaces from earlier periods, that while undergoing the continuous evolution and inevitable change as materials broke down and others were introduced afresh, continued to function and be enlivened through the same processes of weathering and change. Here, weathering established the context of the place.

There is a growing sense by designers that the study of weathering and durability within landscape architecture has become more central to the core of the landscape discipline and its knowledge base. Three issues have brought this about: (1) the growing pressure by clients, municipalities, and site owners to make projects sustainable; (2) the increasing role of natural and cultural site processes as a primary form-making source both in new built work and in guiding any subsequent renditions; and (3) an increasing concern over the limited availability of natural resources. These are not only specific to design in landscape architecture but are to be found in other applied design fields related to the built environment, for example, in architecture, interior and industrial design, and site engineering. Architectural standards for the performance of buildings in terms of energy efficiency and the use of recycled materials and nontoxic components have been introduced. However, there are clear differences between landscape architecture and architecture with regard to the duration of projects, the flexibility or stability of selected materials, and the growth of plant material, to name a few. To demonstrate the unique characteristics of weathering in landscape architecture, let us now examine how landscape architecture and architecture compare with regard to their attitudes to time and change.

2. SIGNIFICANCE

Simply stated, the difference between landscape architecture and architecture is the dimension of time as realized through the medium of their respective built work. In a study on weathering, the authors recognize "the limitations of buildings, inert as they are, to accept the action of the elements. (Mostafavi and Leatherbarrows, 1993). Instead, they pose a more pertinent question: "Is it possible that weathering is not only a problem to be solved, or a fact to be neglected, but is an inevitable occurrence to be recognized and made use of in the uncertainties of its manifestation?" They continue, "our aim is to revise the sense of ending of an architectural project, not to see finishing as the final moment of construction but to see the unending deterioration of a finish that results from weathering, the continuous metamorphosis of the building itself, as part of its beginning(s) and its ever-changing 'finish.'" From the initial design idea to the reality of building concept to implementation, raw material to finished surfaces, built landscapes as opposed to buildings undergo incremental and full-scale changes as part of the growth and maturing of the project rather than as a process of deterioration or neglect. Landscape architecture as a profession, an academic discipline, and a series of design practices has little understanding of how built landscapes in reality decay or change over time and mature. Designers select known site materials and applications in their built work to ensure continuity over time of landscape form as well as from expediency of effort by repeating a limited palette of trusted materials. In this way, "learning by mistakes," "rules of thumb," and other design practices develop over a number of years, to be repeated and elaborated on or misappropriated and lost over time. There is little documentation on the forces that bring about the changes to built landscapes, the form that these changes take, and how this phenomenon can be addressed in design schools in both a descriptive and prescriptive manner to view the durability and change of a landscape as a creative and central activity in landscape design.

In landscape architecture, weathering and, by association, durability, takes on a broad series of meanings and associations. Time and change are implicit in all considerations about weathering in landscape architecture. There are also the daily and seasonal cycles of weathering, growth, and decay to consider in the built landscape. Living materials (one thinks of plants immediately) grow, mature, and die within a reasonably predictable and documented life cycle and, in doing so, alter both their own form and the physical form and structure of the landscapes they exist in. Inert landscape materials may be less visibly altered and appear more resilient to physical change during their life cycle; however, they are also altered by cycles of weathering and decay that are in some cases able to be arrested through repair and replacement.

Genuine permanence in any work of landscape design, however desirable from a client's or designer's point of view, is, with rare exceptions, unobtainable. Plants mature, or die and are replaced; built site elements are, in turn, removed, replaced, altered, added to, recycled, or discarded by successive owners or users. This may be the inevitable result of the regular wear and tear of daily human use—patinas, stains, marks, and altered surfaces resulting from changing seasonal climatic conditions or the single severe weathering event that causes permanent structural alterations to the physical form of the built landscape elements. These weathering events include floods, storms, and winds. Landscape materials break down as others are being introduced anew. It can be said that built landscapes undergo different forms of change in an uneven manner and at different rates of change over time within any single project and not always in the way in which the designer has even considered, may desire, or can control at the outset of a project.

It can be argued that in landscape architecture there are two major types of weathering. The first is cyclical weathering, the constant flux inherent in a living landscape caused by the vegetative, hydrologic, and other natural life cycles with their daily and seasonal variation. The second is linear weathering concerned with the persistent decay and deterioration or alteration of landscape materials and forms over time in a persistent and cumulative manner.

In the discipline of landscape architecture, the subject of weathering and durability has been ignored, assumed to be unimportant or too obvious a subject to merit isolated investigation. For practical as well as professional reasons, the discussion of weathering often extends only so far as it concerns the continuous maintenance operations required on a project. This is unfortunate, as recent cultural and technological developments have made the associations between the processes of weathering and design more important for landscape architects to understand. These developments include an increasing number of manufactured and composite materials available for use in the design of exterior built environments. Developments in the availability, production, and distribution of these material types have encouraged ongoing design exploration of new site design strategies and experimentation in material use and form making such as the temporary use of glass, canvas, and plastic materials and recycled rubber and plastic compounds. Landscape design proposals using contrasting surfaces and forms can bring together untested manufactured industrial elements such as recycled plastics in conjunction with naturally occurring raw materials such as wood and clay tile, resulting in discordant forms and material junctions. It should be noted that this period of material design exploration has been productive and invigorating for the landscape field but has not been without its share of disappointments in the resulting forms or from errors of judgment in material selection and application.

Landscape architecture projects built as recently as ten years ago and intended as "permanent works" are falling into disrepair, some requiring major renovation or even more drastic action such as total removal and replacement. Examples include award-winning projects such as the North Carolina National Bank Plaza in Tampa, Florida, an ASLA National Design Award winner, and now closed off to the public for safety reasons and requiring intensive renovation and reconstruction. For more information on this project, see Dean (1996). Harlequin Plaza in Denver, Colorado, a design project that was significantly invested with experimental material choices and forms, was totally removed and has reopened recently after a design makeover as a more normative open space in both design expression and material use. For an article on the demise and replacement of Harlequin Plaza, see Thompson (1999). Steps have also been taken to advocate for the restoration of the Lincoln Center Plaza landscape in New York. To counteract maintenance changes and alterations by the management, local landscape architects have campaigned to return the Plaza as close to the original design project as possible (Arnold, 1994). Finally, emergency repair and reconstruction is being carried out to the built landscape elements of the Irish Hunger Memorial in Lower Manhattan, which had opened nine months previously in July 2002 (Kay, 2003).

These four examples illustrate some of the ways and situations in which designers and design projects engage the issues of weathering and durability in landscape architecture. These include restricting the evolution of a design project to maintain its original aesthetic integrity, accepting the eventual weathering and destruction of new landscape material applications or forms as part of the evolution of a design project, choosing to trust in the continuous maintenance of a built work to ensure its continued durability, or requiring immediate repairs to quickly address the complex interaction of site systems and materials.

3. CHARACTERIZATION OF THE BOOK

What are the ways in which built landscapes are modified and what are the probable causes? Why do certain material assemblies deteriorate and fail and what can be learned from these failures? Finally, is longevity in landscape design a worthwhile goal for the landscape architect to strive for or is it appropriate for specific built landscapes to be maintained as close to their original condition as possible or to have a limited life? In short, what is the performance desired over time for landscape work and can it be achieved, given the information and means at the disposal of the landscape architect? The field and discipline of landscape architecture has not served this subject of change in the built landscape particularly well. Documentation in the usual sense of predictable or studied change is almost nonexistent. This appears at first to be somewhat unusual, as time, change, and the evolution and growth of landscapes, in general, are embedded in the subjects of landscape design, design theory and history, applied landscape technologies and engineering and natural sciences such as ecology, biology, and hydrology. As the restoration and regeneration of older as well as more recent built landscapes take place at an increasing pace, this is a key moment to examine those approaches by landscape practitioners that directly engage the themes of change in the designed landscape.

Weathering and Durability in Landscape Architecture is conceived as a textbook to introduce landscape design students, academic audiences, and younger design practitioners to the issues and approaches to change in the designed landscape. A broad spectrum of current and emerging design approaches and strategies employed by contemporary landscape architects in addressing weathering and durability in landscape design is described. The book can be used as a text for courses in construction design, landscape theory, landscape technology, site planning, or to support design studios. It is not, however, intended to be a comprehensive handbook or an in-depth reference source on the subject of landscape materials and their physical properties or landscape construction for that matter. It can, however, be read by all those involved in the commissioning, design, or maintenance of contemporary open space and built landscapes.

My conception of the subject of weathering and durability is also not related to the field of material science and the testing, analysis, and characterization of the chemical or biological processes of how materials weather and change, however important that might be for landscape architects. Rather, it is concerned with viewing the subject of weathering and durability through the lens of design and landscape design processes. It focuses on the exchange between design and materials brought about during the design process itself, as well as the patterns of human use over time along with the actions of climate and their design implications. These can range from modest material alterations due to daily wear to temporary but drastic site transformations. In other words, the aim is to give greater influence to the range of design approaches and processes related to durability in the built environment and to emphasize their significance in landscape architecture.

4. FOR READERS

A warning at this stage has to be given to readers, particularly those who are involved as professionals in the design and implementation of constructed landscapes and have lived to see their earlier work subsequently modified, altered, or removed. This book does not attempt to identify or lay blame for the deterioration of current landscapes on landscape architects and designers; in fact, nowhere does the issue of responsibility or, more important, liability directly enter into the discussion unless it has a bearing on a design issue. This is quite deliberate on the part of the author. The intention is for readers to avoid conceiving of weathering and durability as separate from the design process or as an exclusive part of the routines of postcompletion maintenance. Rather, the issues and approaches to the subject are introduced through the process of design and technological thinking. It does, however, appropriately discuss the notion of professional responsibility that the landscape architect must bear in making the correct design choices and decisions with regard to the efficacy and economy of landscape materials, elements, and site assemblies and processes.

The examples of built landscapes featured are predominantly focused in North America. This is not to suggest a lack of interest in other countries, regions, climates, or the landscape architecture of other cultures. Quite the contrary, there are many lessons in material applications and good practices to be learned and transferred appropriately from other built environments. It is hoped that designers and researchers in other countries will study and document their local landscapes, and a more balanced design view of weathering and durability can be gained with their help. Finally, an understanding of the entire subject of weathering and durability of built landscape works, including the physics, material science, engineering, structural mechanics, chemistry, ecology, and microclimatic study of constructed landscapes, will take many years to accomplish.

A number of progressive and productive contemporary designers, including those featured in the case studies in Part Two, introduce and discuss their design work through the complex interrelated processes of microclimate, hydrology, and social and cultural processes at work on the site. Landscape architecture as a discipline is now able to benefit from study of the results of a productive fifty-year period of landscape work completed in North America since World War II. The examples set out in this book will form the basis for the start of a more focused study of weathering and durability as the legacy of other built projects are able to be reassessed in terms of their design and durability. In time, future landscape design work will benefit from what is learned.

5. STRUCTURE OF THE BOOK

The structure of the book moves from a general understanding of the relationship of landscape design with the conditions of weathering and durability to responses by landscape architects to the topic of change and durability as it influences their own design work. The book is organized in three parts.

Part One gives an overview of weathering and durability from a landscape design perspective and introduces the main approaches and principles. The purpose is to locate the subject within the design conception and evolution of a built landscape. Part Two forms the major portion of the book and introduces case studies of contemporary built landscape projects accompanied by interviews with their landscape architects focusing on the relationship between design and weathering and durability. The selected designers deliberately represent a broad range of attitudes and approaches to the work and practice of landscape design. The scope of their work includes the establishment of long-term durable public urban spaces to temporary landscape installations rendered in ephemeral site materials. Part Three returns to the main approaches and principles of weathering and durability introduced in Part One and reassesses them in light of the case studies in Part Two and the lessons derived from them.

Part One: Design for Weathering and Durability

This section forms an overview of the subject of weathering and durability with three short chapters that can be read in sequence or individually and that cover methods, materials, and poetics from the beginning of a design concept to the beginning of the end. Each of the chapters illustrates aspects of weathering and durability, starting with a brief survey of the main causes of weathering and change in designed landscapes and concluding with design strategies and approaches to site weathering conditions. In this way, the reader moves from the general concerns of making landscapes, to the design issues of material selection, and, finally, to specific design approaches to address change and durability in built work. Each chapter starts with a brief introduction to the scope of the essay and ends with class assignments.

Part Two: Landscape Architectural Design Case Studies

The central section of the book illustrates and critiques examples drawn from contemporary landscape practice over the last twenty years. The examples are selected primarily for their range of design approaches, concepts, and principles to built landscape design work as well as attitudes to change and temporality. In addition, the landscape architects, visible figures in the design world of the landscape profession, represent the very best in contemporary landscape design from across the country, each designer having received numerous design awards individually or as part of landscape design firms. Each case study contains an introduction to the project background, reviewing the designer's intentions, the consultants involved, and data from the project files. This includes discussion of the site, the program, and the evolution of the initial design concepts. Interviews with the designers are illustrated with drawings, models, and sketches, as appropriate from the period of design development. Photographic images from initial completion to current conditions and analysis and discussion of the relationship to the concepts and principles of weathering and durability are also included as reference material.

Part Three: Afterword

A final section returns to the main concepts and principles of Part One and reviews the design achievements and failures of the landscape architects in addressing the problems of weathering, time, and durability in their work as illustrated in Part Two. Commentary is also offered on the design challenges resulting from built work and the future research to be carried out in the landscape field on this topic.

6. TECHNOLOGICAL ISSUES AND THEMES IN WEATHERING AND DURABILITY

> Decay is indestructible. So it's not a product of time,
> but a measure of it. *The* Measure.
> *(Dekkers, 2000)*

Design proposes ideas, but it is through the medium of landscape technology and, in particular, "technological thinking" that designers in landscape architecture translate ideas into a material form. As a continuation of that process, weathering acts on these built forms and transforms them into adapted but durable landscapes. Landscape technology is described as "the entire body of methods, materials and poetics by which landscape design objectives are met or the application of these methods or materials" (adapted from the *American Heritage Dictionary of the English Language,* 1971). Landscape technology is quite distinct from other subject areas, such as landscape history, landscape theory, and landscape representation, although many technological issues feature prominently in, and are central to, the development of these subjects. In addition, landscape technology cannot be considered a subset of "technology" in other disciplines, for example, in architecture or civil engineering, even though they may share common areas of interest and overlapping subject matter, for example, in earthmoving, site drainage, and stormwater management principles. As a part of landscape technology, "technological thinking" in landscape architecture addresses how landscapes are made over time and the actions of climate and the patterns of use that bring about an exchange among materials, design, and construction. Therefore, as one of the modes of landscape architectural thought, "technological thinking" encompasses the theories and methods of landscape production as well as the activities and processes of landscape change and durability.

A designer's understanding of the finality of making in the built landscape is vital in a technological sense. There is the initial commitment to conceiving, executing, and then accepting the physical presence of the built work in time for better or worse, however it may turn out. In addition, from the designer's point of view, it is assumed, optimistically, that the built landscape will endure while even from the outset climate and human use acts upon it. The designer must also assume, with a certain amount of resignation, that at a particular point in time the built landscape will no longer exist as it was originally conceived, will be altered beyond recognition by others, or may cease to exist altogether. From a practical point of view, the threshold at which the designer must relinquish control over the design project can be troublesome to those used to guiding the entire effort. This contradictory position of needing to accept change while wishing for longevity is most often expressed at an early stage in the design process through a correct desire on the part of the landscape architect for a proposal that is both durable and robust—a built landscape that is able to endure while remaining adaptive to any number of changes. In this, the designer relies on his or her own experience of previous built work or the work of others to guide the landscape design process from conception. Also, through this process, landscape technology and "technological thinking" in landscape architecture are accepted as a primary activity and a pragmatic force in how designed landscapes are conceived and made. While landscape technology has evolved into a recognized academic field, a field that is researchable, with its own literature and methodologies, "technological thinking" has remained a practical activity reacting to, or describing, the phenomena of change in the built landscape rather than being an active part of design thinking. At present, "technological thinking" is deepening both its knowledge base through much needed research and publishing on the use and misuse of natural and manufactured landscape materials and the application of innovative landscape construction procedures and practices. Through landscape architecture educators and practitioners such as Daniel Winterbottom, Meg Calkins, Liz Gourley, Kim Sorvig, and Stan Jones, landscape technology and "technological thinking" are continuing to expand their boundaries in the new areas of emerging landscape practice, for example, with regard to emerging landscape materials and engineering practices and their use in rebuilding disturbed and contaminated land and water bodies. These include bioengineering techniques to stabilize slopes, the construction of new treatment wetlands, and the recycling of construction materials to be crushed, ground down, remade, and reused.

Designers have to absorb a large quantity of new information about changing methods, landscape products, materials, and codes. At the same time, there is a continued need to define the edges of knowledge in landscape technology—what, for example, constitutes the basic and emerging knowledge cores, and how does "technological thinking" enrich and continue to redefine the landscape discipline. "Technological thinking" and tectonics, according to Carles Vallhonrat, "depends on a few fundamental things in the physical world; gravity, the structure of materials we have or make, and the way we put these materials together" (Vallhonrat, 1988). *Weathering and Durability in Landscape Architecture* introduces "technological thinking" in two areas that connect weathering and durability with design and as a way of relating to the context and place of implementation in the exchange of elements and materials.

- The phenomena of weathering and durability are seen as a method of landscape measurement, a way of determining the passage of both time and activities on the site. Conversely, the built landscape also becomes a record of those actions that have taken place.
- The practices resulting from weathering and durability are employed by the designer as a means of establishing the singularity of context and individual site in a built landscape work through exchanges between elements and materials of the built landscape and the surrounding environment of the built landscape.

Method of Landscape Measurement

Frequent reference is made in the case studies in Part Two to the reciprocal conditions of the physical built landscape and the ongoing actions of weathering and durability. Is the built work responding to the actions of weathering or does the built work make these actions visible? Actions within and to the built landscape by climate and human use are exposed and made visible in the wearing of the form and materials of landscape projects. This is one of the most telling ways of noting the passage of time as well as forming a record of that passage. Here, the built landscape is a measure of the alterations to materials and landscape elements by climate over time. Conversely, the conditions of weathering are, in turn, a result of built work. The formation of a physical landscape project offers conditions for climate and human use to act upon landscape surfaces and materials. The result is the physical processes of weathering and durability within a landscape project. It can be said that, as well as acting as a measure of weathering processes, the built landscape acts on the climatic conditions and may alter them at the microscale and, in doing so, it causes the actions of weathering to be a measure of the built work over time.

Context and Place

Weathering and the actions of climate and use can be viewed as a way of marking the specific context of a particular work of landscape design. No two design projects will change in exactly the same way, and the particular pattern of weathering will be altered in time. Recently, increasing concern has arisen about the environment in which built landscapes themselves exist, which also may directly contribute to the weathering of a built project. These include the environmental issues of acid rain, toxic leachates in the soil, airborne industrial byproducts, and polluted runoff on a site.

Landscape architectural design is based on the belief that landscapes endure and mature over time. The more practical view held by most designers is that landscapes will cease to exist over time in the form they were originally conceived or might cease to exist altogether. In fact, it is not only expected that landscapes will change, but designers deem it necessary in order for the design to become fully formed, although a termination point may never be fully realized.

Weathering and Durability in Landscape Architecture is based on the belief that the main contribution of landscape architects to the built environment is the quality of thought and precision of execution that is brought to this means of producing built landscape works and their continued evolution over time. The content of the book will examine cities and urban spaces, parks and public gardens, synthetic and natural materials, landscapes that are old, some that are juvenile, and others that will last only one summer. In doing so, the immediate purpose is to bring to the fore the concerns of weathering and durability in the landscape field. The long-term purpose is to establish the potential of "technological thought" as a core of landscape practice. Design proposes ideas, but it is through the medium of landscape technology and, in particular, "technological thinking" that landscape architects translate ideas into a material form. As a continuation of that process, weathering acts on material forms and transforms them into durable landscapes. Thus, weathering and durability act together with landscape architecture to create and develop places of timeless quality. It is with this in mind that Part One is now introduced.

NOTES

Arnold, Henry (1994). "Preserve the Present: It's Not Too Early to Protect Modern Landscapes." *Landscape Architecture*, Vol. 84, No. 4.

Calvino, Italo (1974). *Invisible Cities*. Translated into English by William Weaver. San Diego: Harcourt Brace.

Dean, Andrea Oppenheimer (1996). "Modern Master." *Landscape Architecture*, Vol. 86, No. 2.

Dekkers, Midas (2000). *The Way of All Flesh: The Romance of Ruins*. New York: Farrar, Straus and Giroux.

Kay, Jane Holtz (2003). "A Hunger for Memorials." *Landscape Architecture*, Vol. 93, No. 3.

Mostafavi, Moshen and David Leatherbarrow (1993). *On Weathering, The Life of Buildings in Time*. Cambridge, MA: MIT Press.

Thompson, J William (1999). "Metamorphosis." *Landscape Architecture*, Vol. 89, No. 9.

Vallhonrat, Carles (1988). "Tectonics Considered." *Persecta 24, The Yale Architectural Journal*. New York: Rizzoli.

PART ONE

Design for Weathering and Durability

In Part One, the key design topics surrounding the permanence or otherwise of constructed landscapes are outlined through three introductory chapters. The chapters move through the design process sequence of initial conception, development, implementation, and permanence on site as they relate to the issues of durability, flexibility, and adaptive change in the built environment. Chapters 1 to 3 identify the concerns of weathering and durability in landscape architecture, address the significance of change and the temporary or permanent nature of built landscape design work, and discuss the main design principles for landscape architects and designers working in the external built environment.

1

Chapter 1 focuses on the initial aspects of the landscape design process. It examines the relationship of the early conception of design proposals to the subsequent changes brought to a built landscape over time.

Chapter 2 continues with a review of the ongoing design work during the latter part of the landscape design process and aspects of permanence related to the evolution and elaboration of design proposals. An overview of the changes that are brought to bear on design projects is given.

Finally, Chapter 3 features ongoing work related to the permanence of built work and summarizes the range of design strategies and approaches that are employed by landscape architects to anticipate alterations brought about by climate and human use.

Time and the Built Landscape

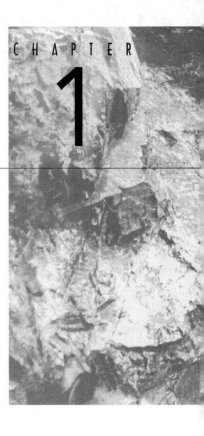

This chapter concerns a broader understanding of the scope of weathering and durability in landscape architecture, focusing on how it influences the landscape design process. It considers decisions made during the early conceptual phases of a project; the levels of performance to be expected from landscape materials and forms; and how attitudes to postoccupancy weathering, durability, and maintenance influence the final outcome of the design. Issues of climate and the effects on materials and changes to landscape elements are briefly reviewed. An emphasis throughout is placed on the nature of weathering and durability as a potential source of design creativity and invention for landscape architects, rather than a continual and exacting condition of site context and environment to be overcome. Students will gain a greater appreciation for landscape design over the longer view and an understanding of the ability of built landscapes and their material form to change or modify while maintaining their basic integrity. It will also reinforce the issue of time as a central concern to consider initially in the development of landscape design ideas and forms.

1. OVERVIEW: THE BUILT LANDSCAPE

> That everything is new is in itself new. There used
> to be more of the old.
>
> *(Dekkers, 2000)*

Built landscapes weather, break down, and are replaced or endure over time. This book is concerned with how built landscapes age. It is about the observation and measure of the process of weathering and durability and its relevance to the work of design in landscape architecture. It is also, in part, an examination of the changes that result from weathering and the range of interpretations by designers of the issues of durability in the built landscape as seen through their design work.

Building the Landscape

A number of key questions arise when considering how built works of landscape design endure: What is the significance of weathering and durability in relation to landscape architecture? Why should designers concerned with the complex task of conceiving and implementing built landscape spaces need to take into account the effects and influence of time on their design projects? Should built landscapes endure? If they do, are landscape architects able to understand the changes brought to their design work by the external forces of climate, by the surrounding environment, as well as by social and cultural forces? Finally, how does a designer extend or add to existing built landscape work or carry out new and original design work in an existing built setting and what are the resulting points of engagement, repair, and replacement?

The image illustrated in Figure 1.1 depicts a new constructed landscape surface of thick sections of iron plates. The iron plates, each weighing seven to eight tons, were placed in the middle of a newly formed public space where their upper surfaces were cleaned of ashes using high-pressure hoses. The pattern of the metal plates creates a central focus of the ground plane within the landscape of the public courtyard—Piazza Metallica—located within the former Thyssen Steel Mill complex in Duisburg, Germany. The resulting horizontal surface continues to weather—rusting and eroding in place as visitors to the courtyard use it. The standard working method over the rest of the site is, as in the example of the metal plates, one of adaptation and reinterpretation of the existing landscape site materials and elements, rather than wholesale change, removal, or destruction. Conceived by the landscape architect Peter Latz, the landscape surface of the project has

Figure 1.1. Iron plates as a new constructed landscape surface. Piazza Metallica, Park Duisburg Nord, International Building Exhibition, Emscher Park (IBA). (Latz + Partner, Landscape Architects. Courtesy of Latz + Partner.)

Figure 1.2. Wealth of materials in various stages of weathering and durability. Metal plates being lowered into place. Park Duisburg Nord, International Building Exhibition, Emscher Park (IBA). (Latz + Partner, Landscape Architects, Courtesy of Latz + Partner.)

become synonymous with, and a potent symbol of, the reclamation and reuse of this industrial site, as well as the durability and recycling of materials on the site, both inert and organic.

In the northern Ruhr area of Germany where the project is located, the former coal, steel, and iron industries have left behind an extraordinary built landscape of foundries accompanied by a rusting infrastructure of rails, roads, bridges, cooling basins and a wealth of recycled waste material in various stages of weathering and durability, as shown in the plates in Figure 1.2 being lowered into place.

Here, it is not a matter of demanding the removal of all traces of the former landscape elements—returning to a cleared site or a "clean slate." Nor was the central issue the use of the new landscape design as a contrast to, or point of departure for criticism of, the site's previous derelict state. Rather, the fundamental design approach was one of adaptive reinvention of landscape materials and forms to make this entire project healthy and attractive again for inhabitation and reinvestment by the surrounding communities. Duisburg Nord is a key project in this regard where the weathered landscape fabric of the former activities on the site is the basis of a series of new landscape elements and forms. The processes of weathering

Figure 1.3. Existing structures, walls, and loose waste materials. Former ore bunkers. Park Duisburg Nord, International Building Exhibition, Emscher Park (IBA). (Latz + Partner, Landscape Architects. Courtesy of Latz + Partner.)

and durability of certain materials on the site play an important role in the reinterpretation of a private industrial landscape to a public recreational and educational site.

The large quantity of existing structures, walls, and loose waste materials, as shown in the view of former ore bunkers in Figure 1.3, could neither be taken away nor be ignored. For example, walls were reused on the site, stone and brick were ground down to become materials for new walking surfaces, and the recycled metal plates became a new public floor. Addressing the weathering and durability of built landscapes such as this requires new design approaches that accept the vulnerability and physical qualities of new materials introduced to the site as well as their juxtaposition with the reused destroyed materials and landscape elements over time.

How does the landscape architect carry out design work not only in postindustrial landscapes such as this, but in the more traditional forms of projects and professional practice? For the designer, are there approaches to conceptual landscape ideas that address durability in all forms of landscape work from the most conventional to the most extreme sites, programs, and climates? Finally, where do weathering and durability lie in the core of the landscape discipline as well as the more speculative areas of design research and practice? The example of Duisburg Nord offers only one direction for the designer in considering the relationship between weathering and durability. Broader strategies of adaptive durability allow for the careful identification and selection of treated and treatable surfaces; for the juxtaposition of new, recycled, and existing landscape materials and elements together; and for a more open-ended approach to the issues of durability, where different "time clocks" are at work on the site. Some of these "time clocks" are permanent, lasting decades or even centuries in the case of our older public parks; some temporary, lasting only days in the case of art installations in the landscape. The task of working with landscapes such as these requires new approaches to the processes of weathering that accept the physical qualities of the built landscapes as well as their altered and destroyed nature and seeks justification within the existing weathered forms. Most project sites, it should be said, however, do not start with such a rich and evocative legacy of degraded forms and weathered materials. Nor is the intention of the designer always focused on temporal and material issues in this way. As an example of working with weathering and adaptive durability, the Duisburg Nord project stands in opposition to more conventional landscape design projects that have less concern generally for the material fabric of the project beyond implementation and completion and are based on a more restricted notion about the life and durability of the project beyond the expected growth and maturity of plants.

Completion and Beyond

Recently built landscape design works of a more conventional nature in terms of materials and durability over time are weathering and deteriorating at an alarming rate. Many projects built over the last twenty years require intensive redesign and reconstruction, and it is clear that the landscape design work under construction today will fail even faster due to the use again of similar materials and forms. Do designers want the results of their work to endure? Based on the repetitive nature and type of these failures, it suggests that they don't. Consider, for example, the North Carolina National Bank (NCNB) Plaza in Tampa, Florida, as shown in Figure 1.4. Designed in the mid-1980s by one of the country's foremost landscape architects, it is presently derelict and uninhabitable. For more information on the NCNB Plaza, see Guthheim (1982), Kiley (1992), and Kiley and Amidon (1999).

Planned as a shady respite from the heat, with a grid of Washingtonia palm trees, canopies of crape myrtle, cast stone benches beside water channels and gushing fountains, it has had to be roped off for public safety. After eighteen years, the sidewalks are in various stages of collapse; fountains are cracked, open, and dry; and plantings are overgrown and unmanaged, as shown in Figure 1.5. How does the physical condition of a built landscape degenerate so quickly to the point of collapse? Would the study of the causes of weathering and durability here avoid making the same mistakes again? And who is asking these questions; is it landscape architects, or is it more likely to be their clients and insurance companies? Finally, do landscapes of this type have a short lifespan by their very nature and should longevity even be expected beyond fifteen to twenty years?

In another more recent example, in nearly one year since its opening in July 2002, the Irish Hunger Memorial in Lower Manhattan was reported to be shutting down for emergency repairs (Dwyer, 2003). This "part hillock, part tunnel," a concrete pedestal for a fieldstone collage commemorating the bitter Irish famine of 1845, was "melting away in the rain and blowing away in the wind" (Kay, 2003). While these two contemporary examples (an urban plaza and a memorial) suggest the swiftness of attack of climate and the weathering of the breakdown of landscape materials and elements, it is likely that they will undergo the necessary repair and reconstruction in order to be returned to their original condition—or, more correctly, the next iteration of their built form.

Figure 1.4. Derelict and uninhabitable built landscape. North Carolina National Bank (NCNB) Plaza, Tampa, Florida. (Photography by Howard Supnik.)

Figure 1.5. Plantings unmanaged. North Carolina National Bank (NCNB) Plaza, Tampa, Florida. (Photography by Howard Supnik.)

Construction and Durability

Addressing the issues of design, construction, and durability was a great source of shared knowledge and investigation for landscape architects in the early days of the profession a hundred years ago. Letters and articles published during the first twenty years of *Landscape Architecture* magazine (1910–1930) passed information among the modest number of practitioners and offices, eventually turning into the basic rules of thumb of landscape professional practice. For examples from this period, see Hayden (1916), Noyes (1925), Peets (1915), and Wheelwright (1915). The durability and breakdown of landscape materials and site elements in the project in Tampa, Florida, are typical of the effects of landscape weathering currently found throughout the country, although they are regionally distinct in their breakdown and durability. It is all too easy to blame these failures of durability on thrifty clients, restrictive construction codes, meager budgets, incompetent implementation, or lack of ongoing care and maintenance. Ongoing care is still correctly applied to a great many built landscapes of note such as the cleaning and annual repair of the spray nozzles and water pipes in the utility chamber below the Tanner Fountain designed by landscape architect Peter Walker, as shown in Figure 1.6.

Figure 1.6. Ongoing care and maintenance: inspecting and cleaning the nozzles, pipes, and utility chamber below the Tanner Fountain, Cambridge, Massachusetts.

The answer is more complex. The landscape profession continues to value success in design (however it is evaluated) through annual professional design awards and honors. The study of the causes, forms, and significance of landscape durability is rarely carried out or discussed, although there have been recent moves to identify these issues in short editorial case studies in *Landscape Architecture* titled "Icons Revisited." Among projects discussed were the decline and impending demolition of Lawrence Halprin's Water Garden on the capitol grounds in Olympia, Washington, from the early 1970s (LeBrasseur, 2003) as well as the ongoing durability of Herbert Bayer's Mill Creek Canyon Earthworks in Kent, Washington, near Seattle (Baird, 2003).

In other design disciplines as well as engineering, business, medicine, law, and the military, the study of durability and failure is integrated at many levels into the education and professional lives of those practitioners. The development and evolution of many of the fields are, in fact, dependent on them (think of bridge collapses, stock market analyses, and drug treatments).

Where does the landscape profession go from here? It is currently responsible for built work that is temporary by default and wasteful of material resources, while ironically advancing or advocating for the design principles of sustainability and the protection of limited material resources.

Landscape architects must consider whether the legacy of the profession's design work in this century will be a collection of crisp transparencies shot on opening day of the project, rather than the project itself over time, or whether the long arduous task of learning from weathering and the many forms of durability is worth the effort.

2. WHAT ARE WEATHERING AND DURABILITY?

> Weathering is not caused by and large by
> the summer sun or winter storm, but the
> drip, drip, drip of an early November day.
>
> *Old English saying*

The actions of continuous weathering work in the background, almost silently (see Figure 1.7). In *The Art of Landscape Detail* by the author (Kirkwood, 1998), a chapter was devoted to the causes and effects of weathering on the built landscape at the detailed level of landscape design. A short summary of that chapter is now given with respect to the changes brought about by weathering and climatic conditions to the larger built landscape.

Figure 1.7. "The drip, drip, drip of an early November day."

Introducing Types of Weathering

Cyclical

Weathering by the natural forces of climate on daily and seasonal cycles is one of the main causes of material change that is addressed by the landscape architect. Climatic weathering such as wind, rain, sunlight, humidity, snow, and ice is one of the most easily recognized and understood factors that act upon built outdoor work, as shown in Figure 1.8. The timing and range of weathering effects act in a cyclical manner and either behave over time as agents of erosion and deposition, altering coatings and applied treatments through fading, crumbling, cracking or blistering, or as the sources of live loads (snow and ice buildup), shear forces (wind) which result in structural and mechanical changes or thermal movement (sun, humidity, and ice).

Serial

Multiple forms of linear weathering occur in built landscapes. They differ from the normal cycle of climatic weathering by occurring as a continuous trajectory or process, each stage dependent on the one before in a gradual

Figure 1.8. Snow and ice buildup. Cyclical weathering: snow and ice are the most easily recognized and understood factors that act upon built outdoor work.

Figure 1.9. Serial weathering of timber landscape structure: breakdown by mechanical damage, loss of material integrity.

but consistent series of changes that are irreversible. The process may be subtractive, each stage an incremental process of decay, as shown in Figure 1.9 in the breakdown of a built timber landscape structure by mechanical damage, loss of material integrity, and the actions of climate (ice, sun, wind, and rain). The process may also be progressive, accelerating exponentially toward total decline and failure.

Episodic

Projects are altered intermittently over time by the client, new owners, or municipal authorities as episodes in the life of a project. These changes may be a result of damage from vandalism; a response to social factors, including stylistic shifts in design expression; or responses and alterations to cultural, legal, or economic concerns such as changes in building codes, energy restrictions, or access laws. This form of weathering is able to be vigorously arrested and altered, but is not reversible.

Absolute

Finally, there is damage to the built landscape that irreversibly alters it, making it unsafe and unusable. This extreme form of weathering is likely to be the result of a total collapse of structural, mechanical, or material integrity, caused, for example, by flooding or as shown in Figure 1.10, a combination of intense storms and fire. It is absolute and irreversible, and initiates a phase of complete redesign or replacement.

Therefore, in the built landscape there are four distinguishable types of weathering, each determined by aspects of time, the period of recurrence of predictable change, and the ability, where possible, to respond to these changes. These are cyclical, serial, episodic, and absolute. It is rare, however, that a single type of weathering occurs in isolation; rather, it is more common that more than one type are taking place concurrently and acting with, rather than against, each other.

Figure 1.10.
Absolute weathering: resulting landscape from intense storms and fire.

Reconsidering Weathering

Durability is concerned with the soundness, constancy, and permanence of design elements and constructed landscapes over different periods of time as shown in Figure 1.11, which are, to some extent, predetermined. Critical material questions arise from this, such as: Who determines the longevity of a particular landscape? How do designers ensure permanence within the continuity of built landscapes, or if not, are they sensitive to the temporary nature of their undertaking? To understand landscape change as a result of weathering, the landscape architect can advocate in three ways for a larger reconsideration within the profession of the relationships between time and materials, material choice, and design assemblies and expression during the process of creating a built landscape.

Figure 1.11. Durability of design elements and a constructed landscape over different periods of time: walls, paving and natural rock outcrop.

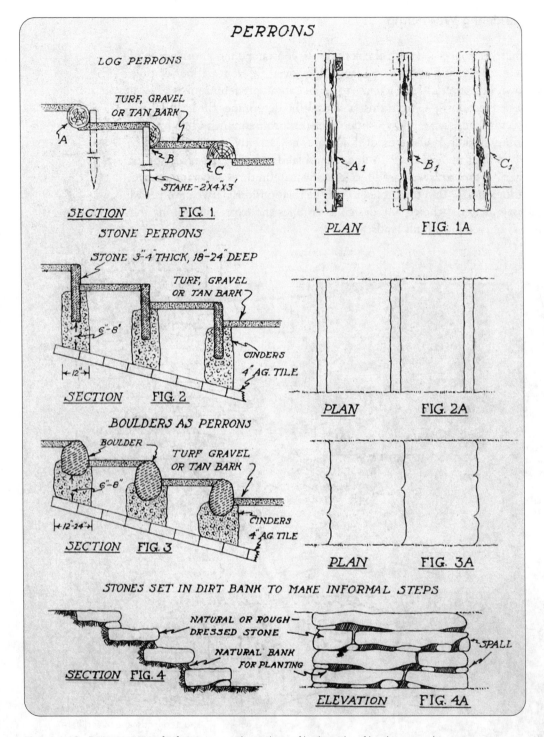

Figure 1.12. Dissemination of information on the making of built works of landscape architecture: *Landscape Architecture* article, 1920s.

Dissemination of Information

To learn from previous actions of weathering and durability in built land-scapes, to be aware of ongoing changes in built work, and to minimize the repetition of failure in the durability of projects, all require the continuation of active dissemination of research and evaluation into the making of built works of landscape architecture, as shown in Figure 1.12, which illustrates an early article from *Landscape Architecture* magazine in the 1920s on perrons, or stepped ramps.

"Don't be discouraged by a failure. It can be a positive experience. Failure is, in a sense, the highway to success," wrote the poet Keats, "in as much as every discovery of what is false leads us to seek earnestly after what is true, and every fresh experience points out some form of error, which we shall afterward carefully avoid" (Keats, 1818).

Development of Innovative Design Forms

Second, the ongoing development of innovative design forms or juxtapositions of contemporary and traditional materials such as metal screens and stone as shown in Figure 1.13, in contemporary landscape work needs to be continued. Many design approaches and their resulting projects rely on standardized forms, materials, and specifications. The introduction of new or untested materials or the deliberate choice to investigate alternative methods of forming or making landscape built forms is important. "New and untested" in a landscape element does not in itself indicate that the breakdown of materials is inevitable.

Figure 1.13. Juxtaposition of contemporary and traditional materials. Shrub and Vine Collection, Arnold Arboretum, Boston, Massachusetts. Reed /Hilderbrand, Landscape Architects.

Figure 1.14. Temporary surface tread on steps.

Figure 1.15. Minor repairs to landscape materials: breakdown of a bluestone band between concrete paving.

The Choice of Where and When

Third, avoidance of weathering in any of its forms is impossible. David Pye has noted that "the designer or his client has to choose in what degree and where there shall be failure" (Pye, 1968) or put another way, to adapt the issues arising from durability to decisions on the site about materials and climatic conditions of built work. For example, as shown in Figure 1.14, laying a temporary surface on the tread during the winter months alleviates wear and traction on the underlying stone steps. In addition, this new tread surface, made from a composite plastic material, is not damaged by frequent applications of salt and sand and provides a firm footing for pedestrians.

However, it may be easier to establish principles and lessons from examples of failure than from examples that appear to perform well at the present time.

3. TYPES AND FORMS OF CHANGE IN AND TO THE BUILT LANDSCAPE

Pervasive Effects

The persistent effects of climatic weathering on landscape materials cause a wide range of results—some major, requiring extensive repair; others minor, needing only simple maintenance, as shown in Figure 1.15 with the breakdown of a bluestone band between concrete. Moisture in the form of rain, snow and ice under the force of gravity as well as driven by capillary action seeps down into microscopic cracks and travels along joints in land-scape materials. From there, it works slowly to break down and dissolve site materials.

In a solid state as ice, it swells, increasing in volume to break and buckle landscape assemblies and elements. More damaging, however, are the repetitive soaking and drying actions in the vertical plane or, as shown in Figure 1.16, in horizontal surfaces caused by poor grading and drainage. Wind and swirling microcurrents attack and mechanically puncture and roughen landscape surfaces using airborne sand and grit. The sun blisters and fades and bakes and splits external wall and ground surfaces. The following section outlines a number of the more common effects of weathering and changes to landscape materials and elements.

Common Weathering Changes

Paving and freestanding walls are commonly found elements in the built landscape. Following are examples of weathering changes to these materials and elements alongside potential causes of the weathering actions.

Figure 1.16. Soaking and drying action of horizontal surfaces caused by poor grading and drainage.

Paving

Surface weedy: *windblown seeds and pods rooted between sand-bed pavers*

Surface dirty or stained: *weather, traffic, pollution; oil, grease, paint spills*

Loose, cracked, or crumbling: *weather and traffic, roots or deicing salts*

Sunken or heaved, as shown in Figure 1.17: *weather and traffic*

Spreading or crooked: *edging misaligned or damaged, no edging*

Edging loose, sunken, or heaved: *weather and traffic*

Walls

Surface dirty, stained, or textured with growth as shown in Figure 1.18: *weather, wear, and pollution*

Figure 1.17. Sunken and heaved surface of paving.

Figure 1.18, Stained vertical brick wall with lichen and algae growth.

Surface efflorescence: *high humidity, poor air circulation, moisture pene-trating joints, insufficient drainage*

Mortar joint loose or crumbling: *erosion and moisture penetration, insufficient drainage*

Mortar joint cracked: *structure settlement*

Brick loose, cracked, or crumbling: *clogged weep hole, blocked drainpipe*

Wall leaning: *structure settlement, damaged foundation or footing*

4. TESTS OF TIME

Design, Durability, and Failure

In landscape architecture, built projects take years before the semblance of any form of maturity is evident (if ever), materials acquire markings and abrasions, and surfaces are worn.

In an article titled "Holding Our Ground" by the author (Kirkwood, 1996), the issues of design and durability in the built landscape environment were discussed and documented. Commentary on the excessive use, aging, obsolescence, and resulting deterioration of many of the built landscape spaces in cities across the country was made. Some of the breakdown in durability was severe, causing the closure of public plazas, promenades, and parks and resulting in legal claims against the designers. Other changes were minor, such as those outlined in the previous section, appearing only as slight cosmetic alterations to surfaces and material assemblies and requiring only regular ongoing maintenance. Accompanying the article were photographs of examples of contemporary design work (urban plazas, waterfront promenades), taken from the author's walks, and their material weathering conditions that illustrated the range and types of deterioration. The short commentary asked more questions about the durability of built landscapes than gave answers; it did, however, hit a raw nerve with certain members of the landscape profession who were less than pleased to see what was termed the "airing of dirty laundry" in a professional organization's magazine. The selection of less than exemplary materials, the development of certain forms, and the resulting weathering and breakdown of landscape surfaces, paving, and elements were introduced not to attribute blame to the landscape profession and individual landscape architects but rather as an examination of how those in the landscape field could learn from their design mistakes.

5. IDENTIFYING DESIGN ISSUES, PROBLEMS, AND OPPORTUNITIES

Over the next several decades, private and public institutions and municipalities will commit millions of dollars annually to repair their built landscapes and sites containing multiple materials, changes, patinas, breakages, and faults. From this there arise a number of design issues, problems, and opportunities for landscape architects to consider:

- How will the weathering of built landscape projects structure the changing needs of scientific and aesthetic knowledge in landscape architecture?
- How will the restoration, recycling, and reconstruction of built landscapes affect how the public perceives and interacts with these places and the built world in the twenty-first century?
- How will the landscape strategies of time and durability in built projects shape the national landscape and influence future communities, towns, and regions?
- How will the design strategies of delay and acceleration be applied to material use to speed up or slow down the weathering process and how will it be measured?

6. ASSIGNMENTS

Exercises around the observation and analysis of weathering and durability form part of a series of assignments to be carried out within the structure of a course on landscape construction or landscape technology or as part of a landscape design studio. Instructors will be able to adapt each part of the exercise to their own regional location, site, or scale of design problem.

EXERCISE 1: TIME AND THE BUILT LANDSCAPE

1. Develop a timeline to describe the potential weathering of elements of a built landscape. Examples of landscape elements are paved surfaces, vertical constructions, drainage structures, and sloped landforms. Establish graphically from the timeline elements that are most durable and elements that are vulnerable to change and alteration. Stretch out the duration of the timeline over one, three, five, ten, and twenty-five years.

   Record these through photographs and notes. Find and compare to project examples of similar landscape elements in age and initial quality of construction, where possible.

2. Select two landscape forms observed in the surrounding local built environment. The forms may consist of several materials or assemblies, and must be located at a significant point of connection or transition within an outdoor space. One of the landscape forms selected should display characteristics to the student that demonstrate durability, and one should display lack of durability. The meaning of success and failure in durability is for each individual student to define and is a central part of the assignment.

   Record the landscape forms through field notes (dimensions, materials, finishes) and freehand sketches. Try a range of drawing media to describe the nature of materials and junctions and how they are used. What were the possible design sources available or used by the designer? What was the cause of the less durable form? Was it related to the initial design sources?

3. Investigate the consequences of extreme climatic forces on the construction of built landscapes in your region. Recent floods, hurricanes, droughts, fire, and ice and wind storms, for example, should be examined for their short- and long-term effects.

   Develop a response in terms of traditional and innovative uses of materials and landscape procedures for future work in the region. Which landscape elements can be considered temporary and which are fundamental to ensure durable built landscapes?

4. Carry out short scientific experiments in the studio or workshop to test the ability of landscape materials to withstand extremes of moisture, heat, and cooling. Examples would include soaking and drying repeatedly small samples of brick, stone, wood, and concrete; freezing samples over longer periods of time; or baking at high temperatures. Groups can be responsible for testing against field or standard samples under normal climatic conditions.

   How can the results be used effectively in the field? Determine in local built projects if designers or contractors carry out landscape material testing to establish local performance and durability criteria.

5. Carry out research through manufacturers' and landscape material suppliers' publications to discover the range of tests carried out in laboratories and field sites.

   Over what length of time are they carried out, what standards do they conform to, and how is that information translated into specifications and site design?

NOTES

Baird, C. Timothy (2003). "A Composed Ecology." *Landscape Architecture*, Vol. 93, No. 3.

Dekkers, Midas (2000). *The Way of All Flesh: The Romance of Ruins*. New York: Farrar, Straus and Giroux.

Dwyer, Jim. "Memorial to Irish Fortitude Comes Undone in New York." *New York Times*, May 7, 2003.

Guthheim, Frederick (1982). "Landscape Design: The Works of Dan Kiley." *Process Architecture*, Vol. 33.

Hayden, Richard J. (1916). 'The Soil Improvement on Boston Common." *Landscape Architecture*, Vol. vi, No. 4.

Kay, Jane Holtz. "A Hunger for Memorials." *Landscape Architecture*, Vol. 93, No. 3.

Kiley, Dan. "A Way with Water.", *Landscape Design*, No. 208.

Kiley, Dan and Jane Amidon (1999). *The Complete Works of America's Master Landscape Architect*. Bulfinch.

Kirkwood, Niall (1996). "Holding Our Ground." *Landscape Architecture*, Vol. 86, No. 2.

Kirkwood, Niall (1998). *The Art of Landscape Detail, Fundamentals, Practices and Case Studies*. New York: John Wiley & Sons.

Keats, John (1818). Preface, *Endymion*.

LeBrasseur, Rick (2003). "Sublime Reglect." *Landscape Architecture*, Vol. 93, No. 6.

Noyes, John (1925). "Shaw's Garden Subdivision Construction and Cost Data." *Landscape Architecture*, Vol. xv, No. 4.

Peets, Elbert (1915). "Street Trees in the Built-up Districts of Large Cities." *Landscape Architecture*, Vol. vi, No. 1.

Pye, David (1968). *The Nature and Art of Workmanship*. Cambridge, UK: Cambridge University Press.

Wheelwright, Robert (1915). "Notes on Stepped Ramps." *Landscape Architecture*, Vol. v, No. 3.

Aspects of Permanence

1. OVERVIEW: CONCERNS OF DURABILITY

2. THE TEMPORARY AND THE PERMANENT LANDSCAPE

3. MATERIALITY

4. PERFORMANCE AND PROGRAM

5. LESSONS FROM LONGEVITY

6. ASSIGNMENTS

NOTES

This chapter addresses the range of concerns that cover the aesthetic, material, and constructional requirements of contemporary built landscapes. It also addresses the more individual aspects of built landscapes as they relate to the particular use of standard and nonstandard approaches to weathering and durability that distinguish the work of one designer or design office from that of another. For landscape architectural students, exposure to the entire scope of activities related to the implementation of built landscape work and beyond may not occur until they have been in a design office for a number of years and have carried out a significant amount of professional work. The reader will be introduced to the conditions and constraints that act upon the development of built landscape projects during the evolution of a design proposal and the design concerns of landscape architects about the processes and patterns of weathering during that stage of work.

1. OVERVIEW: CONCERNS OF DURABILITY

Let us consider why it is necessary to address the weathering of a landscape during the interim design stages of a project, as well as the role of decay and longevity of materials and design elements in the built landscape. In short, what are the design concerns associated with weathering and durability?

Implemented landscape work in the built environment, whether a street, square, waterfront, pedestrian trail, park, or garden, has been carried out with consideration for the most fundamental and crucial design concerns, for example, to provide durable horizontal surfaces, to achieve permanent changes of grade on site, or, as shown in Figure 2.1, to temporarily shed or divert water across a site. These functional concerns are derived from the everyday requirements of landscape use and design performance. For the young landscape architect who wishes to acquire good design practices regarding the durability of his or her built design work, it is important to understand the forces that affect built landscapes and to distinguish them from those forces brought about solely by economic or maintenance concerns. This is in addition to those concerns that are derived from the individual material choice and design expression of the landscape architect.

Figure 2.1. Shedding and diverting water across a site.

Arising from this, the following issues need to be addressed. They also must be considered by the landscape architect during each project:

- How are landscape durability concerns, once they have been established, to be weighed or judged one against another, and, in doing so, which are more important than others?
- Do these durability concerns change over the time of the development of the design project and the duration of the built work?
- Finally, and most important for landscape architects, how are they able to be reconciled together during the later stages of the design process?

In addressing these questions, it is necessary to understand that while the built landscape and the processes of durability in design can be the focus of a considerable amount of effort and energy to a design student or practitioner within landscape architecture practice, the motivations to carry them out are guided as much by forces outside of the landscape profession and industry as by forces directly related to landscape design.

2. THE TEMPORARY AND THE PERMANENT LANDSCAPE

In reviewing the broad range of concerns that affect the built landscape, the subject that is most often overlooked is that of the landscape architect's own concerns of professional growth, particularly those involving development in spatial, contextual, technological, and aesthetic issues. These include the issues of *site, context,* and *climate;* the connection between *landscape construction* and *landscape durability;* and the development of *individual design expressions* toward weathering.

Defining "Site" and "Place" Through Landscape Weathering

The varied actions of weathering on the built landscape are one of the factors that define the context within which the landscape work is carried out. Landscape design materials and forms have the ability to reflect or resonate with the characteristics of the site's context, microclimate, and the subtle shifts of shade, moisture, light, or, as shown in the seawall in Figure 2.2, salt laden air within the surrounding marine environment. The resulting materials in this case are formed as a functional response to continuous attack on connections, joints, and water-edge surfaces from spray and wind. These include walls that sequentially cool and heat and receive lichen, molds, and surface staining from rain and ice and small pools of sunlight or water on paving that alter its visual character and physical nature.

Figure 2.2.
Surrounding marine
environment: reflecting
a site's microclimate.

In addition, weathering on site reveals the nature and properties of the local geology, soils, and vegetation. The specific material qualities and patterns of the local landscape are reflected in the selection of plants and in the choice of the landscape materials, whether timber, metal, stone, or clay with their varied qualities of reflectivity, density, color, surface, and texture.

Connecting Durability to Landscape Construction

Landscape durability is closely related to the many acts of construction proposed on site during project implementation and planned in design development. Among these are the placement and juxtaposition of landscape materials, the fixing of materials in place on site, and the sequence of construction on site, as well as the application of materials and coatings, and the juxtaposition of materials and finishes, as shown in Figure 2.3.

The concerns of landscape durability during the design development phase require an attention to the working of materials and landscape elements and their selection, placement, weight, jointing, and finish. It is carried out as a design activity during the development stages of the project rather than as the final implementation of a design proposal. In that way, landscape construction and design activities are combined in the later stages of conceptual landscape design, where the creative possibilities of landscape materials and forms are allied with the pragmatic concerns of progressive weathering and durability.

Figure 2.3. Juxtaposition of materials and finishes: metal grating and random precast pavers with stone inserts.

Landscape Design Expression and Weathering: Developing Individual Approaches

The results of weathering of built landscapes can be permanent and obvious to the naked eye and the visually acute, for example, through the breakdown and repair of materials and surface textures and hues, as shown in the paving in Figure 2.4, or the wearing of surfaces by skateboards grinding along the edges of plinths, steps, or walls, as shown in Figure 2.5. Or it can be temporary, as shown in a child's playground markings in Figure 2.6, deceptive, occurring almost unnoticed and unobserved within the structure or composition of materials or between joints.

The significance of both the obvious and the unseen for the designer is related to their ability to form, through continued evolution, a broad range of design expressions. In short, they open up a wide scope of approaches for the landscape architect to both generate and represent landscape design ideas.

Figure 2.4. Breakdown of walking surface: decay of landscape materials and surface textures.

Figure 2.5. Wearing of surfaces by skate-boards grinding the edges of plinths.

Figure 2.6. Child's playground markings.

Let us continue by looking at the general considerations and concerns of landscape durability—those related to program, function, and uses; form and material; and the structure of landscape elements and their expression. The durability of a landscape design proposal is related to the emphasis made by the designer on well-considered approaches to the overall future weathering patterns. The landscape architect has to consider the following issues regarding proposed landscape design forms and elements to know if they will remain durable over time:

- Will the selected landscape materials and elements weather appropriately with the rigors of climate, including extremes of heat and cold, wind and water, salt spray, and ice?
- Will the landscape materials and elements continue to function as they were originally intended postimplementation and after the start of the weathering process, for example, by shedding water, preventing erosion, allowing plants to grow and flourish, or supporting the weight and movement of pedestrians?
- Will the selected landscape materials and constructed elements change their structural properties over time?
- Will the weathering and durability of the landscape materials work together as a common group of landscape elements, supporting the overall conceptual ideas and forms of landscape spaces that are produced?

Landscape architects must address these questions as conceptual landscape ideas mature and develop. The purpose here is to understand that landscape durability requires a considerable amount of effort within the landscape design process and continues to exert a considerable influence on how broader landscape design ideas are to be translated into built work. From the specific questions listed above, it is necessary to cover a broader group of detail concerns under which the landscape durability is carried out. These are the basic conditions, related to practice and aesthetic issues, under which planning for landscape durability in the design process is carried out, irrespective of project type, size, or location, as follows:

- Types and Classes of Landscape Durability. The range of landscape durability approaches used in contemporary design practice is identified.
- Landscape Design and Maintenance. How and where the subject of landscape durability appears within the conventions of postoccupancy landscape operations on a built landscape project need to be examined.

- Landscape Durability and Aesthetics. Artistic and engineering design practices are outlined arising from the general concerns of generating durable landscape forms and elements.

To ensure the successful execution of any built project, these concerns must be addressed. In addition, they are a reliable and effective way of carrying out the following activities related to landscape durability:

- Analyzing landscape materials and constructed elements in existing projects
- Reviewing one's own landscape design work or the work of others in an office or studio
- Judging the quality of manufactured elements or prefabricated or off-site landscape members
- Diagnosing potential problems in existing built landscape work

They are also useful as a way of reviewing the work of previous generations of landscape projects and landscape forms and materials to determine their successful and distinguishing features.

The condition of many built landscapes in the public realm of cities, towns, and communities raises serious issues for designers regarding the suitability of their landscape materials and the concerns that were addressed in the previous paragraph. The failure of the landscape elements, the lack of durability, the breakdown of materials and methods of construction have required the recent overhaul and rehabilitation of numerous public outdoor spaces in this country. Clients such as educational institutions, corporations, public agencies, and municipalities have challenged the ability of designers to build outdoor spaces for an expected life of beyond ten to fifteen years and passed responsibility to project managers. Beyond regular maintenance, will a large expenditure of financial resources, including labor, be required to counter the failure in detailing and design detail practices? Of more significance, how can designers start to carry out sound durability practices?

3. MATERIALITY

> I scarcely know which materials to choose. Ideas come to me immaterially, lines on white paper. When I want to fix them I have doubts and they escape, waiting in the distance.
>
> *(Siza, 1988)*

Let us now consider a method by which landscape ideas are developed into built work through the materials that are selected and the concerns of ongoing change and maintenance.

Material Selection and Weathering

For the landscape architect, part of the skill in developing the varied range of landscape forms within a project lies not only in the formulation and development of the initial design concepts, but in understanding how the concepts are to be initially realized and eventually shaped in time through the selection of landscape materials.

For landscape architect Keith Wagner, ASLA, the use of design materials in the landscape and knowledge of their qualities and character are considered central to the design process and key to the experience of and making of meaningful places. "The tactile qualities of materials, their history, evolution and their inherent nature are engaging—a vital part in evoking memory...the way the russet color of rusted metal in sunlight can transport one to another place."* This suggests a closely observed understanding of the organic development of weathering patterns and marks, as shown in Figure 2.7. While he is referring to his background and experience as a sculptor, this has been translated into an approach to everyday practices in his professional landscape architectural office, as illustrated in Case Study L in Chapter 4.

This is not the case, however, with most landscape design students and entry-level practitioners who may lack training in studio or applied arts. The lack of experience of landscape materials and their use and implementation in the field should not hold back a designer from fully developing an understanding of materials over time. This can be achieved through studying the exchanges between landscape weathering and materials and their subsequent use in the development of landscape design proposals. There are research aids for designers in other design fields that attempt to catalog images of the effects of weathering on a range of materials, for example, Judy Juracek's documentation of weathered materials such as marble, stone, wood, and glass in book form (Juracek, 1996).

The relationship between landscape materials and weathering has been seen largely in terms of the functioning of landscape form, for example, the projected life of a granular stone walking surface in a severe climate

---

*Quote by Keith Wagner taken from material prepared by his design office, January 2003. For further discussion of his design work, see Case Study L.

or the ability of a concrete retaining wall to withstand the structural forces and acidic nature of the adjoining soils that would attack the wall's surfaces. Making the weathering of a material visible within the landscape is a design activity that sees the practice of material selection as both artistic and pragmatic. When the weathering of materials is made visible and is articulated by the landscape architect during design development, we refer to the "landscape materiality" of the particular project. ("Materiality is referred to instead of "materials application" to denote a broader approach to the process and phenomena of site materials and their application.)

The materiality of landscape elements and forms establishes how the design ideas are to be made visible in time and the necessary elements and forces that establish and mold the eventual physical form.

Figure 2.7. Weathering patterns and marks: tactile qualities of materials.

Materiality is derived from a spatial and physical ordering brought to any landscape design condition. This allows the designer to develop landscape design ideas in terms of the exchanges of the material parts, structuring the detail parts conceptually, while, at the same time, developing a language of material construction that is both expressive of the main conceptual design ideas and practical in terms of their use and application in the field.

In considering landscape materials, however, there are three significant factors related to the character, exposure, and life span of the landscape material that are relevant to designers:

1. Character of Landscape Materials. Materials will alter and change irrespective of use or operation because of their organic nature and character. These range from larger earth forms and water bodies to plants and natural wood, clay, and stone products. This makes their performance more difficult to codify and specify.

2. Exposure to Natural Forces and Weathering. Landscape materials are especially vulnerable when exposed to harsh conditions, for example, in marine edges or in heavily trafficked urban streets, sidewalks, and parks. Even in unexposed situations, landscape materials and forms are open to changes brought about by constant wear and weathering.

3. Life Span of Projects. Many landscape design projects are temporary installations or form part of larger phased proposals. The implication is that they are expected to have a limited life span and are designed accordingly, for example, in temporary outdoor sculpture areas and garden expositions.

It can be said, quite simply, that landscape materials undergo forms of change, and not always in ways in which the designer can control, may desire, or may have ever considered at the outset of a project. This may be the inevitable result of one of the following:

- Wear and Tear. General changes brought about by daily use and normal climatic conditions. This is differentiated from the more specialized forms of wear and tear as a result of vandalism or deliberate misuse.

- Extreme Patterns of Weather. Occasional but severe storm events that cause total and permanent alterations to the physical form and structure of landscape forms and materials.

- Poor Design. The breakdown of particular landscape elements may occur through poor design practices. Examples include misuse of installations and site assemblies and the selection of inappropriate materials, including plants. This can be made worse by additional general wear and tear or when subject to occasional but severe storm events.

4. PERFORMANCE AND PROGRAM

When considering where you are likely to encounter the process of durability in landscape design, it is useful to briefly review the various stages of the conventional landscape design sequence as they are described through the client/designer relationship and services (AIA, 1993).

Landscape Design Process

Design services are described as follows:

- Inception
- Conceptual design
- Schematic design
- Detail design
- Documentation
- Implementation
- Maintenance and postoccupancy evaluation

While it is most likely that issues of materials and materiality will be addressed within the detail design or documentation phases, there are instances where problems or issues of materials and material form will occur in other phases of the design process.

- Inception. In the preparation of the program issues and scope, as well as timetable, phasing, and initial economic concerns, specific material issues may exist, for example, those concerned with existing materials and landscape forms.
- Conceptual Design. Specialized landscape forms and materials may be part of the initial design concepts or form part of the program elements. Investigations of site conditions require analysis and documentation of existing landscape conditions and the recording of proposed materials and elements to be saved, enhanced, or new ones sited.
- Schematic Design. This is the critical time in the design process for the establishment and formation of the material language of the proj-

ect and the evolution of the precise expression of the material finishes and applications.

- Detail Design. This involves the completion of not only the development of the overall project design, but also the final selection of materials and their assembly into an entire body of constructed design work.
- Documentation. This involves recording the execution and site implementation in drawings and written specifications, and describes the finished qualities and performance, which are required in the material forms.
- Implementation. Observation of the execution of the design on site. Changes to landscape elements and forms arising from inaccurate information on site conditions or issues of craft, workmanship, and quality of materials.
- Maintenance and Postoccupancy Evaluation. Review and alteration to landscape forms that have weathered badly or are required to be changed because of inadequate performance, variation to codes and legal requirements, or as part of regular maintenance.

5. LESSONS FROM LONGEVITY

Returning to the questions identified at the beginning of the chapter to be considered by the designer:

Q: How are the landscape durability concerns, once they have been established, to be weighed or judged one against another, and in doing so, which are more important than others?

A: Of interest to the designer here is how the general concerns of professional practice, liability, and standard detail forms direct aesthetic and design decisions related to those of durability.

Q: Do these durability concerns change over the time of the development of the design project and the duration of the built work?

A: As with other aspects of landscape design, periodic changes will occur to alter concerns about and around the subject of landscape detail form.

Q: Finally, and most important for landscape architects, how are they reconciled during the later stages of the design process?

A: This requires an understanding of the different approaches to design durability that are presently used by designers. This is the subject of the next chapter.

6. ASSIGNMENTS

These exercises form part of a series of assignments to be carried out within the structure of a course or studio on landscape architectural design or as part of a course on landscape construction or landscape technology.

EXERCISE 2: ASPECTS OF PERMANENCE

1. Identify two built landscape projects. The two landscapes should consist of similar landscape types from different time periods *or* locations (e.g., parks from the nineteenth and twenty-first centuries or located in different parts of the country), or two examples of different landscape types from the same time period. Research the background to the project design and the range of material and durability concerns that were addressed in the project for the designer(s) involved.

   By comparing the two precedents, determine the changes or similarities in the durability concerns that designers address over time or between locations and project types. Are certain material concerns related only to specific landscape types? What are the contemporary durability concerns of different landscapes?

2. Visit a landscape architectural project in your locale that is currently under construction in the field (after obtaining official permission to visit the site). Inspect the range of landscape materials and forms being implemented on site and determine which are designed to be temporary and which are permanent.

   What type of materials and forms are found there? The intention is to examine what percentage of each material type is present in different project types. Do certain classes of design projects consist only of temporary materials and forms and others mainly permanent?

3. Carry out a review of the issues of seasonal weathering and change using the precedent examples selected for Assignment 1. What landscape forms were executed as a result of the concerns of weathering as opposed to other concerns? In particular, examine older landscapes where alterations to the overall built forms have been made over time.

   How are these concerns realized on site through landscape design—what forms of weathering are covered and which areas and types of landscape forms and materials are the focus of this design attention? The purpose is to examine basic weathering conditions, related to practice and aesthetic issues, under which landscape design is carried out, irrespective of project type, size, or location.

NOTES

AIA (1993). Document B163.

Juracek, Judy A. (1996). *Visual Research for Artists, Architects, and Designers.* New York: Norton.

Siza, Alvaro (1988). "On Materials." In W. Wang, ed. Alvaro Siza: *Figures and Configurations: Buildings and Projects 1986–1988*. New York: Rizzoli.

Design Approaches

1. TO THE END OF TIME?

2. DESIGN TO DURABILITY

3. INTRODUCTION TO CASE STUDIES

4. CLASSROOM ASSIGNMENTS

NOTES

The key question addressed in this chapter is how to proceed in integrating the issues of weathering and durability in the design process. Where and how does one start? The chapter introduces the approaches to design durability that are used by the landscape architect in the landscape design process. In addition, design approaches to work that are already implemented or adaptive weathering as well as new areas of landscape work are considered. Finally, an introduction is given to the case studies in Part Two, which form a sizable section of the book. These are described in terms of the landscape designers and project types selected for the studies along with the structure employed in their presentation.

1. TO THE END OF TIME?

> Those who make choices with ease are satisfied with glueing together the things that they have thought to be materials, glueing them onto materials about which they have not thought.
>
> There these materials remain, until the first storms lay bare what could have been foreseen. They do not exist.
>
> *(Siza, 1988)*

Nothing lasts forever. Time alters a built landscape by the direct affect it has on the landscape itself, not on the conceptual ideas behind the landscape. Designers can attempt to reverse this change through regular and persistent maintenance and reconstruction, producing a static piece of built work. This, however, is also a form of change, re-creating a built landscape space, at different phases of its design evolution and development. Designers who attempt to register change can do so by deliberately proposing built forms that will fail or will have a restricted or limited life. Ideas about change come from the selection and juxtaposition of materials, the methods of working the materials and their assembly, and the relationship and sequence of joints and junctions in materials.

The most important and, at the same time, one of the most difficult aspects of landscape architectural design and its place in the built environment is the ability to bridge the gap between a fixed idea in site design and the realization of that built idea over time. The attitude of designers to avoid, or at least slow down, the decay or destruction of the built work is a natural reaction to the initial investment of time and money, the expenditure of material resources, and the combined energy and effort of clients and design teams.

In short, the premise of avoiding ruins or ruination of the project is driven by a very human desire for the longevity of the built work. However, this is made more complex by the physical nature of landscape elements such as plants that continue on varying cycles of growth and decline, as shown in the replacement maintenance and, therefore, age differences of the allée of trees in Figure 3.1 or the ground cover vegetation taking over the modest timber walkway in Figure 3.2. Materials such as earth, water, and soft walking surfaces that shift, move, and dissolve as well as the temporary conditions of certain landscape proposals ultimately demonstrate the futility of permanence.

These vary from interim designs for spaces undergoing renovation, for example, temporary structures as landscape elements or are of short duration—a summer, for example, or projects that deal with transient materials

Figure 3.1. Varying cycles of plant growth and decline: allée of different periods of plantings.

Figure 3.2. Varying cycles of plant growth and decline: ground cover vegetation taking over a modest timber walkway.

Figure 3.3. Metal scrim, Krakow Ice Garden, 1990. (Photograph by Michael Van Valkenburgh.)

such as Michael Van Valkenburgh's evocative Krakow Ice Garden project in Martha's Vineyard from 1990 as shown in Figure 3.3, that focused on the poetic but fleeting qualities of ice and mesh scrim in winter and was both intentionally temporary and season specific. For further information on the Krakow Ice Garden and other projects, see Van Valkenburgh (1986) and Hodge (1989).

For the landscape architect to adequately transfer a conceptual sketch or a vague series of roughly drawn images and diagrams to a built work in time requires a broad range of design approaches, techniques, and tools. It is also made more difficult for landscape students or young designers by a lack of experience in completing built work, which is only natural at that stage of their careers.

During the course of the development of a design project, a landscape architect will be called on to select materials and finishes and shape landscape elements to reinterpret or to replicate numerous landscape forms. A designer may also combine and assemble existing and new landscape materials to create hybrid elements or built systems, or, in certain cases, to appropriate, treat, and apply old landscape materials and elements as shown in Figure 3.4 of the Piazza Metalica plates discussed in Chapter 1.

Section 2 will introduce design approaches that will specifically allow built landscapes to be created and evolve over time with due concern for their patterns of weathering, durability, and flexibility. The purpose is to examine the general ways in which landscape forms and elements are selected and the methods available to designers in starting a piece of landscape architectural work.

Three approaches to developing built landscapes that account for issues of weathering and durability will be outlined.

1. Durability to weathering establishes initial principles early in the design process for the use and longevity of landscape materials, elements, and forms and focuses on expected performance and repeated maintenance activities.

2. Weathering to durability focuses on the anticipated exchanges between materials and climate, between landscape constructions and human use, and between the longevity of design ideas and the evolution of the built project. It carries out design strategies that predict or accept temporary and permanent patterns of weathering and, in doing so, builds in a flexibility to adapt and alter.

3. The integrative approach combines the first and second approaches in a method that looks at both the beginning and the potential ending of built projects and works to produce a balanced design strategy. This is particularly used in the addition of new landscape elements or materials

Figure 3.4. Cleaning and treating old landscape materials. Piazza Metallica, Park Duisburg Nord, International Building Exhibition, Emscher Park (IBA). (Latz + Partner, Landscape Architects. Courtesy of Latz + Partner.)

within an existing built project or the incorporation of a new design adjacent to an older project.

Two questions are significant in introducing the range of design to durability approaches and the resultant built landscape forms:

- Is it possible to conceive of the weathering and durability of a built landscape simultaneously at a range of material scales and during various stages of the design process?
- What are the ways in which landscape architects are able to address changes to individual parts of the built landscape while at the same time conceiving of the weathering of the entire design project?

In short, how does any approach to weathering and durability alter or establish a different sensibility between the design process and the built work? In answering these questions, it is necessary to first address a range of design issues associated with landscape design and weathering, a topic that is intrinsically tied to the type and range of materials and assemblies, landscape forms, as well as the processes of conceiving and making built landscapes.

2. DESIGN TO DURABILITY

Part of the process of development of a landscape project involves the comprehension, visualization, and response to the weathering of the final built landscape form over time. The skill of the landscape architect lies in determining the following:

Q: What landscape elements and materials does the landscape architect need to be concerned about and what does the landscape architect need not in reference to weathering and change?

A: In a built landscape, the total scope of landscape materials and forms has to be understood as an integral part of the evolution of the entire project. However, precise design study of weathering and durability is especially needed when the landscape forms are complex in their arrangement or assembly, or the quality of certain materials, finishes, and textures requires them to be more closely studied.

Q: How to identify and address potential areas in the design where there are likely to be weathering and durability problems.

A: This is particularly the case when unknown or experimental materials, finishes, or techniques of construction are being used for the first time.

The landscape architect establishes the pattern of durability that is most appropriate in relation to the location and condition of the site; the client requirements and program uses; and the opportunities and limitations afforded by the budget, local codes, material choice, manufacturing limits, and the abilities of construction implementation in the field.

Let us now examine the three general approaches to durability in design previously mentioned that utilize the results of these investigations.

Approach 1: Durability to Weathering

This is the most commonly understood method of advancing landscape design work, starting from an overall design concept, or concepts, and developing through a series of interim steps a more resolved understanding of the spatial relationships, materials, structure, forms, and dimensional organization of the final built project. This involves an ongoing shift in scale (from large to small) and gradual clarification of the selection, hierarchy, shape, and density of materials and landscape elements based on their known durability. Weathering in the built landscape is, therefore, seen as the processes brought to bear on the project at the completion of the entire design process. Weathering is, therefore, a measure against the predetermined level of durability, as shown in the organic breakdown of a concrete sidewalk in Figure 3.5.

Figure 3.5. Organic breakdown of concrete sidewalk: weathering as a measure of durability.

There are instances in certain landscape projects where the design process can be considered to have been carried on during the implementation phase on the construction site. The designer executes changes to the design due to site conditions or alterations to the original design proposal for aesthetic, material, economic, or programmatic reasons. Here, the reselection of materials or alterations to landscape elements or forms leads to a reevaluation or redesign of the approach to durability. The relationship between the landscape design proposal and its future durability is one where the weathering represents a supporting aspect of the conceptual idea or ideas.

Approach 2: Weathering to Durability

In this approach, the projected weathering pattern of the landscape project becomes one of the initial conceptual drivers of the project, leading eventually to the completed built design work. It starts with a set of weathering concepts concerned with how landscape materials can change or break down and then develops them, moving in size and resolution from small elements to the entire landscape project.

This approach requires, as its starting point, a single design idea, or set of ideas, that has been conceived concerning the projected weathering patterns of the landscape materials. The conventional process outlined in Approach 1 is, therefore, reversed. Instead of approaching landscape development from landscape concept to the built form, it starts at an intimate scale of a single or group of conceptual weathering ideas and landscape forms and then moves and develops to a larger scale, from the part to the whole. This approach proposes that the basic nature of the weathering of landscape materials and assemblies is found within a fragment of the whole landscape and that these material forms become generators for the entire project. From this starting point, these detail forms or detail parts are assembled or reconfigured in various ways, according to site, program, or design aesthetics. What is significant here is the way these details support the evolution of the total project, the relationship between the individual parts and the whole, and the relationship between the parts (how they are configured, the strategy of their assembly); these become the main conceptual idea of the project.

Some of the issues at stake here are the means by which the conceptual ideas in weathering can be expanded. What are the limits and boundaries of expansion and scale change? Can approaches to landscape weathering be conceived at the scale of a single element, for example, a crushed-stone surface or a brick wall, and then expanded to encompass larger features in size across a whole site?

Approach 3: Integrative

The third approach combines both previous approaches to create a multi-scaled and interconnected process. Here, considerations of weathering at the initial scale and durability on the larger site are carried out simultaneously. The ultimate goal in developing aspects of weathering and durability together is to create a unified and integrated built design proposal.

Summary

It is difficult to separate the subject of landscape weathering from landscape design and, specifically, the landscape design process. Designers spend an inordinate amount of time in refining and developing the individual form and expression of landscape materials and elements to take account of the effects of climatic change and human use. This has enabled their work to be of such a consistently high standard over time regardless of project type, program, budget, location, or materials selected. The following summary statements regarding the conception and evolution of built landscape form act as a summary of Part One.

- It is as important to consider durability as it is to design and construct well.

  We cannot design well if the way weathering and durability are considered is not an active part of how we organize and achieve the original design intentions. It is in this idea with the interrelation of design and construction processes where the potential and, ultimately, the form, beauty, and significance of future built landscape space lies. It addresses a concern for the relationship in landscape architecture between landscape and materials, how things are conceived in design, and how they are finally executed on site.

- The care and attention with which landscape materials and landscape forms are shaped, articulated, and made for weathering over time is part of the meaning of landscape durability.

  How the landscape architect conceives and ultimately develops the built landscape, either through shaping on paper with sketches and drawings or with models or mockups, is of primary importance to the final interpretation. Meaning can be found in how an artifact was brought into being, not only through the act of construction, but as a design activity considering the project over time. In short, in the fashioning of an approach to durability, the landscape architect is attributing meaning to each part, through material selection and choice of material finishes and assemblies, whether they are made deliberately or not. In addition, and more important, dura-bility in design is seen not only as the means by which built landscapes are achieved but also as one of the central design concerns of the field as contemporary built work continues to deteriorate rapidly.

- Research into weathering and durability in landscape architecture needs to evolve from sustained efforts to monitor and comprehend existing built landscapes, as well as investigations into new and emerging materials and assemblies.

  Efficient study of weathering might be better suited to focusing on a more limited palette of commonly used materials while deepening an under-standing of their durable possibilities, rather than broadening the selection of materials while working superficially with all of them.

In Part Two, we will look at examples of contemporary projects and landscape architects that represent a range of individual interpretations of these basic approaches and comments.

3. INTRODUCTION TO CASE STUDIES

I have always been intrigued by the idea of weathering because it's one part of the design process that we cannot really control—or can we? So therefore I like to think of that ahead of time rather than later in a project.

(Cheryl Barton, personal communication)

The twelve landscape architectural case studies in Part Two will compare the possibilities, strengths, constraints, and weaknesses of these approaches to weathering and durability in a landscape design project or projects and, by doing so, provide an insight into the motivations and available working practices of landscape design practitioners.

Aspects of Weathering and Durability in Landscape Design Practice

For the student and young design practitioner, it illustrates the types of material knowledge and site experience that has been gained over years of professional work and how it is applied in a variety of project types, as shown in the pedestrian wooden walkway over a stormwater collection and diversion landform illustrated in Figure 3.6, and at a range of scales.

Comments by each practitioner confirm that exposure to the subject of landscape weathering started early in their careers, and that knowledge still continues to accrue and evolve today with each project that is undertaken. In addition, the structure and methodology of the case studies will serve as a basis for students to carry out their own studies into weathering and durability in the built landscape.

Figure 3.6. Wooden path over a stormwater basin, Private summer retreat, western Maine. (Courtesy of Michael Blier/LAND-WORKS Studio, Inc.)

The Use of the Case Study in Landscape Architecture Durability

As background information to Part Two, it is worth noting that the case study has not been an integral part of instruction and practice in weathering and durability within landscape design and construction. This is due to the following:

- The nature of landscape work and the length of time to achieve completion or intended maturity in a built work of landscape design.
- Lack of ongoing postoccupancy evaluations of completed projects as part of normal full service between a landscape architect and a client.
- Absence of available comparative and comprehensive data on the documentation, implementation, and maintenance of landscape architectural projects by professional bodies such as the ASLA.

Selection of Weathering Case Study Designers and Projects

There are thousands of built landscape projects carried out by numerous landscape architects that could form suitable subjects for case studies. They are located throughout the country and represent a range of landscape design work, from the scale of a public park to the smallest landscape space, whether street, square, or public or private garden. In addition, they are sited in varying climatic and cultural regions. The authors of these vary from sole practitioners carrying out all aspects of the design process and working in relative isolation to designers who are part of large multidisciplinary practices. To narrow the choice of projects to illustrate and compare, the following criteria were applied:

- Access to the original designer(s) of the landscape project to discuss and review the background, development, and ongoing maintenance and aspects of the built landscape.

  This was necessary to identify, from a primary source, the evolution of the built landscape project and to discuss the decisions that were made in establishing material choices and other aspects of the durability of the built work. In addition, aspects of the project that were never realized or were altered in mid-development could be examined. The study of these design ideas is as important as those that were finally implemented. It illustrates the search for a suitable response and design expression of weathering and durability under the constraints of budget, codes and regulations and in some cases, a client's preferences or prejudices, all valid concerns of the professional environment in which a designer works.

- Project work had to have been implemented by the designer in the last twenty years and represent the designer's intentions regarding how weathering and durability are addressed through built landscape work.

  The projects and their methods of working fall within the same general time period of implementation and within similar forms of professional practice and construction procedures.

- Each project had to present the highest level of design excellence and attention to quality in terms of the selection of landscape materials and elements.

  The designers selected or identified the projects themselves during conversations with the author. In a number of cases, a group of their projects were identified by the landscape architect as representing the general approach to the subject of weathering in their built work.

- Written, drawn, and photographic project information had to be available from the resources and archives of design offices.

  The background studies, sketches, and completed documentation of the projects, including progress site photographs, are necessary to illustrate the detail working methods and interim phases of the project, which cannot be traced by looking at the final project.

In creating an initial list of designers and their built projects, no attempt was made to deliberately search for and highlight obscure or previously unpublished landscape built projects. For that matter, designers and projects that were well known through constant exposure in magazines and design monographs were not dismissed simply on these grounds. Landscape architects and built landscape projects whose planning ideas and design ideas had already been documented in modest depth were ideal subjects. In addition, the selected landscape architects generally represented a generation of designers who are in the middle period of their design careers, having built an initial body of work, and are now starting to expand their design practice in scale and scope of project rather than through size of office personnel. While a number of the built works may be recognizable through photographic images (usually taken just after implementation was completed), many have not been seen before—for example, temporary works such as art installations that have subsequently been removed or destroyed or projects that continue to be in private ownership such as residential gardens or estates.

What was of greater significance in the selection of designers and their projects was the variety and concern for the passage of time in their projects, their interest in weathering as an opportunistic and positive aspect of their design work, and an ability to work with the many forms of durability in the built landscape.

Method of Presentation

The method of presenting the case studies is intended to respond to the individual approaches of the landscape architects to the issues of weathering and durability in their landscape design work. While they deliberately vary in scope and scale, the case studies are, however, limited in terms of their type of work: They are parks, plazas, or gardens; they are located in urban settings; and they have been carried out entirely by landscape architects from within the private sector.

Any selection will almost certainly fail to include familiar works by a known designer or will include projects that, in the opinion of some, should not warrant inclusion. Many of our more familiar designers or design practices are not represented here, or if they are, the project that was selected is not considered their most significant work. The distribution of projects geographically does not cover large areas of the profession and the country. Offices in the public sector are not represented, as are also the large areas of landscape work that come under the heading of preservation and conservation. It was not the author's intention to exclude or include examples purely on the need to cover every part of the country or every form of work currently carried out by the landscape profession. Instead, there was a careful selection and matching of a range of landscape architects and design approaches to weathering, which would represent for a student or young professional a series of models or exemplars from which they could start to study and develop their own individual methods of working. Also, in time, each young professional would be able to develop his or her own list of approaches based on regional, cultural, or personal interests. It should be noted that it is not intended that these represent, by their selection, the best or the only approaches that are present in landscape architecture at this time or that there are not inconsistencies where the final built work in these case studies does not weather according to the original expectations of the designer and the client. In fact, the most instructive for this subject are where there exists a tension in site design and landscape materials and form between what is desired over time and what is actually possible.

Understanding the regional aspects of weathering in landscape architecture is paramount, as are also concerns for how the durable landscapes under study relate to the larger built environment. The professional practice of landscape architecture has the ability now to extend to wider geographical areas and cross national and international boundaries. It is the hope of the author that a significant increase in case studies of weathering and durability from all regions of the country and sectors of the profession will arise, building into a more comprehensive ongoing collection of work from which all professionals can study and draw inspiration, irrespective of their own scale of operations. This collection will, of course, be open ended as built work continues to expand.

The Structure of the Part Two Case Studies

Each case study comprises seven parts, although the amount of attention to each part will vary according to the designer, the project type, and the available documentation. They are as follows:

- Title
- Project information
- Project description
- Interview with the designer
- Images
    Implementation documentation
    Site implementation
    Postimplementation change and maintenance

Title
This part identifies the main characteristic of the approach to weathering and durability related to the range of approaches and themes described in Part One.

Project Background
This includes a written description of the project, the site, and its location, the program, the client organization or authority, the composition of the design team and consultants, and the construction and completion dates. In addition, any formal alterations or additions to the original design are identified.

Project Description
A selection of projects and images are taken from each designer's own exhaustive collection. Of particular interest are the exchanges between designers and manufacturers or contractors on the nature, specification, and durability of landscape materials, particularly those that require close attention because of their complexity, use of new materials, or need for specialized connections and finishes. In addition, this section refers to previous design works that have attempted to address certain issues of weathering and have been monitored and evaluated.

Interview with the Designer
The author carried out interviews with each designer over a two-year period. Follow-up phone calls were also made to clarify certain issues brought up during the interview discussions. It is important to note that the

interviews have been edited to most clearly represent the designer's point of view. The interview focuses on three questions: What is their understanding of weathering and durability in the built landscape? How do they approach these issues in their landscape design work? Why do they consider it significant in an understanding of contemporary landscape architecture? The results include discussion of previous design influences and comments on the construction processes, environmental and ecological design practices, and legal and professional issues arising from the implementation of built landscape work

Images

IMPLEMENTATION DOCUMENTATION
The precise communication of the information that enables the design work to be executed in the field is illustrated in a selection of pertinent construction drawings at a variety of scales. These include hand-drafted sketches, computer images, and combinations of both.

SITE IMPLEMENTATION
Central to an understanding of the implementation process is documentation of the daily and monthly field procedures through photographic records. These portray the extent of progress in terms of a general sequential group of dated images taken at regular intervals every week or ten days over the whole site area; a specific record of a particular element under construction on site, from inception to completion; or an account of decisions made on site. This includes work to be removed that was not according to the specifications or material mockups made on site.

POSTIMPLEMENTATION CHANGE AND MAINTENANCE
Records of subsequent site visits after occupancy to view the physical conditions and use of the space are outlined. Since the project was occupied, changes may have occurred to use, fabric, or material qualities of the site. Some of these are part of the daily wear and tear of a landscape space; others are more serious, requiring new design work, alterations to the built fabric, or the subtraction of existing elements and the addition of new parts. These are documented as appropriate in relationship to the original implemented project.

4. CLASSROOM ASSIGNMENTS

These exercises form part of a series of assignments to be carried out within the structure of a course or studio on landscape architectural design, or as part of a course on landscape construction or landscape technology.

EXERCISE 3: RESEARCHING DESIGN APPROACHES TO DURABILITY

1. Create a design case study for one selected built landscape within your locality or region. Select a project carried out by a local landscape architect or landscape design office. Follow the structure established for the case studies in this chapter. Interview the landscape architect and, where possible, the individuals involved with the project design. These include the contractor, the client, owner, local site inspector, users, and those who maintain the project. Also, follow the development of the built project through the stages of implementation and document on site intentional and unintentional changes and alterations to the built fabric after completion.

   The aim of this assignment is to clearly establish how the decisions regarding design and weathering were made; what the durability concerns of the client, designer, contractor, and user were; and how the current project reflected the design project as initially documented by construction drawings and specifications? Landscape projects by the same or a number of offices, public or private, can be compared in the classroom.

2. Identify and document the weathering of a single built element in the landscape, for example, a surface type, transition, or site boundary from across a range of landscape work: public garden, commercial plaza, community park, or waterfront terrace.

   Examine how the selection of materials, the scale and form of the landscape element, and the weathering type are altered according to the project type. Do the forms of weathering appear across all project types or are they specific to only one?

3. Locate in the field or develop in the classroom a landscape element that adds to, or modifies, an existing built condition in a local landscape space. The approach is to be based on *one* of the following approaches: The landscape form can be either an existing landscape material or element that is required to be extended or increased in size with the use of a similar set of materials and finishes *or* an existing landscape element that is to be modified with the use of a new set of materials.

   The intention is for landscape designers to become familiar with the variation resulting from landscape materials and elements. Which design approach to durability is appropriate? How does the design approach protect the integrity of the existing built form?

4. Carry out a series of short design exercises for a single landscape element, for example, a bridge, seating area, or building entrance in your

locale. Using an "open" approach to selecting landscape materials and generating landscape form, propose alternate patterns of durability or time periods for the same landscape element.

Compare and contrast the results in terms of their ability to generate original landscape forms and their relationship to the selection of landscape materials. Is the combination of certain materials more appropriate to particular periods of durability in built landscape work? What materials are these and how do they operate singly and with others?

NOTES

Siza, Alvaro (1988). "On Materials." In W. Wang, ed. *Alvaro Siza: Figures and Configurations, Buildings and Projects, 1986–1988.* New York: Rizzoli.

Hodge, Brooke, ed. (1989). *Design with the Land: Landscape Architecture of Michael Van Valkenburgh.* New York: Princeton Architectural Press.

Van Valkenburgh, Michael (1986). "Notations of Nature's Processes." *Landscape Architecture*, Vol. 76, No. 1.

Landscape Architectural Design Case Studies

P art Two addresses, through the works and words of contemporary landscape architects, the issues, ideas, and approaches to weathering and durability drawn from contemporary practice over the last ten years. They are selected primarily for their application to a range of design concepts and principles to built landscape design work and reflect the ways by which they have weathered and changed over time. Each case study starts with an introduction to the project's background, reviewing the designers' intentions, the consultants involved and data from the project files where appropriate. Interviews with the designers will be illustrated with site photographs, drawings, models, and/or sketches from the period of design development. A sequence will document changes to the project over time, including photographic sequences from initial completion to current conditions and analysis and discussion of the relationship to the concepts and principles of weathering and durability. Of particular interest in the interviews with the landscape architects is discussion on the interrelationship between conceptual landscape ideas and the concerns of durability expressed through materials. In addition, individual views on the subject of landscape weathering and durability are shown through comments on the role of durability in daily design practice and the sources and influences of material weathering. They show how these issues can be overcome to produce exemplary built landscape work of the highest order.

Case Studies

CHAPTER

4

In this chapter, a range of contemporary landscape architects from private design practice are interviewed individually and asked to discuss how they value the subject of weathering and durability—what it means to them, why they consider it significant in making landscape projects, how it influences their design work and practice, and at what point(s) in the design process do considerations of the permanence of a design project occur. Through the introduction of a single project or type of project from their portfolio of built work, the selected landscape architects present a broad range of attitudes to, and interpretations and strategies for, addressing weathering and durability through their landscape design work, and they demonstrate a series of design proposals for projects that range from the temporary installation to the private garden, the public plaza, the restored and the reclaimed landscape, and, finally, permanent memorials—all projects that bring their own criteria of material use, program, and expectations for longevity.

1. INTRODUCTION

Designers and Projects

The following projects were selected as case studies for this book, based on the criteria outlined at the end of Chapter 3. The landscape architect, project name, location, and design office (where appropriate) are identified.

A. **Title: EXPIRATION DATE**
Landscape Architect: Julie Bargmann
Project: Vintondale Colliery Park Reclamation, Vintondale, Pennsylvania
Design Office: D.I.R.T. Studio, Charlottesville, Virginia

B. **Title: CONSTRUCTING MEMORY**
Landscape Architect: Cheryl Barton, FASLA, FAAR
Project: A Memorial to Rosie the Riveter, Richmond, California
Design Office: Office of Cheryl Barton, San Francisco, California

C. **Title: THE PERSISTENCE OF SPATIAL STRUCTURE**
Landscape Architect: Edward L. Blake, Jr., FASLA
Project: Mid-America All-Indian Center, Wichita, Kansas
Design Office: Oblinger-Smith Corporation and Edward L. Blake, Jr., Mississippi (now as the Landscape Studio, Hattiesburg).

D. **Title: THE READJUSTED SCALES OF DURATION**
Landscape Architect: Michael Blier, ASLA
Project: Maine Re-Creation/Recreation: A Private Summer Retreat, Western Maine
Design Office: Landworks, Salem, Massachusetts

E. **Title: WORKING MATERIALS**
Landscape Architect: Eric Fulford, FAAR, RLA
Project: Congressional Medal of Honor Memorial, Indianapolis, Indiana
Design Office: NINebark, Inc., Indianapolis, Indiana

F. **Title: DIMENSIONS OF PROCESS AND CHANGE**
Landscape Architect: Mary Margaret Jones, FASLA
Project: Crissy Field Tidal Marsh Restoration, San Francisco, California
Design Office: Hargreaves Associates, San Francisco, California

G. Title: AESTHETICS OF CULTURAL WEATHERING
Landscape Architect: Mikyoung Kim, ASLA
Projects: Moylan Elementary School Playground, Hartford, Connecticut
   Courtyard and Meditation Labyrinth, Chester, Connecticut
Design Office: Office of Mikyoung Kim, Brookline, Massachusetts

H. Title: URBAN LEGACIES
Landscape Architect: Elizabeth Mossop
Project: Cook+Phillip Park, Sydney, Australia
Design Office: Spackman+Mossop, Sydney, Australia

I. Title: EVOLVING ECONOMIES
Landscape Architect: Margie Ruddick
Project: Casa Cabo, Cabo San Lucas, Mexico
Design Office: Margie Ruddick, Landscape Architect, Philadelphia,
   Pennsylvania

J. Title: MATURING PRACTICES
Landscape Architect: Peter Lindsay Schaudt, ASLA
Project: Advantica Plaza and Park, Spartanburg, South Carolina
Design Office: Office of Peter Lindsay Schaudt, Chicago, Illinois

K. Title: PERPETUAL MATERIAL
Landscape Architect: Ken Smith, ASLA
Project: Aluminum Garden, New York, New York
Design Office: Office of Ken Smith, New York, New York

L. Title: COMPRESSED
Landscape Architect: H. Keith Wagner, ASLA
Project: "Compressed": A Temporary Landscape Installation,
   Cazenovia, New York
Design Office: Office of H. Keith Wagner, Burlington, Vermont

EXPIRATION DATE

Figure 4.1. Mountain slope of waste bony material. Vintondale Colliery Park Reclamation, Vintondale, Pennsylvania. (Courtesy of Julie Bargmann.)

Project Information

Project:	Vintondale Colliery Park Reclamation
Location:	Vintondale, Pennsylvania
Landscape Architect:	D.I.R.T. Studio, Charlottesville, Virginia
Project designer:	Julie Bargmann
Artist:	Stacy Levy
Historian:	T. Allan Comp, Director, Southwestern Pennsylvania Heritage Preservation Commission
Hydrogeologist:	Robert Deason, EarthTech, Inc.
Funding:	U.S. Environmental Protection Agency, Office of Surface Mining, and Heinz Endowments

PROJECT DESCRIPTION

The Vintondale site is situated on thirty-five acres of reclaimed mine land next to the South Branch of Blacklick Creek. A washery, power plant, and a battery of 152 coke ovens once stood on this site. The Ebensburg and Blacklick Railroad, a branch of the Pennsylvania Railroad, bordered the site. Today, the riverbed is blanketed with orange sediment from abandoned mine drainage and the streets are lined with dilapidated houses. Hundreds of abandoned coal mines and mounds of mine refuse (called "bony" piles) continue to poison southwestern Pennsylvania with deadly discharges of acid mine drainage (AMD). AMD forms when rainwater and groundwater absorb the minerals exposed by the mining process. AMD drains into streams and rivers, killing all life-forms by raising the acidity level and suffocating the lower ends of the food web under a rust-colored layer of metals (nicknamed "yellow boy"). In Pennsylvania alone, AMD pollutes more than 3400 miles of waterways. In Vintondale, Pennsylvania, Eastern European immigrants joined American labor forces to extract coal in miles of underground tunnels and to process tons of coke at the Vintondale Colliery. Today, all that remains of the ambitious coal works are barren lowlands of mine refuse, abandoned uplands in early succession, and a giant bony pile (see Figure 4.2). A fluorescent deposit of "yellow boy" leaking out of old Mine No. 6 cuts across fields littered with railroad skeletons and ghosts of mine buildings. The existing topography of Vintondale's thirty-five-acre site is carved to form a passive AMD treatment system, a series of retention basins, and constructed wet-

Figure 4.2. Existing site waste bony material. Vintondale Colliery Park Reclamation, Vintondale, Pennsylvania. (Courtesy of Julie Bargmann.)

lands. Situated between Blacklick Creek and the regional Ghost Town Rail Trail, the proposed landscape has three parts: the Treatment Garden with pH ponds and the Litmus Garden; the Emergent History Wetlands; and the Community Uplands, which include picnic and play areas.

In the Treatment Garden,

> AMD flows through the pH Ponds, a series of S.A.P.S. (Sequential Alkaline Producing Systems) and settling basins. Cascading over the Limestone Spillways, the metals (iron, manganese, and aluminum) settle out of solution and encrust the light gray limestone with "yellow boy". The changing water color reflects the progress of treatment in each basin, from acidic orange to pea green to alkaline blue green. After flowing through the two wetland areas, the cleansed water returns to Blacklick Creek. To create the "final rinse" of the AMD treatment system, the flood plain is recontoured into the clarification marsh and emergent wetlands. Earthen and planted forms emerge as footprints of former mine buildings. A long plinth of the excavated soil and bony is inscribed with black discs recalling the 152 coke ovens that stretched 1400 feet across the Vinton mine works. Monitors at the Acid Basin display the deadly acidic level of the AMD at 2.9 pH. The cleansing process is registered by the Litmus Gardens: alternating rows of native trees and shrubs whose seasonal colors of bark, foliage, and fruit vivify the treatment sequence, progressing from deep reds and oranges, yielding to cooler hues of green and blue.

> *(Adapted from Bargmann and Levy, 1998)*

In addressing the weathering and durability issues of this site with its particular landscape materials and applications, it is necessary to look beyond the normal ways and methods of observing, describing, or understanding the actions of climate and change over time. It can be said that this type of landscape project establishes time and change as less an external design component and embeds it as the core factor in how design decisions are to be made. This directly influences what expected alterations to the site and site materials are not only going to occur but are necessary to happen in order for the site and its processes of reclamation and regeneration to continue to function. Here, the issue of who is responsible for establishing the durability of the project is answered clearly: the designer, informed by the scientists, historians, and artists. In reading the interview with the landscape architect, note the continued reference to the driving processes at work on the site and the material design choices by the designer as a reflection of these processes rather than for their own sake. For the young landscape architect or student this design approach will become more common in professional practice as landscape architects are required to address the legacy of postindustrial sites. The issues of weathering and durability will focus not on "expiration dates" but on how designers define the processes and endpoints of built landscape work.

INTERVIEW WITH THE DESIGNER

Discussion with the landscape architect Julie Bargmann took place on June 24, 2002, by telephone and April 28, 2003, in Charlottesville, Virginia. Interview participants are identified as Julie Bargmann (JB) and author (Q).

Q:

Which designer made you first aware that the notion of change was embedded in landscape work?

JB:

One who immediately comes to mind is Dead Fred (Frederick Law Olmsted) as well as the value of artist Robert Smithson's reading of Olmsted. It is all perfectly obvious that Olmsted was talking about absolute change and the whole process of building. Everyone forgot what Olmsted was all about, form as a verb, rather than form as a noun, and we needed Robert Smithson to come along and re-read Olmsted's work and put the verb back in it so to speak.

Q:

Name a project where you saw Olmsted's work doing just that.

JB:

I really flashed to Central Park when you said that, and seeing some of the reconstruction. They had unearthed a bridge where sediment had accumulated over time. It was just so cool to see them unearth it, all muddied and messed up.

Q:

What interested you more wasn't the archeology, rather it was the notion of a site that has been evolving in time, and while it had sediment layered on top of it, they can scrape it away and the project keeps on going—is that true?

JB:

Correct, an ongoing process! It was not the archeology, nor the image of this bridge, it was what Olmsted would have done himself—let's get the bulldozers out and start working. Well, Olmsted did not have bulldozers, so let's get the mules out!

Q:

With that tradition, why do you think there is so little writing or interest in the subject of the permanence or the durability of landscapes?

JB:

One thought that I had about this absence (along with many other designers and cultural critics) has to do with the image of the built landscape.

Landscapes have become an image, particularly a still photographic image, and many designers are more concerned with the way their projects look.

Q:

The perfect camera shot?

JB:

The glamour design magazines just perpetuated that, and all of a sudden the landscape became static because it was created as such (within the design process).

Q:

Did this come from the bias of modernism towards the perfect form and image of, for example, the white concrete residence on the hillside?

JB:

I don't really know how much of that is true. Le Corbusier said that the box on the hillside was really a machine, breathing and churning and belching, and I like to think he thought the same about the landscape in and around the building. I think modernist designers did have more understanding of the land than they were given credit for, but they did not necessarily know how to integrate the two. It's the continuum of the landscape, although landscape architects use different media and configure different spaces. I think modernists were onto that, but I don't think they quite got there with an understanding of what site systems bring.

Q:

Do you think we are there now in terms of a landscape breathing, snorting, belching, sweating?

JB:

We are getting there. Most people think of that expression in a bad way, say, in a landfill, but that's a process, too. I think we are getting there through the environmental crisis and through people's awareness rather than design practice. When you are trying to understand natural processes and systems, it will take another giant step to have people say, "Let's also look at the other nasty processes, the ones that have gone awry."

Q:

Do you distinguish in your own design work between a project that is temporary and one that is permanent, leaving aside the nature of the commission?

JB:

I would not distinguish between them. I see more of a continuum in a landscape that is constructed to last a certain amount of time—I don't want to say permanent, as there is no such thing. There are different clocks on the site, and some are going to be shorter and operate like a sweeping second hand and others are going to be very slow, like geological time. You have to ask: What is the situation in terms of the site itself and the project and what kind of clock is it asking for and what is appropriate? A temporary project I would just call a short-time clock.

Q:

There is no difference (between temporary and permanent). Therefore, they are just different renderings of an idea about a continuum?

JB:

That's what drives everybody absolutely batty. It's very interesting to see how people react to Spiral Jetty going under water; some people it drove absolutely nutty, like uh-oh the work is gone. No—the work is better than ever—you still have design critics going on pilgrimages to see it and I did, too. I was so delighted when I went to a dull architecture conference, did my paper, heard that the lake was down and the jetty was just cresting out of the water, and I made a beeline out there—it's just incredible. The other thing is what the aerial images did not capture of that work. If you go there, just out of your peripheral vision is an old industrial jetty in ruin.

Q:

Which never comes up in the published images?

JB:

Exactly the same angle as the stem of Spiral Jetty, so everybody says, "Well, why is it here?" But you go there and you know exactly why it is there, because Spiral Jetty has another timepiece next to it.

Q:

A measure against it?

JB:

How you measure or register the phenomena is just a different way of saying, how do you show these different clocks?

Q:

Continuing the "clock" analogy, is the context in which a piece of work happens important to you?

JB:

Yes, there are already clocks operative there—multiple clocks, workaday clocks, nine to five clocks, sediment clocks.

Q:

How do you enact that idea in practice?

JB:

You do not accept that there is such a thing as a master plan in the first place—it's just bullshit. That static image is still getting landscape architects in trouble. There is a reuse plan called a master plan, and they take this pretty picture of what this landscape is going to be—in your wildest dreams! What is wrong with showing that landscape over time? It may not ever be that pretty little picture.

Q:

The single fixed image in time again?

JB:

I do not accept a single plan at all. If you ask what year it is, they go, "Well, mmm.... It's really all these different times collapsed into this one plan; now that's interesting, take it apart—what's 2005, what's 2008?

Q:

What happens when 2004 changes something?

JB:

It might have to change, oh-no! That's why I get pretty adamant when clients ask me for master plans—they are just design frameworks. You have to rewire the site, put the bones in, and just flesh it out.

Q:

How do you conceptualize a project, then?

JB:

I am staring at a scribbling on the wall just now. Industrial sites were wired a certain way, and a lot of times they were wired with interesting flows of raw and manufactured materials. So how do you get the flow of the site going? Do you reuse some of the infrastructure of the industrial past? Do you take more of the flow from the surrounding context of the town and insert it into the site? What forces in the past and present are influencing how it currently flows? How do you reset and rewire the site?

Q:

Let's talk further about the materiality of raw and manufactured materials. How in your own work do you address the physicality of the project?

JB:

Materials per se only represent the processes at work. I am not looking at the materials in themselves. I am looking at the processes that the material embodies. For me, that's how you get away from being overly romantic about ruins. A lot of times making it a ruin or a monument for monument's sake is actually quite patronizing as a designer and destroys the thing.

I want to bring up MASS MoCA (Massachusetts Museum of Contemporary Art)* and the Ford Rouge River Plant because of the issue of being able to appreciate the site traces and the patina of materials.

---

*MASS MoCA is on the site of a twelve-acre complex built in 1872 by an international cloth manufacturer, Arnold Print & Dye Works, in North Adams, Massachusetts. The twenty-seven buildings listed on the National Historic Register form an elaborate system of interlocking courtyards and passageways. The site was purchased in 1940 by the Sprague Electric Company, which for the next thirty years was one of the world's most successful producers of high-quality electronic products. MASS MoCA has evolved into a multidisciplinary center for the performing and visual arts.

Q:

Or the misunderstanding of site traces?

JB:

I have to be really careful when I go to industrial sites. The old fence at MASS MoCA, for example, looked very cool to me, but to the town, it represented a very intense strike, a labor dispute, so it had a completely different meaning for them. I had to stop being the artist and say, "Wait a second, what does that fence mean?" It's not about the thing in itself; it concerns what it's associated with.

I got into trouble with the architects because they wanted to import a lot of outside influences to the site. The project was basically how do you take the landscape at the former Sprague Electric Factory, North Adams, Massachusetts, of twenty-seven buildings that formed four primary courtyards and make public space. Incredible—I mean you really don't have to do too much!

Q:

What did they originally make there?

JB:

They made electrical components, and before that it had a history as a mill. The site is twelve acres smack in town—a pretty intimate factory as far as that scale goes. It's a relatively small precinct within the city. People said, "Here's these great volumes to exhibit all this large scale art from the 1970s that's currently in storage. Let's take this material out of storage and exhibit it." I came in late in the game through the chairman of the foundation who was not satisfied with the way that the site was being developed. So he brought Ellen Zimmerman and I in to look at it. Basically, the architect didn't want to play, but I stuck with it. Ellen quit the first day. I asked the question: What is the industrial landscape—what's the nature of it, the spatial qualities, the materiality, what is it?

Q:

How did this eventually evolve over time into the new cultural center?

JB:

I've tried to establish a very distinct pattern of found materials that is about the site traces that are full of time. What I was trying to do was go and put my finger on each one of these pulses or clocks. I wasn't looking for the ideal image to bring onto the site—what is the vocabulary of an art museum overlaid with the vocabulary of this productive landscape. The other thing in this approach was recognizing that the time that was embedded on site was not purely a material concern; there were also social and psychological issues that you can read into these things.

Q:

How would you read these issues?

JB:

That's where you're an absolute slave to having to do your homework; you have to do your research; you have to get people talking—to do the oral history. That's when we found out that the fence that I was completely enamored with was all about a workers' strike that took place there.

Q:

Keeping people out, more than people in?

JB:

It was all about control. It goes beyond any kind of visual design issue.

Q:

What, as a designer, do you do about it? How do you say, "I have an interest in this fence and its material, but it has all these other associations"? Do you back away?

JB:

No, don't interpret it and don't put up a plaque. I will also not do the knee-jerk thing of assuming it has to come down. In the Ford Plant project at River Rouge, Michigan, the entire area housing the coke ovens was steeped in the social and cultural history of the plant and the association for the present and former workers of the remaining coke ovens as artifacts. If you looked at them just structurally and historically in terms of how coke ovens go, they were not great shakes—the run-of-the-mill coke ovens. However, if you put them in the context of the Ford River Rouge, as being part of the very first integrated manufacturing plant, there are no others like them on the earth. That's basically the argument we were trying to make with their environmental office that was getting pressure from the EPA to just demolish them. I mean, no question, "hog and haul." Meanwhile, I was collecting oral histories in a rather informal way. I was pummeling people for information when we were walking through the site. From generations of workers, I heard story after story about those coke ovens and how they were the beginning point for many families and how they would over time move up in the factory. The guy who's in charge of the River Rouge Plant right now, he started on the coke ovens; the bus driver from the airport told me a story about them. Everybody also remembers the powerhouse, with the stacks that the photographer Charles Sheeler* made infamous. Writers say it was Henry Ford's favorite thing—for him, it was the powerhouse and the symbol of what he'd built. Sometime in 1997–1998 an explosion in the power-

---

*Charles Sheeler (1883–1965) is recognized as one of the founders of American modernism and one of the master photographers of the twentieth century. His work includes a series of views dating from 1927 of the Ford Motor Company's River Rouge Plant.

house killed six, so the powerhouse is slated for demolition because of that moment in its history. Wait a second, you know, that is one moment in 100-year history, and those stacks are a visual and symbolic continuum from all around. That's what the huge debate on site is about just now; there's the environmental criteria for removal and we said, "Where is the criteria for the curatorial understanding of the site!"

Q:
They couldn't just take down part of it, open it up?

JB:
You get into that dilemma that I run into all the time—the lack of differen-tiation. In our plans we showed the demolition of the byproducts area and retaining the coke ovens and the batteries. It isn't either–or; it's curating.

Q:
Let's talk about a piece of work you are doing just now in which all these issues—clocks, time, process, and materials—are evident in your day-to-day design practices. What is the relationship between the conception of these ideas and how they are actually carried out at the reclamation project in Vintondale, Pennsylvania?

Vintondale Colliery Park Reclamation, Vintondale, Pennsylvania

Q:
Can you briefly describe the context for the project? (See Figure 4.3.)

JB:
Here, we dealt with a site that was demolished—just plowed to the ground. There was very little evidence of the past 100 years, in terms of

Figure 4.3. AMD. Vintondale Colliery Park Reclamation, Vintondale, Pennsylvania. (Courtesy of Julie Bargmann.)

the coke works. The cleansing part initiated it. The historian called me and said, "Listen, part of the legacy of this coal mining district is acid mine drainage (AMD)." I said, "Absolutely, it is." He introduced this great idea of "finishing the work"—I would call it "continuing the work"—and now it's our turn to do something about the acid mine drainage, which was a process that the mining companies knew about. The tunnels were going to fill up with groundwater and spew out nasty stuff (AMD), but it was more important to make steel to win the war. The real driving force of the project was this way of introducing a new process of production into the landscape—the production of cleansing AMD. I kept on saying, "How is this different from another passive-treatment system that an engineer or scientist would do?" The difference is we tried to really give form to making the process evident.

Q:

As opposed to just the engineering process?

JB:

Yes, we asked questions of its legibility. Stacy Levy, the artist, and I wanted to make the process legible. What form does that take, how does it show the flow, how does it really show the "yellow boy" material of the AMD?

Q:

So you have built a instrument in the landscape to register this?

JB:

It is a giant apparatus. The key question in this particular landscape is: How do we superimpose this new system of flow and production while recalling past industrial processes. We almost got into fistfights with the historian about how to reconstruct buildings on the site or evoke them. Stacy and I constantly wanted an evocation of these structures, not a literal reconstruction. The original enormous buildings (see Figure 4.4)—the powerhouse, washery, ammonia plant, and the coke ovens were bulldozed. The historian wanted whatever footprints we suspected were beneath this big pile of bony (mining waste) and lime refuse to be accurately rendered. When we created the earth workings and reconfigured the flood plain to be the final rinsing wetlands, our intention was to evoke the scale of labor of the former building structures. The bony was pushed into these earthen forms to be a long, thin evocation of the coke ovens. It also doubled as a hummock in the wetlands and, in time, will become a wildlife habitat. One moment we would be talking science, the next art, then ecology, then history, then economic development—all the components of a complex landscape. We were obsessed with the passive treatment wetland system, the new system we were putting on the site. We were toying with the idea of

Figure 4.4. Historic image of Vintondale colliery buildings. Vintondale Colliery Park Reclamation, Vintondale, Pennsylvania. (Courtesy of Julie Bargmann.)

how were we going to make that whole process visible on the site. We didn't want the treatment system to be a juxtaposition against the past production on the site, a new clock against an old clock. We were basically saying, we are restarting an old one. Stacy and I were interested in the evocation, particularly spatial, of the occupation of this forty-acre site by the coke works over 100 years. How do we evoke any sense of those pasts, that past century of labor on the site? When we anticipated needing to excavate for the treatment wetlands, we said, "Let's basically not count on finding the footprints perfectly, but in fact grade the wetland to leave some evidence of them." With the Sanborn Maps, we figured out, to the best of our ability, the long footprint of the coke ovens, the machinery, to guide the excavation and make this topographic relief in the wetlands. (See Figures 4.5 to 4.8.)

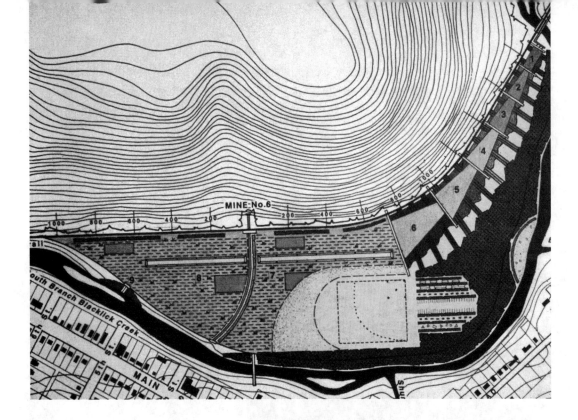

Figure 4.5. Landscape plan with descending litmus ponds. Vintondale Colliery Park Reclamation, Vintondale, Pennsylvania. (Courtesy of Julie Bargmann.)

Figure 4.6. Systems of AMD treatment: pH ponds and limestone spillways. Vintondale Colliery Park Reclamation, Vintondale, Pennsylvania. (Courtesy of Julie Bargmann.)

Figure 4.7. Emergent history wetlands: earthen and planted forms. Vintondale Colliery Park Reclamation, Vintondale, Pennsylvania. (Courtesy of Julie Bargmann.)

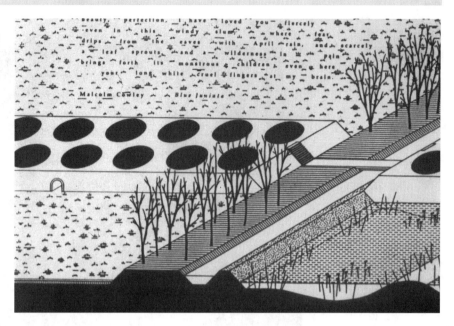

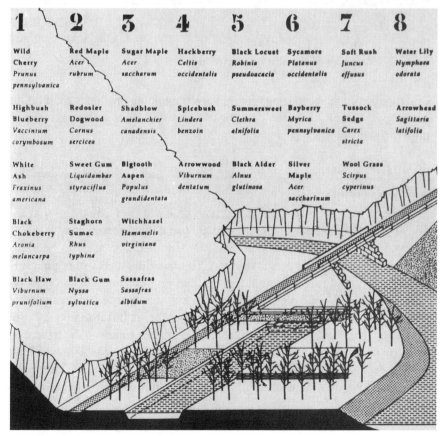

1	2	3	4	5	6	7	8
Wild Cherry *Prunus pennsylvanica*	Red Maple *Acer rubrum*	Sugar Maple *Acer saccharum*	Hackberry *Celtis occidentalis*	Black Locust *Robinia pseudoacacia*	Sycamore *Platanus occidentalis*	Soft Rush *Juncus effusus*	Water Lily *Nymphaea odorata*
Highbush Blueberry *Vaccinium corymbosum*	Redosier Dogwood *Cornus sericea*	Shadblow *Amelanchier canadensis*	Spicebush *Lindera benzoin*	Summersweet *Clethra alnifolia*	Bayberry *Myrica pennsylvanica*	Tussock Sedge *Carex stricta*	Arrowhead *Sagittaria latifolia*
White Ash *Fraxinus americana*	Sweet Gum *Liquidambar styraciflua*	Bigtooth Aspen *Populus grandidentata*	Arrowwood *Viburnum dentatum*	Black Alder *Alnus glutinosa*	Silver Maple *Acer saccharinum*	Wool Grass *Scirpus cyperinus*	
Black Chokeberry *Aronia melancarpa*	Staghorn Sumac *Rhus typhina*	Witchhazel *Hamamelis virginiana*					
Black Haw *Viburnum prunifolium*	Black Gum *Nyssa sylvatica*	Sassafras *Sassafras albidum*					

Figure 4.8. Acid basin and litmus gardens: alternating rows of native trees and shrubs. Vintondale Colliery Park Reclamation, Vintondale, Pennsylvania. (Courtesy of Julie Bargmann.)

Figure 4.9. Litmus ponds under construction. Vintondale Colliery Park Reclamation, Vintondale, Pennsylvania. (Courtesy of Julie Bargmann.)

Q:
This is the last part of the mining operation?

JB:
Exactly. So it's acknowledging that through the mining production the AMD began to be produced, so the cleaning of the AMD water is the next part of the process.

Q:
How do you see the project in fifty years? What's going on—still cleaning?

JB:
It's for perpetuity because the acid mine drainage isn't going to go away. They'll have to clean out the basins that are part of the treatment system and the wetlands will be backwashed. They are designed over time to be inundated and disturbed; it's preset that way. The one thing that I'm hoping survives actually, and this may sound a little perverse, are some of the scars on the landscape. This one big trace of "yellow boy" (AMD) we're channelizing and purposefully hoping to leave a scar. I hope it stays, but it may not. I love this thing that students talked about in one of the studios—an expiration date for memory. I loved that. This landscape is there for however long someone's there to tell those stories, the structure of those mine footprints, and the passive treatment system, but it may get replaced with other stories. (See Figure 4.9.)

Q:

It's, therefore, about the legibility of these processes where the work of landscape architecture lies?

JB:

Yes, and it's not new. I'll never forget when Peter Walker would say, "It's all about making the landscape evident." He looked to artists to inspire him with form (as a noun) to make a landscape evident. I think earlier the landscape was not evident it was just background; he had the guts to say, "Let's give it some legibility, some form." He bulldozed the way clear for others to start to really look at artists' work and look at form as a verb in the landscape.

NOTES

Bargmann, Julie and Stacy Levy (1998). "Testing the Waters." *Landscape Journal*.

CASE STUDY B	CONSTRUCTING MEMORY

Figure 4.10. Detail of structure. Rosie the Riveter Memorial, San Francisco, California. (Courtesy of Office of Cheryl Barton.)

Project Information

Project:	A Memorial to Rosie the Riveter
Location:	Richmond, California
Client:	City of Richmond, Redevelopment Agency
Landscape Architect:	Office of Cheryl Barton
Project designer:	Cheryl Barton, FASLA, FAAR
Project manager:	Zoee Astrachan
Artist:	Susan Schwartzenberg
General Contractor:	Oliver and Company
Landscape Contractor:	Shooter and Butts
Specialty Fabrications:	West Edge Design (steel)
	PMA Photo Metals (steel photoetching)
	Winsor Graphics (porcelain-enameled panels)
	Chapman Monument (sand-etched granite pavers)
Design Phase:	Complete
Date Completed:	October 2000
Project Cost:	$600,000

PROJECT DESCRIPTION

The Rosie the Riveter Memorial, honoring American women's labor during World War II, is the first in the nation to celebrate and interpret women's contributions to the home front. Sited at the location of the former Kaiser Shipyards, the memorial was completed in the summer of 2000 in Rosie the Riveter Memorial Park, in Richmond's Marina Bay neighborhood. The project was dedicated on October 14, 2000. The Memorial sculpture design, by Cheryl Barton, pays homage to the scale at which the women and men at the Kaiser Shipyard worked. A 441-foot walkway, reflecting the length of the liberty ships constructed at the site, includes a home front timeline with quotations from former women shipyard workers. Sculptural elements evoking features of a liberty ship are positioned along the walk and hold porcelain panels with photographs depicting the range of labor women performed. At the water's edge, a lookout leads visitors to a view across the bay to San Francisco's Golden Gate Bridge.

In this project, the recognition, celebration, and cultural associations of a particular external landscape material — stainless steel — is the vehicle for a design exploration of weathering and changes. In particular, the attention paid to the material itself, the patinas, the potential for rusting, and the breakdown of the steel surface with pit marks and imperfections as well as the ideas and associations of the material with the processes of construction and making are explored through one particular historical period. Of interest here is the in-depth research carried out on the material, the processes, and the working conditions as well as the efforts to find a suitable means to memorialize people and events. This presents particular difficulties to the designer in attempting to work in a durable material that will succumb to weathering processes caused by the imperfection of the material while ensuring longevity for the project as a public memorial. The design issues of material selection, the symbolic aspects of the selected material as a substitute for the original material, the need to provide a series of workable public spaces that surround the actual memorial are balanced against the designer's careful understanding of the effects of the passing of time on both the landscape elements and the memory of the event itself. For the younger landscape architect or student, the lessons of this project demonstrate an approach grounded in solid background research that offers sculptural and spatial possibilities as well as a curatorial strategy to the sculpture element. Only in time will we be able to judge whether the projected effects of weathering on the steel's surface will have a detrimental effect on the public's perception of the memorial and, in turn, will devalue the project as a symbol of "constructing memory."

INTERVIEW WITH THE DESIGNER

Discussion with the landscape architect Cheryl Barton took place on June 15, 2001, and April 3, 2003, by telephone. Interview participants are identified as Cheryl Barton (CB) and author (Q).

Q:

Based on your own travels and professional practice what other places or the projects of others have you been drawn to that specifically feature how their landscape changes as central to the project?

CB:

I was greatly influenced by the environmental artists of the late 1960s and early 1970s whose work dealt with the play of many phenomena and weathering, both intentionally and unintentionally. Also, there is the specific issue of patina that I find particularly interesting, and the first place that comes to mind is Ryoanji Temple in Kyoto. The central feature is the raked gravel and the stones. However, my eye kept wandering to the wall surrounding the garden and to the painted stucco wall that was flaking irregularly and deteriorating. In other areas of the wall, moss was literally growing vertically from the wall. It added an extraordinary beauty and resonance to that place. I have always been intrigued by the idea of weathering because it's one part of the design process that we cannot really control—or can we? I like to think about that phenomenon ahead of time rather than later in the design of a project.

Q:

What you were talking about in the Kyoto example is a natural process of staining and moss inhabiting joints. This starts to suggest the question of what is weathering and can we control weathering in any way?

CB:

We can also ask: What outcomes of the design intention can we (as designers) predict? I am interested in places that express a certain geometry that weathering or the evolution of simply plant material completely changes over time. The temporal quality and the marking of time I find extremely evocative. We have the opportunity to play to that "marking"—it's part of our medium.

Q:

How in your own design work is that actually done consciously or in a subliminal way?

CB:

It is conscious to a point—depending on client budget, site characteristics, and so forth. Yet there is a subconscious acceptance that one cannot control deterioration. I used to think about weathering and change much less, but now I am more attuned to it as part of the design process as my work evolves. I have not explored all the ways of controlling it, or thinking about it, or integrating it into the work largely because I don't have the scientific knowledge of how things will weather. It is quite a site-specific phenomenon. For example, if you are working inland as opposed to near the ocean, there are very different forces at work; for that reason, every design is still somewhat of an experiment or a research project for me.

Q:

What sort of research would that be, literally erecting mockups on site and leaving them for a few years?

CB:

That would be a very beneficial demonstration project! I have had fabricators and contractors working with me on such issues as the stability of color in concrete or the character of a weathering rammed earth wall. One contractor, who has done extensive work with very powerful integral color in concrete, has placed samples of color on his shop roof; they have been there since last summer. This experiment happened almost accidentally. We had designed a boldly colored concrete wall for a project that was not constructed due to "value engineering"—a delightful oxymoron. It will be interesting to see the stability of the color after a year or two. Of course, that is a very short period in the entire life of a project. It does, however, provide a datum of the relative stability of that particular blue or yellow over time. Designers need the benefit of hundreds of years of experience—that's why travel and looking at other projects is critical.

Q:

Some people have suggested that weathering has two movements. One is cyclical or seasonal and that brings almost a circular movement, and the other is the linear, cumulative like a patina, accretions, layers on materials or the removal. How do these two movements play for the duration of a project? Are they eternal from the beginning?

CB:

I interpret weathering as the latter. It is part of a patina or palimpsest. Eternal is a big word—I don't necessarily believe that any material we use can be eternal. I like to think of my projects as enduring as opposed to temporal, although I have done temporary installations I do like to think "long term," but I am not sure that eternal is the right word!

Q:

Maybe eternal is a bad choice of term.

CB:

The concept of eternal collides with issues of budget and the kind of extraordinarily tough materials that endure, for example, stone. Public clients such as mine don't always have a budget for stone. The question is: What can be done to concrete to make it eternal?

Q:
What, for you, would be the difference between a temporary project and a project that is not temporary?

CB:
Typically, a designer can be more experimental if a work is temporary; it can be one of the research projects in durability that we spoke about earlier. Temporary installations can give more latitude in the use or range of materials—if one pushes the envelope. Sculpted fabric, glass pellets, "found" materials and objects, painted fiberboard or even cardboard can provide a great range of short-term possibilities. Because most of my work is in the public realm, I provoke the "durability" questions early in the design process. I want to know who will be maintaining the project and what their budgets and technical capabilities are. I make an effort to engage whomever will be involved in long-term maintenance at the very beginning of a project. My intent is to raise the client's awareness of place and elevate the level of commitment to maintenance. I am looking for a "curatorial" attitude toward place. This dialogue also tempers the palette of materials as well as my knowledge about the location and climate of the site.

Q:
Looking at your local geography in San Francisco, what would you categorize as the limits of external built work in terms of weathering?

CB:
What do you mean by limits—elemental forces such as wind, sun, salt or air pollution?

Q:
I was quite surprised when you said "cardboard" as a temporary landscape material. I am interested to know how where someone works affects them as designers and creates limits.

CB:
I have seen—not used—folded cardboard elements used in temporary art installations. When I worked in the eastern United States, the freeze-thaw cycle and an abundance of rain and snow governed my design. Here, in coastal California, I have to design differently. The temperature is milder; the marine environment with constant on-shore winds creates saline conditions in the air and soil. In urban areas, there is the smog, which does both wonderful and nasty things to materials. I have done several projects at the water's edge where one has little control over combinations of salt and pollutants in the air. Depending on the material, these elements either weather, corrode, or add deposits. That process of addition and subtraction is fascinating to me.

Q:
Have you ever deliberately or forcefully made that a central focus of a piece of built landscape work?

CB:
Yes, in the Constructing Memory project north of San Francisco. It is a piece that extends into [and even under] the water at high tide, and over the water at other times. We have deliberately not "finished" the #316L marine stainless steel [a grade of stainless steel that weathers more slowly in coastal environments]. We have not put a high polish on it, nor have we buffed out the imperfections from the mill. It has what is called a "mill finish," with scratches and pockmarks. It is not a completely distressed finish but it has a rougher looking overall surface. That "look" was intentional to this project because it commemorated shipbuilding. I had to convince the client that this was a desirable and symbolic effect and that those scratches are places where the finish is broken and where rust will appear.

Q:
Are you able to control the rust in these limited areas and will it have a controlled marking?

CB:
Yes, the rust will take the form of and enhance the mill marks. We had many intense conversations with materials conservators to let them know that we did not want anyone to polish out these blemishes or sandblast them away. We wanted these nicks and scratches to be as visible as they would be on any worked piece of metal.

Q:
There is a narrow definition of weathering in landscape architecture and most people talk about it in terms of how a finish is altered either for better or worse. But what about the role of cultural weathering?

CB:
I like that terminology. Contemporary design is about preparing ourselves physically (and psychologically) for cultural incidents that are bound to happen, particularly in urban work.

Q:
Is the built landscape, then, a canvas for this form of weathering through preparing surfaces for change through, say, graffiti?

CB:
Yes, in the case of public work. There is another popular form of cultural weathering right now, which is more prevalent than graffiti: skateboarding. This activity is one of the key "weathering factors" for any public design work we do now in San Francisco. It is everywhere, and the impact is extraordinary from skateboarders as well as from others on mountain bikes

with steel wheel axle studs. These popular street activities are very effective at grinding up the "eternal" stone walls we are building! We have just finished a plaza for the Gap on the waterfront in San Francisco. The seat walls are made of black granite, and the plaza's ground surface is constructed of three-inch-thick precast concrete pavers on a pedestal system. Cyclists ride on the top of the walls and, where they land on the plaza, the pavers have cracked because of the continual impact.

Q:

The client is now probably trying to ban activities like that?

CB:

Yes, but these places are difficult to police around the clock. The client initially boarded up the walls, until we could design and install bronze fins in the walls. As a footnote, we learned that there is now a company that makes skateboards as well as skateboard deterrents, playing both sides of the market, as it were!

Q:

However, designers go to an old waterfront and are fascinated because of the rope marks rubbed into the stone edges after hundreds of years of loading and unloading ships. They talk about this evidence of the wearing or working down of the stone edge as an evocative memory of the waterfront and its former activities. Yet will designers ever accept a skateboard working down a stone edge?

CB:

We are not yet that enlightened. Perhaps in a few hundred years!

Q:

Why do we look at the same physical action (working an edge on stone) in these different ways?

CB:

The idea of the palimpsest is something that has motivated me from my earliest awareness of landscapes. I think of landscapes as strata, as a layering of natural and cultural materials and markings. I suppose that skateboarding is simply the newest layer. This new layer will take some time to comprehend or to become romanticized. The passage of time often brings about a romanticizing of the past. Perhaps, this is the reason for the apparent difference in attitude.

Q:

Materials or materiality is a common thread throughout the subject of weathering and the durability of built work. Are you drawn to certain materials for the material itself that you are drawn back to in your design work?

CB:

I have always felt a deep connection to stone. My other interests before landscape architecture were geology and sculpture. Stone is a basic and very tactile material. Metals are also intriguing materials for landscape architects to explore. One of the reasons that the Constructing Memory project was so interesting was that we had to understand the material and its properties and really work at detailing it. We are currently working on another public park (near the bay) with a series of arcing seat walls. Skateboarders will love them! I strongly resisted the notion of eliminating the walls or adding off-the-shelf fins. We are now contemplating clusters of bronze sea creatures—crabs, turtles, octopi—that would be attached to the edges of the wall to discourage skateboarding but permit sitting. The project has a "percent for the arts" requirement and the city client has requested design elements that can be "discovered" by children. We have just identified a local artist who works in bronze—a material that will weather beautifully in the marine conditions at the site. And, as evident with ancient bronze sculptures around the world, the material weathers in a very interesting way over time as it is touched by a human hand.

Q:
There are specialists who spend their lives working with one type of metal or even one way of working with metal or one type of metal finish. Was that your experience on this project?

CB:
As landscape architects, we can collaborate with these specialists, but we must understand and design with their processes in mind. Bronze fabrication is particularly compelling. The making of maquettes and molds, the heating of the crucible, and the pouring of white-hot metal is still a medieval technology.

Q:
What is durability in terms of your design work?

CB:
There are two aspects of durability in my view: the durability of the *material* and the durability of the *idea*. Both are critically important to me. I try to employ the most durable materials with the full understanding that weathering will change these materials in some way. I like to think I am controlling that change, but I am also thrilled by the notion that I don't really have ultimate control. The interest for me is observing this process over time. I return to many of my projects specifically to observe change.

Q:
What are you looking for?

CB:
Principally, I want to see how a particular material expresses (or no longer expresses) my original design *idea*. When one returns to a project and sees that a particular stone that expressed a watercourse has been changed out

for petunias by the new gardener, it is very disturbing. On the other hand, you can go back to the same site and see a concrete wall that has taken on a different color and texture because it has weathered. If that wall was intended to enhance the presence of the structure, for example, the enhancement has intensified. It's thrilling to see; the weathering process has become part of your design. It expands your work in a way that you had not anticipated. As a designer, I want to say, "I meant to do that," but it was done intuitively. Those are the significant moments when design takes you to another dimension. You file it away for the future, calculating how the effect can be replicated.

A Memorial to Rosie the Riveter
San Francisco, California

CB:

This project, which has to do with memory, expresses the memory of place as well as the memory of the inhabitants of a place. The selection of material does two things: It recalls the use of a material from the past, and, in certain ways, it makes it more tactile in the present. It then carries the idea into the future. Obviously, if it's a durable material, the idea will be enduring. I think the choice of materials is an incredibly important decision. Motivating clients to budget or fundraise for certain materials is critical to the formation of the idea that, ultimately, is what interests me in my work. (See Figures 4.11 and 4.12.)

Q:

Do you think it's a very unusual commission in the sense that one could read what it's attempting to memorialize in many different ways? One reading of it would be it is the actions of a particular group of women entering the war production era, and the enormous debt the country owed to them. On the other hand, it's a social memorial to this group of people, who maybe didn't get the recognition that other groups did after the war—is that true?

CB:

It was a commission that was "loaded" with multiple readings. There were many social implications at the time: The civil rights movement, the women's movement, and many of the social labor movements were incubated on this site.

Q:

From a landscape design point of view, is there not an undeniable association with the material that gave you an incredible starting point?

CB:

It did. We absolutely had to use metal.

Figure 4.11. Site axonometric. Rosie the Riveter Memorial, San Francisco, California. (Courtesy of Office of Cheryl Barton.)

Figure 4.12. Model study. Rosie the Riveter Memorial, San Francisco, California. (Courtesy of Office of Cheryl Barton.)

Q:

You had to research the differences between the metals that were worked then and the fixings and rivets. Clearly, there's been a passage of time that has happened, and did that enter into your early discussions regarding practices available to you now? (See Figure 4.13.)

CB:

We spent the first several weeks of the project exploring ships anchored in a "mothball fleet" in a remote part of San Francisco Bay. We were looking for parts and photographing details; we climbed down into the engine room to understand how the ribs and sidewalls were joined. You mentioned rivets and, although the women were called Rosie the Riveter, the World War II ship construction technology had changed to welding so that ships could be mass produced quickly. These women actually welded; they did not pop rivets (the "rosie" term was intentionally demeaning). To our great surprise, that

Figure 4.13. Historic photograph, ship skeleton. Rosie the Riveter Memorial, San Francisco, California. (Courtesy of Office of Cheryl Barton.)

dictated no rivets in our work. We used weld connections, so the detailing of the metal components was quite important. Having spent time on the rusted hulks of the mothball fleet, my initial response was that Corten steel would be the most appropriate material. It would most powerfully recall the look and feel—even the smell—of a ship under construction. Rusted steel is what the women actually touched. The ships were painted after the women assembled them.

Q:

Unlike the more common use of Corten steel, which is not treated and is allowed to oxidize to become the protective coating?

CB:

Exactly. During the process, we conducted workshops and design presentations to several "Rosies"—now in their seventies and eighties—who were our ad hoc review committee. We were compelled by their harrowing experiences. They called welding "stitching with fire." We talked at length to the women about materials, and they recoiled at the thought of Corten. To them, it was an old rusty decrepit material and not at all an appropriate symbol of their war effort.

Figure 4.14. View to memorial. Rosie the Riveter Memorial, San Francisco, California. (Courtesy of Office of Cheryl Barton.)

Figure 4.15. Memorial in context. Rosie the Riveter Memorial, San Francisco, California. (Courtesy of Office of Cheryl Barton.)

Q:

What were they looking for, then? Was it another type of metal?

CB:

I don't think they were necessarily looking for metal: I think they were looking for a typical "object" monument—such as a bronze welder on horseback! As we worked with them, they began to understand that the design idea was about the place and the scale of their work. (See Figures 4.14 and 4.15.) They became comfortable with metal once we showed them the stainless steel. It seemed more precious and more jewel-like to them, and it had a more elegant look and feel. We struggled with the city agencies to get them to agree to retain the mill finish. As I mentioned, the steel had scratches and pits that would accumulate rust. This aspect of the weathering of ships was what I wanted to capture; it was fundamental to the design idea. Ships had to be painted every year, and weathering has always been part of the process of shipbuilding. I was arguing for selective degradation—a difficult concept for public agencies to grasp. This was a public art; consequently, the art commission required maintenance specifications. This document was instrumental in negotiating the use of the preferred steel finish and other materials. It contained photographs of every type of metal, stone, and with recommendations from conservators as to how to maintain (or not maintain) them.

Q:

Was that difficult to get by the various committees?

CB:

Extremely! I think they assumed that the memorial was going to rust very, very quickly. As a public entity, they were also concerned that citizens would think they were not upholding their civic responsibilities.

Figure 4.16. Memorial. Rosie the Riveter Memorial, San Francisco, California. (Courtesy of Office of Cheryl Barton.)

Figure 4.17. Memorial detail. Rosie the Riveter Memorial, San Francisco, California. (Courtesy of Office of Cheryl Barton.)

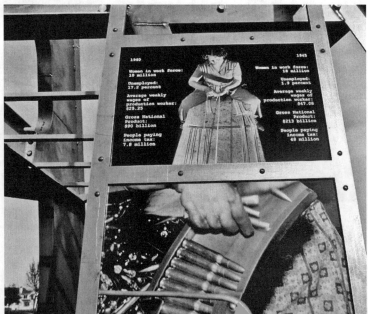

Figure 4.18. Memorial detail. Rosie the Riveter Memorial, San Francisco, California. (Courtesy of Office of Cheryl Barton.)

Q:

Were you able to recall any precedents in landscape design terms that you could turn to that could have helped you build the case or give you confidence—I'm thinking of maybe Gasworks Park in Seattle?

CB:

Gasworks Park was not the type of project that would have inspired confidence in this client. We referenced other regional public art installations.

Q:

Was this project a break in the way that you had normally approached landscape architecture projects and could you apply these ideas now to a more normative design project?

CB:

It was a break primarily because it was public art. (See Figures 4.16, 4.17, and 4.18.) These were not new ideas for me, but I had more leeway because the client was prepared for something different than the norm. As for more "normative" design projects, much of the work we do with cultural landscapes embodies the notion of selective deterioration, i.e., leaving elements in place that will continue to degrade while creating new interventions for contemporary use.

With other projects, it is a tougher sell. There is great initial interest in the permanence and durability of materials, but it is not backed up with a commitment to budgeting for or maintaining them. This absence of long-term thinking seems to me to be symptomatic of a deeper cultural denial of the passage of time.

What I have learned is to be rigorously strategic with clients early in the design process by decoding what they fear and what truly motivates them. Ironically, this ultimately gives me more freedom in my work.

CASE
STUDY C   THE PERSISTENCE OF SPATIAL STRUCTURE

Figure 4.19. The formal geometry of tree planting adjacent to the center and the transitional scale between building and site have encouraged the use of these areas for outdoor exhibits. Mid-America All-Indian Center, Wichita, Kansas. (Photography by Edward L. Blake, Jr.)

Project Information

Project: Mid-America All-Indian Center

Location: Wichita, Kansas

Client: City of Wichita

Landscape Architect: Oblinger-Smith Corporation
Edward L. Blake, Jr., Project Landscape Architect
(now practicing as The Landscape Studio)

Design Phase: 1975

Date Completed: 1976

PROJECT DESCRIPTION

The center is a multifaceted nonprofit organization, whose mission includes providing social services to Native Americans in need and serving as a center where Native Americans can practice their cultural traditions and pass them on to their children. The center is located at the confluence of the Big and Little Arkansas Rivers, on land where the Wichita tribe camped more than 100 years ago. The building was a bicentennial gift to all Native Americans from the people of Wichita. The Indian Center is part of the cultural triangle that includes the Wichita Art Museum and the Old Cowtown Museum. The *Keeper of the Plains* is a forty-four-foot-tall Indian sculpture by Native American artist, Blackbear Bosin. In the shadow of this sculpture, you find the Indian Artist Walk of Fame, a series of small gardens, each dedicated to a famous Native American artist.

The project represents one of the oldest in the case studies, and, as a result, the issues of change, maintenance, and weathering of the landscape forms are all present. However, there are significant lessons for young landscape architect and students in the designer's approach to how the landscape might change, the desire to be flexible to achieve the best framework or structure to hold the project together and the acceptance that over time certain elements will be altered or removed.

INTERVIEW WITH THE DESIGNER

Discussion with the landscape architect Ed Blake took place on January 18, 2002, and April 23, 2003 by telephone. Interview participants are identified as (EB) and author (Q).

Q:

As a designer, when did you become aware, maybe for the first time, that certain landscapes endure and last and certain landscapes do not endure?

EB:

When I got out of design school in 1970, I worked in Campbell Miller's office in Louisville, Kentucky. I interned for two summers during school and worked for three years right after school. The Olmsted firm had developed a system of parks in Louisville as well as parkways. I lived very near to these parks, and they made a lasting impression on me, particularly the infrastructure of the roadways and bridges and the network of open spaces and woodlands. I remember the scale of those things and their integrity with the larger topography and landscape. The local ASLA chapter was initiating activities making people aware of Olmsted's legacy. Olmsted's landscapes were close to a hundred years old at that time, and I was impressed at the foresight that had gone into thinking at those scales as well as thinking about the materiality of the place that would last so long. Clearly, people were still using these spaces. I compared this to newly designed and built landscapes that I was seeing with life cycles that seemed so short.

Q:

How would you categorize the contemporary condition that you were comparing to Olmsted at that time?

EB:

This was long before the Louisville Riverfront Park by Hargreaves Associates was created. In the early 1970s, Louisville's riverfront was a patchwork of abandoned industrial infrastructure. I thought, why was nobody thinking as far ahead as Olmsted did about this place and designing an urban riverfront park?

Q:

What was important for you — that the Olmsted landscape had lasted a hundred years or was it important that Olmsted had a vision about this landscape in a hundred years and, in addition, that it was flexible and could change over time?

EB:

I think anyone is impressed that something is still working a hundred years down the road; I have walked through the entrance at the Biltmore Estate that was designed by Olmsted. I am amazed at how well he knew that place, particularly with applied ecology and the earth sciences still in their infancy. As I look back at Louisville's park systems, I admire Olmsted's ability to understand the geology, landform, and vegetative systems and that he was successful in selecting distinctive park sites exemplifying the major plant communities existing in the Louisville area. From a more technical point of view, he understood how to build and had people around him who were so good at what they did that the built work has lasted as long as it has.

Q:

When you go back to your own work now, what do you look for?

EB:

With me, it started when I was asked to direct the development of Pinecote at the Crosby Arboretum.* I was asked to do this immediately after collab-

---

*The Crosby Arboretum is the premier native plant conservatory of the southeastern United States. Through the Crosby Arboretum, aesthetic, agricultural, scientific, and industrial contributions of native plant species and ecosystems can be examined in a real-life setting. The Crosby Arboretum began as a living memorial to L. O. Crosby, Jr. (1907–1978). The arboretum provides for the protection of the region's biological diversity as well as a place for the public's enjoyment of plant species native to the Pearl River Drainage Basin. The Native Plant Center of the Crosby Arboretum 64 acre Interpretive center south of Picayune, Mississippi, serves as the focus of arboretum activities and development. Additionally, the arboretum manages over 700 acres in seven associated natural areas. The vast assemblage of carefully selected and protected lands nurtures over 300 species of indigenous trees and shrubs as well as wildflowers and grasses found in the Pearl River Basin of south-central Mississippi and southeast Louisiana.

orating in the initial schematic design work with Andropogon Associates, Landscape Architects, Philadelphia, Pennsylvania. I had also spent three years researching arboreta, preparing a program, and had spent a summer on site documenting its patterns of habitat and community. The day after I accepted the invitation to become the arboretum's first director, I walked through the site, and the enormity of this undertaking really sank into me. I wondered: How are we going to do this and what moves are we going to make first? We had just been through the conceptual design process—and so much had to be done to implement it. I remember starting to really think particularly about how we were going to develop the plant habitats and communities so they would evolve over time and be true to how we visualized them. My mind stretched to visualize a forest growing like a slow-motion video. Seeing this required me to explore as many of the habitat and plant community types as possible that would mature at Pinecote. I visited many places in the region that were similar to Pinecote as fast as I could and in as many stages of successional development as possible. This experience sensitized me to the structure of the living collections of the arboretum. One issue arose immediately: How were we going to maintain the structural integrity of the living plant community collections over time?

Figure 4.20. Nearly two decades of growth surrounding Pinecote's one-and-one-half acre freshwater wetland exhibit is transforming savanna into wooded bottomland. Crosby Arboretum, Picayune, Mississippi. (Photography by Edward L. Blake, Jr.)

Q:

To clarify by structure, you mean?

EB:

Anything that is built out of the landscape medium itself, whether it is a lake or a wooden structure built from trees harvested on site. Seeing the landscape in these terms did more than anything else to give me a long-term focus. Today, in my work, I find that many of my clients are startled by the idea of the long-term view and have seldom considered thinking that far ahead. I compiled an archive of over 20,000 images of the Piney Wood's mosaic of habitat and plant community structure. I developed a series of designer's notebooks documenting what I saw and learned.

Q:

In the case of the Crosby Arboretum, it was just you; there were no other forms of recording, whether writing or photography, of the different types of plant communities?

EB:

When you read the Master Plan Report for Pinecote that I authored ten years after initiating Pinecote's development, the essence of the work comes across, even though the poetics of the language may not have revealed it explicitly. The challenge was to condense ten years of insight and experiencing and seeing a landscape in twenty-nine pages, so that reading the text and looking at the images clearly conveys one's vision. This was what Olmsted was so good at. Those big sweeping moves that he made testify that he saw the scale, duration, and the form of the processes that constituted the landscapes he worked with. He put his thoughts in place to realize them and wrote vivid descriptions of what he had seen and done.

Q:

There are different types of change in the landscape you talked about there, the ecological and vegetation development of communities as they age through succession. There is also the cultural weathering, changes brought to a site by use or misuse. How do you, as a designer, think about cultural weathering or is it just part of the design process?

EB:

It's too early to tell in the case of the arboretum, as it is only twenty-five years old. Mississippi exists in the popular imagination as a mysterious, undeveloped, and brooding frontier. The reality is that rapid growth has transformed the state and region within the space of a single generation. When I look back twenty-two years ago when we started our work at Pinecote, our landscape had more of an undiscovered, rural piney woods character. Now, an airport has been built only a mile away from the Pinecote. At night, the view of the horizon from Pinecote Pavilion is pulsed by a light beacon. So, clearly, we are seeing rapid cultural changes in the immediate landscape. When beginning my work at the Crosby, I walked through the Arnold Arboretum in Jamaica Plain and imagined it as the sheep field that it used to be. Now, it is a wooded green fragment of the Arcadian ideal. Aware of the changes that have transformed the context and content of the Arnold Arboretum, it will be interesting to see how the Crosby holds up over time. Ironically, the more archetypical it becomes as a native landscape, the clearer it will become. Today, Pinecote looks too much like the surrounding landscape, with the exception of its built structures, that it is too often taken for granted.

Q:

So, in a sense, once the contrast is emphasized, it will become more legible?

EB:

I hate to say it, and I don't think it should be like this, but in the popular imagination, it is a scale issue. I don't think the majority of the public will see the forest until only a remnant remains.

Q:

Do you ever in your design work carry out individual projects that are temporary or known to be short lived?

EB:

I would say that this consists of many of the urban or suburban projects that we are doing today. I tend to use larger clusters of smaller plants. Looking at how real estate changes each time a property is bought and sold, I view urban landscapes as places of continual disturbance. As such, these sites often remain in very early and youthful stages of ecological succession.

Q:

Like a floodplain?

EB:

Yes, that is a good analogy to a very weighty landscape with thin soils stripped by lots of heavy forces moving through it and causing big-time changes. In areas frequently altered by humans, I design with vegetative structures appropriate to the scale, rhythm and duration of these forces. Today's landscapes are so different from those Olmstedian landscapes characterized by big stable areas where individual specimen trees were amply spaced to reach their maturity in 80 to 100 years. We will seldom see that approach used designing our public landscapes today. Planning and design is now more open ended and fluid. Today's landscapes must endure more frequent and diverse disturbances. The Lake Terrace Convention Center in Hattiesburg, Mississippi, is a good example of changing the enduring emphasis to the built infrastructure and giving it a permanence that will last to register the vegetative and cultural changes that flow through it. This infrastructure is placed as a measured instrument of documenting change. (See Figures 4.21, 4.22, 4.23, 4.24.)

Figure 4.21. The geometry of the cascade reveals the differing sedimentation patterns left by storms. Lake Terrace Convention Center, Hattiesburg, Mississippi. (Photography by Edward L. Blake, Jr.)

Figure 4.22. Lake terraces were planted with tree species that grow along the region's floodplains and terraces. Lake Terrace Convention Center, Hattiesburg, Mississippi. (Photography by Edward L. Blake, Jr.)

Figure 4.23. Weir and cascade make visible the frequency, intensity, and duration of Gulf coastal weather patterns. Lake Terrace Convention Center, Hattiesburg, Mississippi. (Photography by Edward L. Blake, Jr.)

Figure 4.24. The center's constructed wetlands serve to filter and treat runoff generated by the center's impervious surfaces. Lake Terrace Convention Center, Hattiesburg, Mississippi. (Drawing by Edward L. Blake, Jr.)

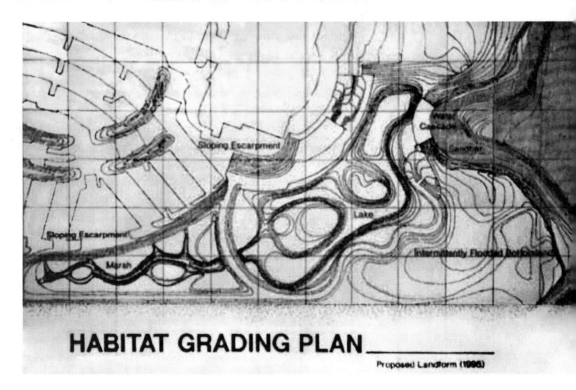

HABITAT GRADING PLAN

Proposed Landform (1995)

Q:

So there again, we have the contrast between the work of the infrastructure and the fluid or vegetative growth, change, and succession. How do you, then, bring your office to think about inert materials?

EB:

They offer so much hope and promise today. The landscape profession too often looks at the living landscape as being its only medium. Most often, it is represented or re-presented so that the human hand is evident and maintained through time so that the designer's intent is always seen. This yields landscapes that evolve over time with individual components simply getting older within a very static setting. The arboretum experience and my collaboration with Andropogon Associates showed me the creative potential of landscapes evolving through time. I now think that the future challenge lies in getting the infrastructure built that allows the creativity or the life force to move through it in ways that you can't imagine. Much of our knowledge of the biological structure of a place can be designed into the constructed infrastructure, so that it amplifies the essence of its living context. As we come to know and see the biological functioning of a place, we will be able to read its constructed infrastructure and interpret its built structure as a signature of a place's ecological structure.

Q:

I'm wondering if there's a certain type of material choice that you keep going back to in your constructed work other than plants?

EB:

We work with a lot of concrete, because we work on the coastal plain and there's not large stone here. Concrete is man-made stone. So we look at ways that we can structure and pattern it to make its form a signature of its place. Exposed aggregate is very prevalent here, as a lot of south Mississippi is a gravel outwash plain from the last glaciation. With ample gravel pits, we often use exposed aggregate finishes. It is an indigenous expression, one that is most often mindlessly used. We have a number of projects underway that use timber and metal. We are designing an office campus on the site of an old sawmill that was built a century ago by one of Hattiesburg's pioneering lumbering families. The sawmill site is being developed as a headquarters for a timberlands management company with properties clustered in four or five states surrounding Mississippi. We are using materials and forms that are expressive of the railroads and timber-harvesting processes that were the genesis of the sawmill. There are metal cattle guards at entrance points, and parking areas have metal wheel stops. The front entrance piers were inspired by the stacked forms of sawed timber that was left to dry. A metal roof covers these stacks to keep them dry and free of pine straw from the towering longleaf pines.

Q:
You're doing research of your own in seeing what the material can do, how it changes.

EB:
In 2001, I taught a studio at Auburn University. I asked the students to focus on the materiality of place. They cast different concretes by adding indigenous stone from the area and experimented with wood and metal. In the Landscape Studio, we're putting more emphasis on placing the infrastructure. That is, how might we choose and form the materials that form a place's development so that it amplifies our cultural understanding, makes visible the origins of place, and is permeable to life's creative evolution?

Q:
Which brings up the issue of designers who practice locally and designers who practice nationally.

EB:
I'm running into this right now as our studio is working with Coleman Coker's Building Studio, planning a retreat on a ten-thousand-acre ranch in Texas and a hundred-acre canyon along the front range in Colorado.

Q:
How do you feel about that, now?

EB:
That's the thing that I was most uncertain about. Let's consider Rey Rosa Retreat, the Texas project. In the early 1970s, I worked in Kansas for four years. I came to understand the prairie system. In the late 1970s, I moved to the blackbelt region of northeast Mississippi. Living there, I saw many of the same plants that I came to know in Kansas. As I began to put the pieces together, I realized that Mississippi and Texas were parts of the same big inland sea that once covered America's heartland. The geology of this sea is the genesis of our prairie, although regional expressions vary due to precipitation quantities, fire frequency, and so forth. As the seabed was lifted and eroded by the newly forming Mississippi River, its floodplain divided the prairie. From the vantage point of Mississippi, it's like seeing Rey Rosa as the distant shoreline of this sea. I found the biggest difference to be cultural. Mississippi was once the frontier of Anglo-Saxon agriculture, and as this frontier moved westward, it was transformed by the nomadic culture of the plains. These are some of the similarities and differences between these two places. I'm finding that as you listen to local people and involve them in your work, the original approaches you used locally stay with you. One of our

consultants in Colorado put us together with a restoration ecologist living in Boulder. All of this resembles my early days at the Crosby Arboretum as I listened to all the botanists, ecologists, writers, musicians, architects, and engineers describe the particularities of a place in detail. My work was one of putting all the pieces together in a way that gave strength and unity to the existing integrity of the place.

Q:

So the only thing that doesn't change is your ability to read the landscape?

EB:

Yes, and your commitment to place, particularly to a place that has a structural integrity to the region. Whatever is designed and built must not obscure a place/region's structural complexity.

Q:

Can you choose one of your own designs, which you have returned to as a case study in weathering and durability? (See Figures 4.25 to 4.27.)

Mid-America All Indian Center
Wichita, Kansas

EB:

I would like to go back to projects that I worked on almost twenty-five years ago when I was in the Midwest. They were small, traditional urban parks, a quarter acre to several acres in size. I had a chance to go back and visit them recently.

Figure 4.25. A quarter century of maturing locust trees provide a shaded retreat in the heart of Wichita's central business district. Heritage Square, Wichita, Kansas. (Photography by Edward L. Blake, Jr.)

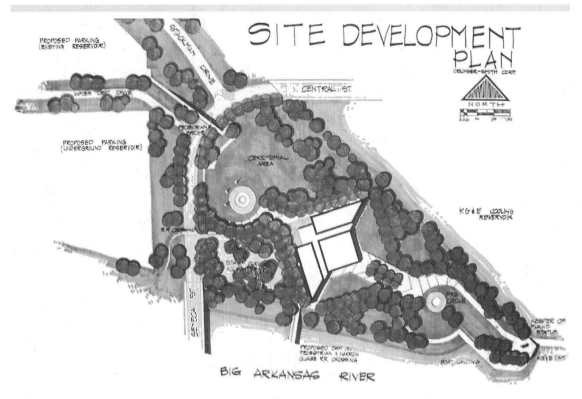

Figure 4.26. Much of the center's peninsula has been left open to encourage ceremonial performances ringed by shaded areas for spectator comfort. Mid-America All-Indian Center, Wichita, Kansas. (Drawing by Edward L. Blake, Jr.)

Figure 4.27. Grasses and trees covering the Center's ceremonial ring were chosen for their ability to adapt to and endure harsh growing conditions. Mid-America All-Indian Center, Wichita, Kansas. (Photography by Edward L. Blake, Jr.)

Q:

What were their names?

EB:

One was Heritage Square and another was the Mid-America All-Indian Center. Both are located in Wichita, Kansas. The Indian Center is a community center for local tribes and a place for their hosting powwows for visitors. It is located on the settlement site that the original peoples of the area had lived on. The land is a peninsula at the confluence of two rivers. From its point, you are only blocks away from Wichita's central business district. The previous thirty years have witnessed an incredible amount of development along the river corridor immediately adjacent the center.

Looking back, it was my first use of a large amount of indigenous plants. I could not install site irrigation, and a lot of the land was made from construction fill that had been dumped from demolition sites. One of the things I did was to use buffalo grass, which is native to the prairies and extremely drought resistant. During a recent visit, I was elated to see how it had established, spread, and thrived.

Q:

Can you describe very briefly, what the park's landscape was made from?

EB:

The project included a building that spanned from river to river and divided the peninsula into two parts. This created a public landscape, extending between the center and the public street. The rear portion extended to the point of the peninsula where the two rivers come together. The peninsula point is dominated by a huge sculpture of a Plains Indian made from Corten steel. From the point to the center are formal plantings of sycamore, elm, mulberry, and sweet gum. Parking was placed in the front, adjacent to a ceremonial area where, during powwows, tribes dance. The city was tearing up the street close by and used the rubble from this street for the majority of the fill for an ampitheater berm surrounding the ceremonial dancing ring to a height of twenty feet. The asphalt and concrete rubble was covered with a soil layer and planted with grass and pines. The dance ring was circled with lace bark elms.

Q:

Do the elms have a special significance to the tribe?

EB:

No, they are just a tough tree that thrives everywhere I've planted it. I chose it because of the soil conditions that I was working with, and these elms have really performed well. I tell our folks in the studio that part of the reward of returning to a project site is to remember the original sketches or the images that flowed from hand to tracing paper during the design process and the spatial structure that these represent. I'm just flabbergasted when I've gone back and visited these sites and found that the spaces are maturing as envisioned a quarter-century ago. Landscape architects must have the patience of Job as we wait at least twenty years (middle age) for trees to grow large enough to form the envisioned spatial structure.

Q:
I'm assuming you left a very clear way of how it would be maintained?

EB:
It has been maintained by the local parks department whom I had worked with in choosing the plants, but I did not leave any maintenance instructions.

Q:
What do you attribute the longevity of the project to?

EB:
I think it's getting the right plant in the right place, as there wasn't a tree missing after all these years. It was my first use of formal plantings; I used sweet gums, an early successional and riparian species, and they have grown beautifully as a formal planting. I also used hardy junipers as small trees in the plains, and scotch pines, a species that is naturalized to the plains.

Q:
So the trees were all healthy when they went in and they had some maintenance and pruning and they established a structure that stood the test of time?

EB:
Yes, I think one of the things I've learned is the importance of getting a good spatial structure in place and to think about trees as being the most important element that forms that structure. Everything else might come and go, but if the tree structure stays in place, the site spatial structure will basically hold together.

Q:
Were there specific examples of that structure on the site?

EB:
Along the peninsula behind the center, I laid out a fairly simple circulation system. A sidewalk goes out to the point where the *Keeper of the Plains* statue is located. I planted avenues of trees on both sides of the peninsula triangle so they would emphasize the triangular perspective to the confluence of the rivers. I planted trees in bosques along the rear of the building, to create more of a shady place for people walking and sitting outside, and as a transition between the scale of the city, rivers, and peninsula to that of the building. They've put picnic tables out under those shaded bosques and also used

these shady spaces as a framework for outdoor exhibits. These bosques have provided enough of a flexible framework that a lot of things have been added beneath them. The planting framework, though very precise, has provided the flexibility for a diverse pattern of things to happen. In hindsight, I think the simplicity of the planting design is a large measure of its endurance.

As I get older, I spend more time editing things to their bare essentials. Simple things are those that are going to be the most flexible through time and will stand up to unanticipated uses. Anything too complicated is often not cared for and often vanishes through neglect.

Q:

Do you think that goes for projects that are of a different type? How about a more sensitive landscape in terms of susceptibility to change?

EB:

Sensitive landscapes and sensitively designed landscapes persist whenever their managers are highly trained, understand diversity, and are funded adequately. It is very difficult to sustain diverse systems over long periods of time. Accomplishing this is the foremost challenge that we face today. Over the last four years, I've been making garden study trips to Europe. As I've walked through Italian gardens and the gardens of France, I see a very limited palette of trees used in their gardens.

Although this is an unconventional view, I would be willing to bet that they have "messed around" with plants long enough in one place to choose plants that have persisted through thousands of years. America is such a young country and our perspective is fresh and young. As a strength, it can also be a weakness as we have not experienced the long haul. I mean, 300 or 400 years is fairly short in the longer scheme of things. Finding those plants in America that persist will lead us to using them as more of the structural backbones of our plantings. As I drive through cemeteries in the South, I see a plant that was once used on every foundation planting of a house, Arborvitae. You don't see it used anymore because it has been so abused and overused. When you see old ones in the cemeteries, they're beautiful and have persisted long enough to obtain this status. I've begun to think about using Arborvitae again in some of my designs because of the longevity of it. The native species has a similar longevity even though it is seldom used because of limited commercial availability.

Q:

In a sense, you're learning from your own work and also from this continued observation of other projects. I was really surprised by your comment that there were no maintenance instructions left in place for the Kansas project, but it was still maintained. Were you surprised to see it in such good condition?

EB:

Yes, I was, and all I can attribute it to is one thing—flexibility. That is, you put a recognizable and simple structure in place. At the twenty-fifth anniversary of Mississippi's School of Architecture, Chris Rischer told a story. He talked about a man buying a suit, and the person that waited on him sold him a suit one size bigger. The man was very flattered because he had lots of room to move around. It lasted him a lot longer than if he had bought one that fit him right now, as it allowed him room to grow. Chris made the point that while we're younger we tend to design very stringently towards the parameters as we understand them. The trick is to design more broadly and leave plenty of room to accommodate the quirks to take place.

Q:

Or the weathering?

EB:

Yes, since hearing Chris' story, I've never forgotten its wisdom. When I say flexibility, I mean not trying to design something that the designer tries to imagine everything that's going to happen. We must conceive designs that are open ended enough and yet provide a strong organizing structure. The challenge and reward is to let it go and hope for the best. We must choose the materials to build this structure from those that we know or have seen to persist.

Figure 4.28. Timber path as bridge over stormwater detention pond. Private summer retreat, western Maine. (Courtesy of Michael Blier/LANDWORKS Studio, Inc.)

Project Information

Project: Maine Re-Creation/Recreation:
A Private Summer Retreat

Location: Western Maine

Client: Worcester Theater Group, New York

Landscape Architect: Office of Michael Blier
Project designer: Michael Blier, ASLA

Date Completed: Ongoing. Phase 1 completed Fall 1998

PROJECT DESCRIPTION

This project site is located within an existing white pine forest canopy on a pristine lakefront in western Maine. The site slopes westward toward the lake and is flanked by cabins, constructed during the 1920s as summer rental retreats. When purchased, the forest opening was severely compacted and eroded, lacked articulated circulation, and conveyed deleterious stormwater to the lake below. The primary focus of this project is to restore ecological and cultural integrity to this neglected lakeside retreat.

The master plan for the site included the following: containment of stormwater runoff, revegetation of the forest canopy, planting to introduce and reestablish mammal and bird habitats, organization and articulation of different scales of pedestrian movement through the site, structure and limitation of vehicular access and parking, and creation of an environment for the owners and their guests to experience direct and meaningful landscape events.

REVEGETATION

Birch Forest

The birch grove provides a filter between the cabins to the north and the primary residence and work spaces of the owners. The birches also serve to mitigate the scale of the pines and to provide a textural foil to the coarse fiber of the original forest.

Spruce and Red Pine Forest

A mix of pine and spruce utilizes the contrast of texture, color, and growth rate of the two species to establish a dynamic forest. The thickness of the grove also provides a sense of privacy for the adjacent cabins while these remote cabins also become linked spatially and experientially to other areas and cabins on the site.

STORMWATER MANAGEMENT

Corkscrew

The owner mandated that no large equipment be used, that the stormwater management system should be finely scaled responding to localized areas of erosion, and that the maximum amount of runoff is retained. Drawing from the nature of the existing undulating context, the construction began with several flexible crescent-shaped earth forms and retention basins. These earth forms are sited to collect water along a curving line and deposit it in a retention basin at the terminus of each crescent. The path systems are strategically placed to engage these crescent-shaped forms at critical moments within the site. While the summer heat places more stress on the wild grasses of the fields, the retention basins, because of the added moisture, have begun to establish a vastly different plant community.

The Basin

The severity of the stormwater erosion problem that could not be addressed by the corkscrew was addressed by the construction of a basin. Located somewhat eccentrically on the site, its position engages and informs pedestrian and vehicular movement. The path sits as a boardwalk on the ground; however, as this path engages the basin, it becomes a bridge, lifting the user above the ground. During a storm event, the basin fills with water and restores the path's relationship to an adjacent horizontal ground plane—now water—if only temporarily.

PEDESTRIAN CIRCULATION

North/South Boardwalk

Movement in this direction links cabins along a line, as well as one end of the site to the other, and in this direction emerges as efficiently as possible as straight lines that allow direct connections between proposed and existing forests.

East/West Serpentine Path

Movement in this direction is toward and away from the lake up and down the slope. Paths in this direction are never straight, meandering slightly to divert water into a newly planted massing of grasses along the path. From an experiential point of view, the contrast in path types creates two clearly distinct types of movements on the site and contributes to the variety of experiences, cadences, and views at and through the site.

The adjusted or readjusted scale of landscape forms, program, and experience on this site is the result of a careful and creative approach by the designer to the ideas of time and duration. This approach and the strategies and technologies employed in handling stormwater runoff, movement, new patterns of vegetation, and microscopic adjustments of land surface come from a close working relationship with a remarkable client. Ideas of long term stewardship of the land and the social and cultural exchanges on site find expression at a detailed scale with landscape materials and forms.

INTERVIEW WITH THE DESIGNER

Discussion with the landscape architect Michael Blier took place on June 20, 2001, by telephone and January 30, 2003, in Cambridge, Massachusetts. Interview participants are identified as Michael Blier (MB) and author (Q).

Q:
Can you describe an example of a designed landscape where you were aware for the first time how the actions of weathering and durability have acted on the built landscape?

MB:
It's a highly archetypal landscape—areas of Central Park, New York. I think the interpretation and transformation of the contour line to be so responsive to not only the physical language of the park, but also to the complex geophysical, hydrological, infrastructure, and social aspects of this space. It's probably not a fancy answer, but it's where the idea of technology overlay on the landscape and the processes of constructing that landscape have resulted in a unique way of experiencing space over time. The study of this park has greatly influenced how I think of landscape; that is, looking at the complexities of the topography—the terrain, let's say, the built wall, the transition through vertical space, and then the introduction of vegetation. The different types of circulation are, I think, an example in the broadest sense of a way to address the relationship of pieces that are sustainable in time. For example, the Bethesda Terrace in Central Park is a nexus of two movements, both in section and in plan.

Q:
And it was in a sense designed to evolve and weather over time?

MB:
As a landscape, even though it is a highly articulated and artificial construction, it still has had to absorb those factors governing actual wild lands and the elements of a New York winter. What is really so remarkable about this park is the ease with which the unpredictable elements of weather over time has served to enhance the reading of the park as an evolving naturalized artifact/organism. Patina, I think it may be called. However limited it was by the technological capacity of that period, the park still works; storm drainage and other technological systems such as field drainage still work today and continue to stand the test of time. I am awed by it on each visit. Most amazing about this project is that it represents a kind of hope, through the sheer scale of thinking beyond what is current, perhaps for the longer view in time. That's what makes it meaningful and special today for me.

Q:

Is that longer view relevant or even achievable today?

MB:

I would not think of it in the same terms. When designers think about longevity in the landscape today, they talk about landscape sustainability. Because I am not an environmentalist per se and know comparatively little of the associated bedrock underlying sciences, I think a more generative word for me, as a designer, would be "duration." In light of the radical changes in technology that have been taking place in the last 100 years, I find that thinking of what we do as landscape architects as having duration, or many durations for that matter, is more productive. Viewing the life of a landscape in episodic terms as opposed to the concern of being *sustainable* yields, for me, more possibilities for design expression in/on the land. It is a subtle distinction, but one that I feel begins to provide honest and meaningful fodder for contemporary design. I would say that the question of the longer view is a critical one. Though, I think of the *longer view* in more conceptual terms; that is, *the longer view* is the conscience of the designer that provides the system of metes and bounds (defined differently by each designer) in our work. The actual direction of the way things pan out is contingent on factors yet to be determined in a dynamic world.

Accepting the inevitability that all things are going to change, for many possible reasons, either because of emerging technologies outmoding others, shifting cultural values, demands brought about, in some cases, purely by extreme and rapid growth. In my own work, at least the work in our office to this point, an appropriate analog for registering this sort of change would be the function/technology of water and the utility of water migration existing on a site or present within a proposal.

In the past, one of the primary ways in which permanence or sustainability in the landscape was expressed was through the overlay of a very clear, identifiable formal language on a site. The original site may or may not have had much at all to do with the superimposition of the overriding language. I am thrilled to be a part of a generation of designers who have questioned this strategy of reliance on imported external references to the site. The rejection of this previous model means that, today, we are increasingly going to the site and to its context to find meaning/form. In this way, perhaps sustainability in the sense that we have been talking about is more achievable. However, this strategy doesn't mean or necessarily lead to the creation of natural forms and cozy naturalistic conditions. In fact, freed up from the overt rigor of recognizable formal languages, site interventions have the opportunity to be more inventive, outrageous. For example, the study of the migration of water across a site or the movement of water in the vertical dimension within a site is an obvious source of great design fun. Understanding just this about a site will provide, I believe, a meaningful, if not sustainable, response. Ultimately, it will lead to one. If you think about rainfall, it begins to be suggestive and descriptive of all sorts of things; including the ground plane, vegetation, cultural use, geotechnical information.

Q:

Apart from water, could you cite some other examples where material choice and durability organized a built landscape?

MB:

I think the trend in the aesthetic of landscape is now less visual and more experiential. Additionally, the language and materials of design are emerging differently. We are working on projects now where we are required to deal with water, but it's not just dealing with water; it is looking at the program through the lens of a heavy rainfall or a wet lowland. You then begin to talk to the hydrologist, soil scientist, and civil engineer and engage the sciences in a way that makes the three-dimensional space essential and meaningful. For example, we are working on a project with a very high groundwater table; you don't really see the water, but you understand that it is there. What does that mean? I think it can have really meaningful conditions on the ground plane. In one of our projects, we have started to look at how the ground can push up in places, and we have been able to capture some extra water in specialized containers. It's not an aesthetic for me that is driven by an overall pattern of landscape or a geometry of repetition, rather a product of understanding exactly what's happening under the ground.

Q:

And also possibly a series of ideas embedded in materiality?

MB:

Exactly. A good example of this would be a discreet area of a project we have ongoing in which we are trying to establish a variety of ground plane conditions without altering the actual planting material on the ground, which is field grass. Therefore, we have been looking at special soil specifications to create alternating percolation rates, hoping the grass will appear differently over the course of a season. Obviously, in this case, it is not about what we can do that will last forever. It is more about what can we do that is responsive to the condition of the site that will optimize your experience in that condition and memory of the place. As a designer, I am more impressed by a work when, after having experienced a new garden or seen a particularly compelling painting or performance, that I see those things around me in everyday life differently because of it; that in some way I have been altered. This phenomenon is at the core of relevant work.

Q:

You are happy to accept how it might change and weather and evolve in ways you might have little or no control over?

MB:

Yes, you have to design it, understanding how it may change or how the direction of change may take it one way or the other. The design problem is more about how effectively the inevitable changes have been incorporated into the *longer view* to which you were referring earlier. Why would we not want it to evolve? This phenomenon is exactly what makes landscape architecture so much more interesting to me than other creative professions. We get to design dynamic places outside in the world for human beings to experience that may be beyond the day-to-day experiences for most. This is a great opportunity.

Q:

As you described, then, the ideas that emanate from the site and the fluctuating conditions of the place are embedded in the materiality of the built landscape. Design decisions are made that have profound implications not only of the experience of walking along the path, but also its possible duration and ability to change. How do you in your design work start to look at materials in this way?

MB:

Oftentimes in landscape architecture, the culture/nature paradigm manifests itself through the juxtaposition of materials: natural versus synthetic. I have to say that I am also moved by this dialectical compulsion. However, I am also cautious about how we, as an office, are moving this thinking forward in our own work. The risk, of course, is that the thinking moves so far out in front of available materials or that the tolerances become so high that technology lags, that the requisite reference is never made, and the project flattens. With so many new materials out there now, the temptation by many young designers has been to gobble them all up and put them into the landscape. I am not interested in juxtaposition of materials for the visual shock value. This is not fashion and I do not want to be a fashion victim.

Q:

Could you explain what you mean by "fashion victim"?

MB:

I respect the pushing of new materials in current landscape practice and appreciate greatly the emergence of the influence of contemporary gallery art and artists as a source/resource in the profession over the

Figure 4.29. Study cross section, trellis. International Garden Festival, Chaumont-sur-Loire, France. (Courtesy of Michael Blier/LANDWORKS Studio, Inc.)

Figure 4.30. Detail installation, trellis. International Garden Festival, Chaumont-sur-Loire, France. (Courtesy of Michael Blier/LANDWORKS Studio, Inc.)

past decade or two. However, when we, as designers, reduce the meaning of these new materials to their visual characteristics only and use them accordingly, relying on the shock of seeing them in the landscape, we miss out on so much more. As landscape architects, we are charged with creating environments to be experienced. For me, this suggests that each material selected is working with the next to form a series of relationships that build three-dimensional complexities that exceeds the visual effect of any particular material. In our project for the International Garden Festival at Chaumont-sur-Loire in France's Loire River valley, for example, we were looking for this juxtaposition of materials to articulate and link the science of the garden to the experience of the place. (See Figures 4.29 and 4.30.) However, the choice of materials was a result of understanding the tectonics of plastic hydroponics tubing and willow trees. We first began to explore a range of different materials, looking for one that would withstand the heat in the summer and hold its rigidity, and one that would be able to handle the weight of the willows once they were grown. Finally, we investigated what the relationship between the two would be—we wanted to maximize the material contrast between the plastic tube and the willow. In a sense, we wanted the willow to read in section as one layer, the tubes to read as a second layer, and the structure a third layer. We needed the plastic of the PVC tubes against the willows in order for the garden to work. You never saw the water, just the contrast between the two materials together.

In another project, a residence at Marblehead Neck in Massachusetts, we are trying to create a canopy which is both to provide shelter and which also expresses the idea of vertical water—whether rain or snow. We are trying to work on the creation of a "bladder" as a canopy that would be, to a certain extent, permeable and able to absorb rainfall, that would begin to emit water after the actual storm had passed. The idea is to bring you up next to the rainfall and to challenge the whole shelter/rain relationship so that the shelter, then, could become a shower of rain.

Q:
Like a small microclimate?

MB:
Yes, it returns to the notion of duration that we have been looking at—stagger it, re-create it, make it fresh again. This is an ongoing challenge in our office. I find it creatively challenging and rewarding.

Q:

Like arrested time?

MB:

Yes. One can squeeze more experience out of the landscape. Rather than saying let's provide a structure and sit underneath and watch the rain, we try to break apart and recompose the typical cadences associated with natural events. Often, this requires that we research and incorporate high-tech materials, often beyond the immediate bounds of any of us in-house here. The owner has been teasing us about the provision of a container of plasma screens somehow out there, which we are also trying to figure out how to incorporate. On the one hand, I said I did not want to be a "fashion victim," but we are incorporating this advanced technology into the landscape as a means of thinking about how we can extend, alter, or radically reinterpret the idea of duration that's seasonal and annual. We had three and a half inches of rain in forty-five minutes here recently. I wish I had found a way to capture and re-present that event.

Q:

When you return to your own projects at times, what are you looking for, and are you surprised or depressed? By that I mean, in returning to your work, are there pieces of the built landscape that you had worked out but surprised you in other ways, or if you see something working well, do you wish you had pushed it a little bit further?

MB:

Yes, of course. We are a young office and sometimes we try to do too much. I admit this much, though I am unapologetic about it. My response to this problem is related to how we address it in the next project. In my earlier work, there was an overreliance on geometry, or the superimposition of something that was maybe too complex. I would go and see the site and I would observe and understand how the shadows of adjacent buildings hit the project and I would say, "I've missed it; the pattern is now too complex." The complexity of the shadows is more interesting. On another project, we had a great reflection created by a fence we had designed. The fence has glass panels set into it, but I did not anticipate it being as compelling as it was and if I had, I would not have put all the panels on the same plane—I would have staggered them back into the landscape. I look at them and think that we missed an opportunity to do something truly special. Perspectively, it could have been far more agitated. By locating them all in one plane, one is either inside or outside. In some ways, the experience is over as soon as one crosses the threshold. These sorts of things are lessons for me.

Figure 4.31. Site section down to lake. Private Summer Retreat, western Maine. (Courtesy of Michael Blier/LANDWORKS Studio, Inc.)

Q:

Can you give an example where you broke from this over-reliance on geometry?

Maine Re-Creation/Recreation: A Private Summer Retreat
Western Maine

MB:

For the past several years, we have been working on a very special project in western Maine. Sited on an irregularly sloping site on the shores of a pristine lake, the site, with its twenty or so cabins, is environmentally quite sensitive. Of immediate concern to the owners was the erosion of organic matter making its way down the hill to the lake. To address this, we came up with a strategy of creating small earth scrolls, as it were, that we could build by hand with wheelbarrows. They are "eyebrow" shaped, and they have a pit or basin at one end. We can build these where we have water erosion problems, and over time they begin to be populated by grasses. (See Figures 4.31 and 4.32.) In the summertime, the upland condition dries out and the grasses turn a yellow color. The little basins at the lower end of each of these eyebrows produce a wetland condition and, therefore, you get contrasting upland and wetland plants, not entirely controllable; one can only hope to choreograph it. In this case, we also established a system of circulation moving down the hill that was curvilinear to shed water left and right, and the movement parallel to the contours across the site was a straight line raised up off the ground. It changes every summer I go up there, either through typical maintenance or the forms themselves get a little softer, the edges become a little more muted, but the pathways don't change.

Figure 4.32. "Scroll" earth form for storm-water movement. Private Summer Retreat, western Maine. (Courtesy of Michael Blier/LAND-WORKS Studio, Inc.)

Q:
Who are the clients?

MB:
A husband and wife who are prominent in the performing arts own the summer retreat. Situated on the entirely deforested and compacted site were the cabins. For decades, cars were permitted to park anywhere; roadbeds were carved into the ground all over the place. No longer using the cabins as weekly rentals, the owners sought to develop a master plan to reforest the site over time and to provide a place for their friends to spend time during the summer.

Q:

How big is the site?

MB:

The entire site is about forty or fifty acres. Our primary intervention occurs in a fifteen-acre opening in a mature pine forest located adjacent to the lake. There exists a thirty-five-foot grade change from the road, which you can imagine as a center spine on a peninsula down to the water, and their site rests in the middle of that slope. Stormwater from area farms migrates through the forest, and organic matter runs through the site down to the water. So their objective was twofold. One is the restoration of the ground so that it can have usable spaces; the second is to protect the lake water from runoff.

Q:

Runoff with pesticides?

MB:

Yes, from area farms, the water makes its way to this very pristine lake. In our master plan, our strategy for addressing this problem has been multi-layered and consists of reduced and more considered pedestrian paths and trails, limited auto access and parking areas, strategically positioned earth forms to capture and then release stormwater, and patterns of revegetation. The use of the cabins over the course of the master plan implementation has evolved to respond to the quality of the emerging landscape spaces. The idea was to begin to establish a cohesive master plan that tied the cabins together somehow but was loose enough to allow the variation that exists between them to remain. We began to address circulation in ways that engaged the movement of the water but also to counter it and to create a range of spaces, for example, one for a garden and another for Wiffle ball. They have owned it for about ten years and we've been on the project for about eight years, and as the client's reading of the place changes, so does ours. We planted a birch grove of about 100 trees, a mixed grove of paper birch and river birch, on the hillside. When the trees went in, they didn't quite touch canopies; they were just hanging out on the edge of the site and they engaged a couple of the pathways.

Essentially, the land that we came upon was a big open space within a thick pine forest of trees 130 feet tall. What we wanted was to create a condition within the envelope that was scaled between the development and this vast pine forest that can be occupied. In addition, it can create screening for a few of the cabins and also create an edge where the softball area is located. The trees are really big and have been in the ground about six or seven years now. Operations can now begin within the grove with overlays of other elements such as these smaller corkscrew-shaped earth bumps that collect localized water. We just planted a rye grass, a real ordinary material.

At one end of the earth roll, there's an eight-foot-diameter basin. The crescent-shaped earth form is about thirty feet to fifty feet long, and the basin is at one end of the crescent. The water comes down and meets the earth form and travels to the basin.

Q:
And does it clean the water while in there or is it just holding or slowing it down?

MB:
It essentially percolates because, at this point, it's relatively sandy soil. What we're seeing now is the grass on the earth form growing; it looks like an upland condition. The basins themselves are almost like lowland conditions. So you start to get this contrast of the plant material that we didn't really anticipate, to be honest with you. Again, through the emerging organic juxtaposition, one's experience of moving through the slope is altered and cadence interrupted.

Q:
How did you, first of all, sort of describe what you were proposing to the client?

MB:
Let's say, members of the group are motivated by a sense of timing, movement, and performance. To a certain extent, the verbal description was easy, conversational. The idea of threshold, cadence, and another scale of duration from the beginning was important. The convergence of conditions had forced multiple cycles and durations to cross at this point, at critical experiential moments: paths, bridges, etc. Because of their environmental and ecological concerns, and also because of their intellectual involvement in the project, I think that the clients have really enjoyed this aspect of the project. Also, the connection to the larger landscape is palpable to all of us. A glance at the aerial photograph describes the movement and the organic matter that winds down to the lakefront, right where the site is located. And they understood that. Prior to this, I don't think the clients ever saw an aerial photograph of the lake, but they understood fully what was going on.

Q:
Your placement of these earth forms was based on what was already happening?

MB:
Exactly. We looked at the site, and we basically knew we wanted certain types of movement but we didn't want to just paste down something on the site. We began to look for the localized ecological reasons why we do certain things and where elements needed to be, and we found that the plan shifted away from maybe how we were going to do it in the drawing.

Q:

Were there other places where you were able to deal with maybe different durations of time? Some that would be only daily or yearly?

MB:

We took one edge of the site that was particularly barren and dry and was within the project envelope. In the short term, the client was interested in filming some short pieces there, but for the future use of the space it needed more spatial enclosure. We introduced a spruce grove and then within the spruce grove we introduced an overlay of red pine. When the trees were first planted, not surprisingly, the conical nature of the spruce defined the understory and the red pine provided a fuzzier backdrop mixed throughout. Well, that was five or six years ago. What's starting to happen is that the pyramidal shape of the spruce is being reinforced, as they get stronger and tall. The growth rate of the red pine is much faster than the spruce and, as a result, they are outpacing the spruce with the lower branches dropping out. The idea is to establish an oddly layered forest by registering tree growth rates and textural qualities against each other. As a result, a more complex spatial condition is created. Because the red pines grow twice as quickly as the spruce, we're starting to see the relationship between these two species yield a bizarre forest in the woods of Maine.

Q:

Do you get any storm events there in Maine where occasionally you'll get some trees blown down?

MB:

There was an ice storm a couple of years ago, and the whole birch grove was just lying on the ground. At the time of the storm, the trees were twenty-two to twenty-four feet tall. We just assumed that they would not recover, that they would never stand up again. And it was just one of the saddest things I've ever seen. However, they came back and we haven't lost one tree, not one tree.

Q:

In what would be considered a somewhat hostile environment?

MB:

I think so. Within the birch grove, there's a little red Buddha about eighteen inches tall. The client claims that it looks after his birch grove, that's what really saved it. I tend to believe him. There's another part of the site where the erosion problem was even greater, and slowing the water down with these smaller earth forms wasn't going to be enough. Every spring, the water would come down the hill, hit the buildup of ice, and go right into one of the cabins, whereas in the summertime the water is able to go underneath the cabin. In this area, we created a bigger earth form as a kind of a large gravel basin, and the pathway is in most cases a boardwalk slightly suspended above the basin. The pathway becomes a bridge across the basin that we made, and it fills up with water after heavy rain. After the heavy rain, the pathway is inches above the surface of the water, and in dry conditions, it's a bridge that's about three and a half feet above the ground. Every couple of years, it is taken care of by maintenance; it will be dredged and cleaned out of whatever material has been deposited there. We're trying to ratchet up these different timescales on the site.

Q:
Play with the different timings.

MB:
The clients have their own process of rejuvenating the cabins in quirky ways, so that there's this layering of changes going on all the time. Never obliterating what was there before, just changing pieces of it so that it looks altered in some ways—that's what we're doing, too. One example of this is where there's a weaving serpentine pedestrian walk set against a flight of nontoxic pressure-treated lumber set in the ground. The pathways are never straight, but the lines set by the lumber are straight and you set up two different kinds of movement.

Q:
These are oversized steps?

MB:
Yes, huge, and when the grade change is bigger they don't quite align. They're spaced so that you can get grass growing between them, and it's very interesting to see people moving down the hill through the tall grass. (See Figures 4.33 and 4.34.)

Q:
Is there a choreography of circulation at night as well?

MB:
Often, the diners at the dinner cabin have to get home in the darkness carrying candles or flashlights, and you can make them out walking on these pathways. They have to stay on the pathway because they don't want to walk in the tall grass if it's damp, and so they end up doing this different kind of movement at night and it's quite interesting in that way. The language is more specific to the site, and I wouldn't necessarily want to have to meander like that every day of my life. So there are certain things you can get away with up there that I couldn't someplace else. There's a kind of a letting go or readjustment that they make when they go there.

Figure 4.33. East-west serpentine path. Private Summer Retreat, western Maine. (Courtesy of Michael Blier/LANDWORKS Studio, Inc.)

Figure 4.34. East-west serpentine path detail. Private Summer Retreat, western Maine. (Courtesy of Michael Blier/LANDWORKS Studio, Inc.)

Q:

You're slowing people down when they go there to focus on certain things?

MB:

Right. These people come to the camps to get away from Manhattan for a few weeks or months. Embedded in the strategy for the site is the desire to create a counter to the city, but also to challenge their notions about the Maine woods and how it can be experienced—a reorientation of sorts. (See Figures 4.35 and 4.36.) Not turning the brain to the off position, but rather

Figure 4.35. Timber path as bridge with stormwater basin full. Private Summer Retreat, western Maine. (Courtesy of Michael Blier/LANDWORKS Studio, Inc.)

Figure 4.36. Timber path in winter. Private Summer Retreat, western Maine. (Courtesy of Michael Blier/LANDWORKS Studio, Inc.)

creating a refreshing experience that evolves a bit each year, as the next piece of the master plan gets implemented.

Q:

Do you feel eventually in your own work that you could transfer these strategies to a public landscape or would that be too difficult?

MB:

I hope so. Why not? Basically, all we are trying to do is to get people to be more engaged with their surroundings. The forms and materials would, no doubt, emerge differently, according to the site and program. I have found this project and client so refreshing. In some ways, there already is a public component to this work. I mean, there's no private estate with a tennis court here. At great personal expense and counter to conventional wisdom of property values, the clients are addressing the conditions of the lake as a whole and doing what they can do about it. They declined to go in there and put up million-dollar houses lined up along the waterfront, which they could have done. Instead (for example), they removed each individual outmoded and polluting septic system and replaced them with one larger centralized system hundreds of feet from the water (also at great expense).

Q:

So this is a stewardship?

MB:

Exactly, and they have forced us to think about that as well. We're asked to keep the construction techniques simple. Trees are brought in with wheelbarrows from the ridge road and planted by hand. The environmental group that watches the lake has written about this project in their publications, too, and have adopted some of the construction techniques that we used in terms of pathways. So, it's a big, ongoing experiment with a different kind of long view.

Q:

I am wondering about the cumulative nature of observations about constructions and how the information gets transferred—say, about what a material can do or how joints work?

MB:

We are working on a project now where there is an eight-foot stone wall—not totally freestanding but acting as a retaining structure. The town was not going to allow us to do a concrete wall, so we did a stone veneer wall with real stones ten inches thick applied to it. The concrete wall has joints and, for me, I did not want to pretend it was a fieldstone wall. We took these joints in the concrete wall and expressed them on the surface. We used a tile material used on the building, brought it out into the landscape, and expressed those joints just out back from the face of the wall, where the tile does not batter, but the wall does. At the top of the wall, the reveal is about an inch; at the bottom, the wall reveal is about six inches. The shadow line grows along the height of the wall, the thought being that the structure was able to affect the reading of the wall. When a person drives by, they will see a lovely fieldstone wall. A person walking by or looking at the wall more closely will understand there is something more at work in this wall. The joints also happen to have the weeps and also the lighting for the base of the wall.

Q:

It is ironic that the order of a fieldstone wall which, let's say, a cow bumps into and knocks a few stones off, a farmhand comes along and puts them back up—it's the nature of a loose-fit, sustainable construction. Does your wall proposal play both sides in addressing the question of authenticity?

MB:

Tough question. In this case, the *loose fit* is expressed in the joint and the programming of the joint. A cow would be unable to knock a stone off this wall. However, our position relative to the issue of authenticity is the same. Only the requirements for the wall have changed. Therefore, we looked back to the technology of the wall as a means of finding a way to deal with what it is going to look and feel like. This wall was not about fooling people. The intention was about a wall that was going to say something about the owners and the designer's attitude to making this construction.

Q:

From your point of view, what are weathering and durability?

MB:

Obviously, the possibilities of weathering are what separate what we do from most architecture and most architects. The reality of weathering and decay and, from decay, new growth is a fantastic world in which to design. I can think of no more interesting media with which to work. Weathering is the product of change that occurs as a result of the interaction of similar or dissimilar materials or actions to or upon one other that results in the creation of a third condition, which is less predictable and far less stable than the original materials. This third condition is where the appropriateness of the initial association is proved to be either interesting or not so interesting.

Durability is a relative term. In a way, I think sustainability is about introducing a logic, a process of design, on a site. It is not necessarily about the preservation of the figure of the thing—but, rather, a way of thinking about a site. I am not so interested in how it will be in 100 years, I have to say. It could be that something is designed intentionally to not be here in 100 years. Sometimes, landscape architects are too preoccupied with being monumental. I think this has to do with wanting to be remembered for whatever reason.

If the project in Maine is still there in, let's say, 100 years—and I hope that it is—it will be so because, at its core, the outline of the master plan is rooted in an understanding of place and that somebody in the coming decades has figured out what is needed to keep it meaningful and responsive to its place in those years and to those ecological issues yet to come.

I have come to believe that those projects that are stuck in rigid geometry, without factoring in a *malleable contingency* and that are resistant to change, become almost too fragile and too susceptible to all sorts of possible misreadings, including the aspect of boredom. However, of course, I am a strong proponent for, and love to visit, landscapes that are defined by formally compelling and aggressive spaces. However, I don't think in those terms necessarily, as a point of departure, as though we set out to make something monumental. This office is just making its own way, exploring those things that emerging technologies can provide for us as a means of creating culturally responsive and fun new spaces. Technology just hands us things, and we find meaningful things to do with them.

CASE STUDY **E** **WORKING MATERIALS**

Figure 4.37. General view. Congressional Medal of Honor Memorial, White River State Park, Indianapolis, Indiana. (Courtesy of NINebark, Inc.)

Project Information

Project:	Congressional Medal of Honor Memorial
Location:	White River State Park, Indianapolis, Indiana
Client:	IPALCO Enterprises
Landscape Architect:	NINebark, Inc., Indianapolis, IN
Project Designers and Manager:	Eric Fulford, FAAR, RLA; Ann Reed, RLA

General Contractor:	Hagerman Construction Corp., Indianapolis, Indiana
Custom Glass Fabrication:	VitraMax Group, Louisville, Kentucky
Custom Metal Fabrication:	Tarpenning-LaFollette Company, Indianapolis, Indiana
Custom Porcelain-Enameled Steel:	Windsor/Fireform, Inc., San Jose, California
Specialty Glass Artists:	Fred di Frenz and Mark Fowler
Structural Design:	McComas Engineering, Indianapolis, Indiana
Lighting Consultant:	Cross Light, Sunman, Indiana
Electrical Contractor:	Miller-Eads Company, Indianapolis, Indiana
MOH Recipient Graphics:	Trive, Indianapolis, Indiana
Informational Graphics:	Rowland Design, Louisville, Kentucky
Landscape Contractor:	Sundown Gardens, Indianapolis, Indiana
Design and Construction Phases:	I and II
Date Completed:	June 1999 (Phase I, Memorial)
	June 2000 (Phase II, A Gathering of Flags)
Project Cost:	$3.5 million

PROJECT DESCRIPTION

The Congressional Medal of Honor Memorial is located on the north bank of the Central Canal in the Indiana White River State Park in downtown Indianapolis. The site is adjacent to Military Park, which was a camp used for the recruitment and training of troops during the Civil War.

The memorial is a group of twenty-seven curved glass walls, each between seven and ten feet tall. Rather than glorifying war, the memorial is a celebration of courage, heroism, and the human spirit. The walls represent the fifteen conflicts, dating back to the Civil War, in which acts of bravery resulted in the awarding of the Medal of Honor. The names of the recipients are located on the front side of the front layers, where visitors can touch them. The branch of the military service and location of their actions appear within a ring of thirty-four stars on the back. Each day at dusk, a sound system plays thirty minutes of recorded war stories about medal recipients and their acts of heroism. As each story is told, lights illuminate a portion of the memorial to highlight the war or conflict being discussed. Medal of Honor recipients have recorded most of the stories.

The materials consist of the following: concrete base, curved blue/green glass panels, aluminum and stainless steel supports, and Indiana limestone in shades of buff, gray, and pink. Each of the twenty-seven glass sails has two parallel layers of three-quarter-inch industrial glass erected twelve inches apart. Information about the 3433 medal recipients is etched into the glass walls. Steps, benches, and a grassy area provide seating for visitors.

The careful examination of materials and their application in a tactile and symbolic way is balanced by the need to push technological barriers in using light, sound, and reflective surfaces in a public memorial within a park. For the designer, the issues of durability are related to the specialized attention to surface finishes, cleaning, and maintenance, all informed by a sensibility to robust and functional landscapes from the historical past in Europe.

INTERVIEW WITH THE DESIGNER

Discussion with the landscape architect Eric Fulford took place on June 19, 2001, and March 3, 2003, by telephone. Interview participants are identified as Eric Fulford (EF) and author (Q).

Q:
When did you first become aware of how a built landscape, a designed landscape, changes over time?

EF:
I was born into the urban South and grew up in the Pacific Northwest so I had two entirely different landscapes that left me with deep and powerful visual memories. However, my conscious memory of materials, designed landscapes, and urban design was first awakened living in Portland, Oregon. It was with this acquired curiosity and awareness that I entered new landscapes, such as the Midwest or Europe. First, there were the agricultural landscapes and the historic river towns I found in Illinois when I studied at the University of Illinois, Champaign-Urbana. Later, attending graduate school at the University of Edinburgh in Scotland, I was captivated by the derelict and, at times, bold industrial landscapes scattered throughout the countryside; in particular, I was drawn to the nineteenth-century mill and company towns, to the early twentieth-century power plants, and repeatedly to the Union Canal that stretches between Glasgow and Edinburgh. All these encounters strongly influenced me, particularly regarding my sense of materials: weathered stone, rusting metal, water, and their interplay with light. Since that time, my interest in how a designed landscape changes over time continues to be informed by two separate sources: first, the beauty of the agricultural landscape and its enduring quality, which despite the ravages of time and man always nourish; and secondly, the monumen-

Figure 4.38. Union Canal, Edinburgh. (Courtesy of NINebark, Inc.)

tal built reminders of man, whether in ancient ruins or in the more recent past, abandoned industrial works. (See Figure 4.38.)

Q:

At the time, did you make the connection between them as works of a designer or designed works?

EF:

No. The only individual standout was Robert Owen's New Lanark mill and company town; beyond that, it was more about the "hands of man." To this day, that continues to humble me. Flying across the countryside, looking out the window, and seeing the network and patterns of cities, small towns and agricultural fields spread out below, you realize how little impact "designers" really make on the landscape. It is a much broader band of people, whether they are engineers or farmers or conservationists, who have a far greater impact on the land we witness, an impact of regional proportions one must respect and try to draw inspiration from.

Q:
You mentioned in the introduction that what struck you about the Union Canal was the sense of materials or the material quality of it. What did you mean by that?

EF:
I meant the striking contrasts I often felt on the Union Canal between the surrounding agricultural landscape and the canal's utilitarian but artful purposefulness. Another dramatic but simple example of this contrast is the urban/regional/geologic change that occurs between one end of the canal where Edinburgh was built of yellowish limestone and at the opposite end where Glasgow was built of red sandstone. Those layers of different materials, the engineering and straightness of the waterway, the crossing of valleys with aqueducts, the sky reflected in the line of water, seeing how all these things tie together seamlessly, *that* is an expression of material quality.

Q:
In terms of the ideas of weathering, was it the fact the canal had endured for so long that drew you to it?

EF:
Yes, it was there, intact, and still respected. Obviously, it has been maintained, but one must not forget that, at the time it was built, it was meant to endure the centuries. When they built the canal's aqueducts, they used heavy masonry arches, much as the ancient Romans would have used. There was, however, the contrasting thinness of the "modern" material of cast iron plates forming a channel that actually carries the water atop the masonry piers. As you traverse the aqueduct, no guardrail exists on the water side; only a narrow strip of metal separating the water from thin air — that is drama. Later, after returning to the States, I worked with several historic canals in northern Illinois, each with aqueducts of similar width and visual power, but their metal water channels had rusted, suffered neglect, and the water had leaked away in recent memory. You now walked across the dry bottom, your views of the surrounding landscape obscured. That sad moment spoke to me about the continued importance of people, not only in terms of physical maintenance but in the protection of a community's memory.

Q:
How do you work with the notion of progressive and cyclical weathering in your design work?

EF:
First, I must confess a fascination with the powerful image created by abandoned, weathered, and ruined buildings, industrial structures, and their sur-

rounding landscapes. Stripped of the echoes of the past, what I see are the honest, simple use of common materials and the beauty they create. That honest expression, the almost monumental quality of masonry and aged concrete walls, inspires and makes me strive to seek similar expressions in our work. So it begins with the selection of durable common materials, the use of expressive and sculptural forms to capture space or express topography, and the gradual stripping away of the design till it captures that beauty we see in weathered and abandoned structures.

Q:

Do you actually think about that in the design process?

EF:

Yes, there are a couple of things that are involved, first understanding the changes that might occur to the material itself, whether inert stone, metal, or a skin of paint. Then there is the living plant material that you want to see grow and change, and will have to be adapted, modified, and tended to over time. Some design elements or materials you want to try and maintain in a pristine way. Other elements you do not mind seeing evolve, age, or have moss grow on them. You need to think critically what the end product will be, the durability or life cycle of materials, and how the client will or will not maintain things. You must take these things under consideration as you design projects. Simultaneously, our curiosity is always pushing the edge on material selection and their application to both visual and functional issues we seek to solve. To do this and be able to implement what we conceptualize, you have to rely heavily on those that actually work with the materials, like metal fabricators, glass artists, and stone masons. These are the people whose repeated experiences over a long period of time you have to rely upon to successfully achieve what you are attempting to express or capture in your materials of choice.

Q:

If you were commissioned to do a temporary built landscape, would that alter the way you worked and in what way?

EF:

All built landscapes are inherently temporary, even the so-called permanent ones. So in the instance of a "temporary" commission, we would worry less about the durable nature of the materials chosen and experiment more with ideas or notions important to us. However, some of the practical things we have been trying to do recently have dealt with this issue of working with local neighborhoods and unsightly vacant lots. In these efforts, we create a transitional landscape, working with plants that grow far more rapidly and so are short lived. We are also dealing with inexpensive inert materials,

materials that can come off the shelf and may have themselves a short life of three to five years before they need to be either upgraded or removed. Knowing you are looking at something that has a life span of only months or a few years obviously affects your choice of materials, how they are attached, and the selection of plants you use.

Q:

Are you saying, therefore, that the temporary nature of the built work gives you more freedom because of a broader palette?

EF:

I wouldn't say it gives us more freedom, because we are always exploring ideas and materials in our permanent works. It simply reflects a more casual approach, using different types of materials for creating transitional experiences. The thing about temporary works, whether they're expressions on paper or actually built, is they allow you to experiment with forms, processes, and materials that may find their way into our permanent works. For example, a temporary work entered for the Chaumont-sur-Loire Garden Competition in France focused on water. In particular, it was concerned with the global scarcity of water, the way rainwater is captured for use, and the critical link between moisture and plants. Through a process of discussion and experimentation, we developed a series of fabric sails, stone cairns, and cisterns that captured and held water, which then released it through weeps and then transported the water to individual planting pockets. A truly fun exploration, it was fairly inexpensive, constructed of recycled materials, and temporary, of course, but it did lead to a commission for a permanent feature at the Eiteljorg Museum of the American Indian and Western Art in Indianapolis, Indiana. Here we developed a fountain system that used similar concepts to the proposed temporary installation, but now as an integral component of a much larger traditional fountain.

Q:

Even though it was a slightly different design evolution and process, you were able to elaborate it into your permanent work?

EF:

Yes. What we created was a "green" fountain, more a celebration of plants than a water display. We proposed a large stone cairn to serve as a cistern from which water would seep out its surface and feed a shallow earthen depression. That depression, intended to always be moist, was planted with a wonderful display of sedges. This "fountain" sat adjacent and attached to a larger fountain with rushing, splashing water and sculpture, which, in turn, was embraced by a prairie-style native landscape. What we were attempting was to visually play up the contrasts between the two fountains and as such the natural experience of water — one, the abundant display of flowing water; the other, water working its invisible miracle. All this resulted from our design of a temporary landscape installation for an international garden competition.

Q:

You mentioned working with fabricators and manufacturers. How do you collaborate with them in testing how a particular material will evolve over time?

EF:

My primary interest in materials rests in three areas — metal, glass, and masonry. In each area, we have been able to find very creative, imaginative, and knowledgeable people and rely upon their willingness to experiment to accomplish the work we design. Beyond them, in particular, are the concrete contractors working in the field — constructing formwork, pouring concrete, and grinding and finishing the exposed surfaces of concrete. We all derive a certain amount of pleasure from what is being built and share in the commitment to the work and the project. Each group are craftsmen who bring a knowledge and experience of how far we, as designers, can push materials and still maintain their integrity. Questions continually arise, such as: How can a design approach capitalize on quarry extraction marks and tooling? As well as: How do we use rejected overburden blocks, with their roughback finish, to capture the spontaneity and the natural character of broken and weathered stone and avoid hand-finishing everything? The same questions arise in working with glass and those craftsmen who bend, mold, cast, and form this colorful and translucent material. With the Medal of Honor Memorial (in Indianapolis), we were trying to push the technology of how to create multiple effects on a single piece of glass, without destroying what we had done previously. That process relied tremendously on not only artistry, but also on the skilled technical and business experience of the fabricators. We were very fortunate in finding people who took as much pleasure in creating those elements as we did, who equally loved to push the design and technical envelope, and who also understood the limitations of their chosen material much better than we did. As a result, there was always a wonderful give and take that happened. We were always questioning, learning, and being inspired and vice versa for them as well. In many ways, it has helped both of us to grow.

Q:

When you go back to see your built work, what are you looking for — surprises and the little "delights" of weathering you had not thought about at the time of design conception and implementation, or is there deep disappointment with what you see?

EF:

Sure, there is always a tinge of disappointment when one goes back. But there are also pleasant surprises, and I think that is integral to the experience of design. The surprise comes from the way people use designed spaces and make them their own. How they respond to something you have created in ways unexpected, both emotionally and physically. They are generally not doing dangerous and stupid things, like kids pushing each other off a high wall into a plant bed, but are playing, gathering, or using the space in ways you never imagined that gives not only them but you pleasure as well. In one project, we had designed a 150-foot-long linear fountain, which was, in essence, a canal, eighteen inches deep. On our frequent trips to the site, we had often noticed footprints on the bottom of the canal. We had imagined people were jumping in and playing around during the day. However, late one evening, near midnight, we had gone down to check that the underwater lighting was working properly. As we were sitting there, a group of about fifteen to twenty students arrived and three of them jumped in at the very far end and began a foot race down the length of the canal with the others cheering them on. It was like an initiation rite for a fraternity or club, one they obviously enjoyed, and one that appeared to have been going on since the canal was built. We have experienced similar surprising twists at other fountains we have created in the past. Simply put, people interact with the water in ways that you never quite imagine, which is really quite wonderful. They use their imagination and experience fountains that way.

Q:

What about the other side of the coin where you come across graffiti, the skateboarders?

EF:

I guess I have never encountered graffiti nor the use of skateboards I did not mind. We have never experienced skateboards really damaging anything other than the edge waxing on low walls. The biggest thing that is disturbing has been the inevitable changing attitudes and staff related to a built work. Even if you have tried to be up front with an owner or client about the need for maintenance during the life of a project, a lot of times that commitment falls by the wayside. When maintenance or repairs are performed on materials or components of the design following this failed commitment, it is often not put back in the same considered fashion as originally constructed. A quick patch job is carried out, and, as a consequence, you see the integrity of a project slowly deteriorate and that cycle just seems to feed on itself. This institutional neglect has, in our mind, bigger negative consequences on a built work than occasional youthful vandalism. I guess it comes from a failure during the excitement of the creative process of an understanding between designers and owners of what is being built, how it's put together, how it's meant to work, and the institutional commitment entailed to maintain this shared vision.

Q:

What do you think about the contemporary body of built landscape work, the work that was produced postwar, and how little of it appears to remain in good stead and, again, how do you consider the needs of future generations of designers where this built work is only preserved through photographs?

EF:

That's a difficult topic. Designed landscapes have always been subject to changing fashions and abuse. I know we have always strived to promote a timeless quality and appearance in our designs, especially with public spaces, but you can't always escape the influences of the times nor neglected maintenance. This is certainly true of the past's contemporary works. Several brilliant works inspired me to travel, to either witness their construction or to experience the spaces personally. Sometimes, I was fortunate and these works were built in my own community. Revisiting these places now can, at times, be sad, but landscapes are organic and you should expect change; however, the true success can be found in how people embrace, love, abuse, or reject these maturing works. Photographs are for memory; these spaces were meant for living. Each time you begin a design, develop concepts, or work on the construction detailing, you try to remember the lessons you've learned from your own projects and any failings. You also remind yourself of the larger body of work that does not seem to be maintained and was destroyed ten, fifteen, twenty years after it's completed. No matter how permanent you try and make something, it's only really here by the grace of the people that maintain the spaces. That's what impressed me most, if I may diverge for a moment, about a single temple in the Roman Forum. What originally upset me were people's attitudes about the Temple of Antoninus and Faustina. Today, it is dismissed as an ugly building and visitors would rather focus on some of the more prestigious ruins in the forum itself. What was important about this building is the fact that it is still basically functioning after 1500 years. Over that period, people made very conscious decisions to keep, preserve, and adapt it for whatever use they needed at the time. You do not see that happening with a lot of the landscapes that were built twenty-five, thirty even fifty years ago.

Congressional Medal of Honor Memorial
Indianapolis, Indiana

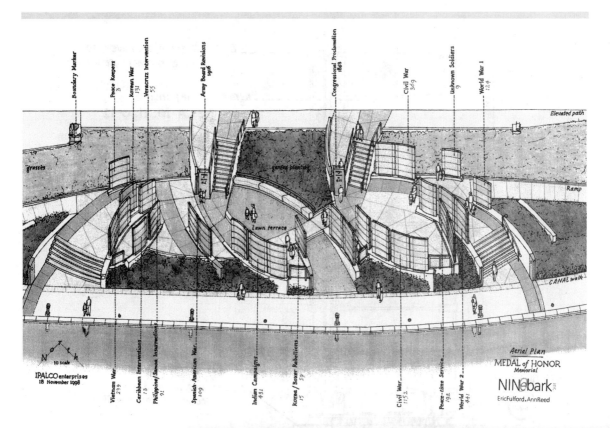

Boundary Marker
Peace Keepers *3*
Korean War *131*
Veracruz Intervention *55*
Army Board Revisions *1908*
Congressional Proclamation *1869*
Civil War *309*
Unknown Soldiers *9*
World War 1 *124*

Elevated path

grasses

garden planting

Lawn terrace

Ramp

CANAL walk

North
10 scale
IPALCO enterprises
18 November 1998

Vietnam War *239*
Carribbean Interventions *13*
Philippine/Samoa Insurrections *91*
Spanish-American War *109*
Indian Campaigns *431*
Korea/Boxer Rebellions *15 59*
Civil War *1152*
Peace-time Service *192*
World War 2 *441*

Aerial Plan
MEDAL of HONOR
Memorial
NINebark
EricFulford.AnnReed

Figure 4.39. Layout plan. Congressional Medal of Honor Memorial, White River State Park, Indianapolis, Indiana. (Courtesy of NINebark, Inc.)

Figure 4.40. General view. Congressional Medal of Honor Memorial, White River State Park, Indianapolis, Indiana. (Courtesy of NINebark, Inc.)

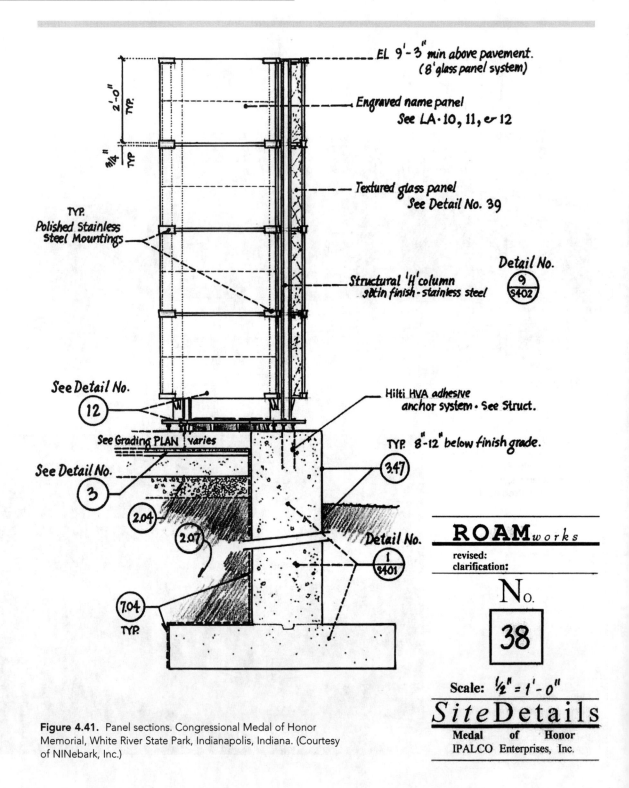

EL 9'-3" min above pavement.
(8' glass panel system)

Engraved name panel
See LA·10, 11, & 12

2'-0" TYP.

3/4" TYP.

Textured glass panel
See Detail No. 39

TYP.
Polished Stainless
Steel Mountings

Structural 'H' column
satin finish - stainless steel

Detail No.
9
S402

See Detail No.
12

Hilti HVA adhesive
anchor system · See Struct.

See Grading PLAN varies

TYP. 8"-12" below finish grade.

See Detail No.
3

3.47

2.04

2.07

Detail No.
1
S401

7.04
TYP.

ROAMworks

revised:
clarification:

No.

38

Scale: 1/2" = 1'-0"

*Site*Details

Medal of Honor
IPALCO Enterprises, Inc.

Figure 4.41. Panel sections. Congressional Medal of Honor
Memorial, White River State Park, Indianapolis, Indiana. (Courtesy
of NINebark, Inc.)

Figure 4.42. View of panels. Congressional Medal of Honor Memorial, White River State Park, Indianapolis, Indiana. (Courtesy of NINebark, Inc.)

Figure 4.44. Memorial at night. Congressional Medal of Honor Memorial, White River State Park, Indianapolis, Indiana. (Courtesy of NINebark, Inc.)

Figure 4.43. Grass planting areas at memorial. Congressional Medal of Honor Memorial, White River State Park, Indianapolis, Indiana. (Courtesy of NINebark, Inc.)

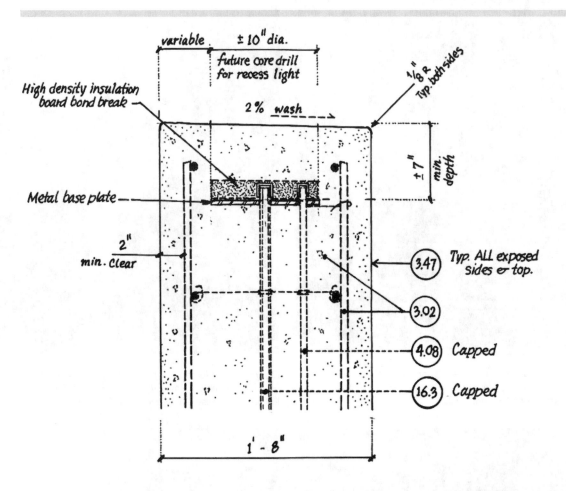

variable · ± 10" dia.

future core drill
for recess light

High density insulation
board bond break

2% wash

1/8 R
Typ. both sides

Metal base plate

± 7" min. depth

2"
min. clear

Typ. ALL exposed
sides & top.

(3.47)

(3.02)

(4.08) Capped

(16.3) Capped

1' - 8"

Future Light SECTION

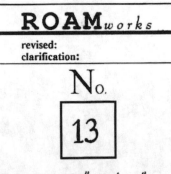

ROAMworks

revised:
clarification:

N_{o.}

13

Scale: 1½" = 1'-0"

*Site*Details

Medal   of   Honor
IPALCO Enterprises, Inc.

Figure 4.45. Future light section detail. Congressional
Medal of Honor Memorial, White River State Park,
Indianapolis, Indiana. (Courtesy of NINebark, Inc.)

Q:

By way of an introduction, can you describe the materials you worked with on the project?

EF:

In terms of materials for the memorial, we chose concrete, stainless steel, aluminum, porcelain-enameled steel for the signage, and, most importantly, glass for the etched names of the medal recipients. (See Figures 4.39–4.45) An issue with using glass as a primary material was its consistent need for washing and cleaning. This is a required weekly ritual that must occur, just like windows on an office building. For Ann and I, this was meant to show, amongst other things, that the memorial and the recipients it honors are cared for. Of course, if that ritual of cleaning the glass stops, the glass gets dirty and that commitment can be seen to immediately fall away.

In addition to the chosen materials, there were three critical groups of people who were important with regard to this project: the metal workers, the glass artists and workers, and the project manager and crews for the general contractor. I've always felt it important to talk and work with the people who actually know the material and who supervise the construction. You need their perceptions as you conduct these interviews, not just the designers. They add such valuable insight to the work we're trying to create and give us such help based upon their experience about how things can and might be built.

Q:

Do you go back to the project very often just to see how it's doing in situ?

EF:

Yes, partly because Ann, my partner, is a member of the foundation board that oversees the maintenance of the memorial and whose annual meetings we attend. It requires us to be familiar with issues involving public perceptions and weathering. As a result, we recently helped to propose and negotiate a contract for a professional gardener to take over the care and maintenance of the memorial's landscape. So instead of having a commercial landscape contractor maintain it, we now have a gardener who works with the plants, dividing, removing, adding new color, which gets back to our original intention of the landscape itself being a garden.

Q:

Would he do both living and nonliving elements?

EF:

No, only living plant material. We originally created a complex layering of ornamental perennials and native plants that gave the landscape a sense of vitality, interesting seasonal color, and texture. Generally, this has worked out well, but like any garden some plants grow more aggressively than you imagined, other plants haven't been as successful as you had hoped. What we're trying to do now is to help the landscape evolve, again with guidance from a gardener who had worked with the botanical garden at the Indianapolis Museum of Art for the last decade. His knowledge, care, and creative spark about the use of annuals, perennials as well as native plants will be invaluable for the memorial. What we've begun is a small series of changes to the garden itself that really brings back the vibrancy that complements the hard landscape elements.

Q:

How many years has it been since it was first implemented?

EF:

This is the memorial's fourth year. Most of the plants that we had specified were drought tolerant. We did install an irrigation system to get an initial growth spurt, but, to everyone's surprise, the native plants did three years' worth of growth in one season. They simply outperformed the ornamental perennials, which I think partly scared our client. It's like any garden or any designed physical space, it always needs that personal touch. It's what people responded to initially with the garden; the husbands would go off and look at the memorial, while the wives would linger around the garden. They'd point out plants and say, "Have you tried this?" "This is a lovely combination!" or "I wonder what this is?" These conversations are ongoing at the memorial and that was always one of our design intents. Now that the board has taken care of some of the other maintenance issues, they are investing time and money again on the landscape.

Q:

Major design issues or problems?

EF:

Within the first year, the main issue that needed attention was the lighting program for the memorial. Our problem was that we had tried to push light-dimming technology a little too far. We are using ground-burial metal halide lights to illuminate the memorial's glass "sails," which have performed well providing the light coverage we wanted. This was, however, coupled with a patented ballast system from a company in Louisville, Kentucky, that allowed us at dusk to program a light-dimming sequence coordinated with our audio system in a choreographed telling of individual Medal of Honor recipient stories. It was an event people would make a special trip to the memorial to witness.

Q:

This was a secure method, that you could just lock in?

EF:

Yes, the programming worked well except for initial problems with the internal clock that fired the light and audio system. The trouble was the clock was having difficulty exactly matching the weekly changing time of sunset. After several clocks, the system seemed to work fine. The thirty-minute light and sound display at dusk involved a sequential raising and dimming of the lights, highlighting specific conflicts whose Medal of Honor stories were being told. It worked well during the spring, summer, and fall, but during winter months, because of the extreme cold temperatures, it was deadly to the lamps. Instead of extending their life, which is what dimming generally promotes, it was actually shortening lamp life.

Q:

It actually achieved the opposite to what you hoped was going to happen?

EF:

With the lamps burning out during winter, the electricians initially thought it might be the current or the temperature sensitivity of the lamps being used. The patented ballast company from Louisville worked in conjunction with the electricians for more than a year, trying to figure out what the problem was. Ultimately, the experimental ballast system was completely removed, replaced with standard ballasts, and the dimming program elimi-nated. We haven't had any problems with lamp life since then.

Q:

You lost the ability to dim the lights?

EF:

Unfortunately, yes. This was one of the initial concepts that captured the client's imagination, something they were willing to spend the extra money to make work. The sequence had all the lights come on full at dusk and then drop down to thirty percent illumination. Then a Medal of Honor story would begin, say with a recipient from World War II, and the World War II "sails" would come up at full brightness. When that story finished, the light level would drop and then the next story would begin, this time the Civil War, then those lights would come up. It was a dramatic device to help draw people through the memorial. It only happened once in the evening, and people would take their friends down at that particular time, whether it was seven o'clock, eight o'clock, or nine o'clock, whenever sunset was. People seemed to find the experience very evocative and emotional, but it all hinged on the fact that the dimming would work, and in the long run it just didn't.

Q:

I think that's a very good example of how a good concept or intention can go awry and necessitate being worked through or corrected on site. If you look ahead now, what changes do you think might happen to the project?

EF:

There is the potential that future conflicts or wars may occur and, as a con-sequence, there may be a need for erecting additional glass "sails" (with the inscribed name, rank, and battlefield of each new MOH recipient). In planning for such an event, we have already included in the original construction a series of curved and polished concrete walls to serve as platforms for these future "sails." Should Medals of Honor be given, these platforms could be "activated," as each has been wired already for sound and lights. The metal halide lighting back boxes with electrical and drain conduits are already entombed within the walls; however, looking at them today, you would see no evidence of this and the walls appear similar to the others except solid on top. We have recorded the coordinate point location for all of the back boxes, so, should the need arise, we can relocate, core drill the concrete, hit a layer of protective rigid foam, remove both, and then install the specified lights. All conduit runs feed back to the buried electrical vault where the computer controls and ballasts are located. I imagine, when erected, this new addition would make a dramatic change to the familiar appearance of the memorial. There are at least four to five walls available where additional "sails" could be installed. For three of these locations, additional pavement and retaining walls would be required so visitors, comrades, and family could easily walk up to and touch the names on these new "sails" in the landscape.

Q:

As a broader question, would you say, then, that your approach to the subject of weather and durability is based on your knowledge and experience of materials and trusting in your own professional judgment that it will sustain and be durable and will change?

EF:

Yes, and I am always hopeful, but there are never any guarantees except one. Anything we typically do as a landscape architect will involve plants, and they are one designed element that is obviously going to change simply because of their growth habits and response to environmental stresses. But looming over everything is the issue of maintenance and accountability. For any public landscape that is built, say, for a university or an institution, executive officers change, maintenance staffs depart, new board members are appointed, and each new arrival brings a changed perception to that landscape. So the landscape and the design intent itself is always vulnerable and susceptible to change either from a loss of institutional memory, why the landscape was designed and built in the first case, or from neglect or maintenance cutbacks. This can happen two years, ten years, or fifty years down the road; it seems almost inevitable and there's no way to control that.

Q:

So, in a sense, yours is much more an integrating of the concerns of materials and change?

EF:

We try to educate our immediate clients; we also try to carefully introduce gardens into the work we do; the complexity, vitality, and wonderful texture that plants bring to a specific work is important to us. They're also the most fragile and the most vulnerable to change. We try to design resilient landscapes or encourage hiring a trained landscape gardener that would hopefully have an ongoing contract to watch that change, to push that change along, and to help the garden grow and mature.

Q:

In a stewardship role?

EF:

Only sometimes are you allowed that opportunity. On more complex designs, we don't see the landscape as being a static element that you plant once and walk away. It is an element forever changing, growing over a long period of time into the design vision first imagined in your mind. Particularly with the memorial or, more recently, a veteran's cemetery, our thought process on the type of plants that we select and the combination of materials that we use is dramatically different from, say, a commercial project.

For the inert materials that make up the backbone of any work, such as the walls, pavement, steps, and railings, we try to think in terms of their lifetime durability and the effects of weathering. Here you're looking at a work that will hopefully endure for seventy-five years and beyond. So we try to take into account the effects of time, both enduring and endearing. On the memorial, the glass is as strong as it ever will be. It will endure for a lifetime, but there is also the endearing human touch that's required each week to come and actually clean the glass, to maintain that wonderful transparency. The porcelain-enameled steel used for the informational signage just needs to be occasionally wiped down, but even with a coat of dust on it, you can read it pretty well. It doesn't require the kind of regular attention that the glass does.

Q:

It is quite remarkable to consider someone cleaning the landscape surfaces weekly.

EF:

Obviously, in the winter, they probably go out every couple of weeks and check the glass. However, during the summertime, they may go out as often as twice a week and clean it because of spider webs, birds, Memorial or Veterans Day weekends, or any other special events. The big cleaning issue initially with the memorial was the huge construction site across the canal from us. It was stirring up a lot of dirt and dust that meant that we had to clean the glass much more frequently than we initially envisioned. With the completion of the new Indiana State Museum, the glass is basically cleaned once a week.

Q:

Can you attempt to define, therefore, within your design work the whole subject of weathering and durability?

EF:

Weathering is climate specific. One aspect that has been driven home to me time and time again is the power of water on a horizontal surface versus a vertical surface. We have several large-scale monumental projects that were built in Indianapolis early in the twentieth century where you can see that impact. Plazas made of granite pavers have seen their horizontal surfaces moved, broken, and disrupted by weathering. The durability of granite as a material is unquestioned. But when you factor in differing expansion and contraction rates for granite, mortar, sealants, and concrete, factor in that once water penetrates the horizontal surface joints and works its way underneath and freezes with more lifting power than the weight of the granite itself, you understand the importance of routine maintenance and the critical impact of temperature. In our Midwest climate, the deep freezing temperatures and moisture we experience in winter can be extremely destructive. As a consequence, we work closely with structural engineers to help prevent the heaving that can happen with any retaining wall, stair, or built structural element.

In terms of durability, we look closely at the materials we select and how durable they are in our climate, not only to rain and water but also to sunshine and heat. Many times when working with aluminum, we specify an anodized finish rather than a paint finish. When a painted finish is required, we look to the most durable, non-color-changing process, such as enameling or powder coating, and then we are careful about the colors we select. From experience and observation, we also try to avoid certain colors that seem more susceptible to fading and chalking. Every new design, we consider and debate all these issues and more.

There is an excellent book of before and after photographs that I used recently to illustrate the temporary nature of even "durable" built works with a client. It focused on the lost buildings and spaces of Philadelphia. When first shown these images, our client misunderstood, reversing the after with the before images, missing the initial point of the story being told. Historic photographs showed elaborate homes and garden designs that were built between the 1880s and 1920s for the wealthy, where tens of millions of dollars were spent. Photographs taken during the 1970s and 1980s now showed the same scenes that had become abandoned landscapes with a few visible ruined walls. When working with clients who have money to spend on landscapes, it's a great awakening to realize that everything they spend here could become derelict or even demolished in a short time. My question for them was: What kind of legacy did they want to leave? Is this landscape something temporary, meant to give them immediate pleasure with no thought to carrying it forward, or did they want to leave something perhaps more important to future generations? What about the larger picture, how did they perceive the landscape as a legacy once it is handed down? They had never really thought about that, only the act of building, creating something great in their image. When armed with photographs documenting the fleeting nature of designed landscapes and the knowledge you carry within you of sites around the country that have met a similar fate, it gives you pause and makes you wonder a little about what you do.

<table>
<tr><td>CASE
STUDY F</td><td># DIMENSIONS OF PROCESS AND CHANGE</td></tr>
</table>

CASE STUDY F | DIMENSIONS OF PROCESS AND CHANGE

Figure 4.46. Crissy Field Pier. (Courtesy of Hargreaves Associates.)

Project Information

Project: Crissy Field: A Tidal Marsh Restoration

Location: Golden Gate National Recreation Area, San Francisco, California

Client: The National Park Service and the Presidio Trust

Landscape Architect: Hargreaves Associates, San Francisco, California

Principal Landscape Architect: Mary Margaret Jones, FASLA

General Contractor: Ghilotti Brothers Construction, Inc., San Rafael, California

Date Completed: 2000, opened May 2001

Project Cost: $32 million

PROJECT DESCRIPTION

The Golden Gate National Recreation Area (NRA) is the largest urban national park in the world. Approximately twenty-eight miles of coastline lie within its boundaries. Golden Gate NRA comprises numerous sites, including the former Presidio Military Base of San Francisco where the Crissy Field site is located.

When the Crissy Field project began in 1998, the prevailing site condition was that of a derelict concrete and asphalt paved airstrip, surrounded by miles of rusting chain-link fencing, left to decay since the facility closed in 1973. The program introduced a twenty-acre tidal marsh, a one and a third-mile promenade along San Francisco Bay, dedicated bike lanes, and a twenty-eight-acre grass airfield to be used for large public events or daily recreation. Since 1998, the National Park Service and the Presidio Trust, a special public-private governmental agency tasked with making the park financially self-sufficient by 2013, have jointly managed the Presidio.

The conversion of the U.S. Sixth Army's military installation at the Presidio into a national park encompassed the restoration and rehabilitation of the natural landscape of wetlands and dune fields along the San Francisco Bay waterfront. The landscape architects reintroduced and amplified the convoluted landforms generated by wind and waves. Crissy Field attempts to integrate a diversity of public recreational uses within a dynamic landscape environment, all within the context of an enduring landmark.

As a landscape design in the public realm addressing the passage and change of a fragile landscape over time, the project was intended to accomplish several widely divergent goals. These were to restore a naturally functioning and sustaining tidal wetland as a habitat for flora and fauna currently not in evidence on site, to restore a historic grass airfield that functioned as a culturally significant military airfield between 1919 and 1936, and to expand and widen the recreational opportunities of the existing mile and a half of San Francisco shore to a broader number of residents and visitors to the Presidio. As a case study in weathering and durability, the Crissy Field project presents the broader dimensions of cultural and natural processes and change over time. Of particular interest is the insistence on working with, rather than against, the recurring processes of tides, wind, and microclimate as well as the clear connection of the durability of the landscape processes and the ideas of landscape design. For the younger landscape architect or student, discussions on the rigor of testing the projected weathering and changes in the marsh restoration attest to the amount of background research that is needed by the designer when considering altering or restoring any built landscape to a point in time.

INTERVIEW WITH THE DESIGNER

Discussion with the landscape architect Mary Margaret Jones took place on December 18, 2001, by telephone and August 21, 2002, in Cambridge, Massachusetts. Interview participants are identified as Mary Margaret Jones (MMJ) and author (Q).

Q:

How do you distinguish between the temporary and permanent with reference to built landscape work?

MMJ:

Where other designers talk about the difference between temporary and permanent, I would talk about the difference between process-oriented landscapes and landscapes designed as set pieces. In our work, we are very interested in the process-oriented landscape. So our work is not so much set object pieces or precious landscapes that are intended to stay as originally built; they are instead intended to change, to evolve, and to be shaped by natural forces.

Q:

When you say process, you are not only talking about ecological and other physical processes but cultural processes — is that true?

MMJ:

Exactly. Crissy Field is a project that comes to mind as exemplifying both of those conditions. For the wetland and tidal marsh in the project, we did a grading plan and that was what was built. The plan was based on an optimal tidal prism to ensure the right exchange on a daily tidal basis and ensure that the mouth would stay open as long as possible before the National Park Service would have to clean out sedimentation. You need a certain exchange, a certain flow, so the tidal prism calculations ensure that. The grading plan then accommodates these calculations. But you know very well that the shape will change over time, and, in fact, the hydrologist can predict how some of that reshaping will occur based on sedimentation process modeling. Some of it is unpredictable, and that's really the beauty of it. The landscape of the fringes, of the mudflats, and the upland vegetation on the edges of the wetland will be volunteer. Although we also planted wetland species, there will be considerable change to these plantings as the wetland evolves over time. Already, the mouth moves quite a bit in the first few months.

Q:

Referring to work that is not your own or the work of the office, when were you aware of the notion in a designed landscape that this landscape would weather or change or that the ideas of durability were in the mind of the designers when they were doing it?

MMJ:

Certainly, visiting Europe is an easy answer. Rome, in particular, has all those time periods still existing in pieces and literally in layers. I grew up in one of the first houses in a new neighborhood in southeast Texas, and when we moved in it was all woods, bayous, gullies, and bay-edge wetlands near Galveston Bay. So there were incredible woodland and water-edge landscapes that I was able to play in. Then the houses expanded fairly rapidly, as it was a growing community. By the time I was in college, most of these woodlands were gone. I would still walk the remaining woods to see how they changed and evolved and maintained, in some respects, their integrity even after development happened. The teacher in my first design class at Texas A&M had designed the chapel on the campus, a really lovely piece of architecture. I remember he was beside himself because the university was changing it as they claimed it as their own. It made it past the point of being his and became theirs. I think, in particular, the issue was an alteration to the carpet color of the chapel. He talked about how hard it was for him, as an architect, to see that happen and to be so close to your own most significant works. I remember thinking that in landscape the ideas of change might be more interesting and less heartbreaking. He talked about the architect's creation of the perfect thing, perfect the day it was finished and from then on never perfect again; it does nothing but degrade. It was one of the reasons that I was much more interested in landscape architecture than architecture. I felt that landscapes change but often for the better or at least they simply undergo change for neither better or worse, and that type of change in itself is interesting. Certainly, the maturing of a landscape is something that is usually positive and beautiful.

Q:

You mentioned different types of change — in your childhood environment and in the designed object, in this case, a piece of contemporary architecture. In landscapes, there are changes that can be considered linear and cyclical in nature. In terms of the experience of a natural and a designed landscape where you are intervening in some way, how do you, as a designer, consider these types of weathering and weigh one against another?

MMJ:

In cyclical weathering, the best thing one can do, especially in the big landscape, for example, the park landscape, is to keep those man-made elements or objects simple and made from the best possible materials. So, for example, long seat walls at the shore edge might weather better made of stone rather than concrete or metal or wood. You might do them more simply to last as well. I find it more interesting to have a contrast between a few moments that are simply designed and will hold through time juxtaposed against a landscape that will change. So the contrast between the two is something that I am really interested in.

Q:

How do you, as a designer, actually work with this means of contrast, setting one up against another to basically heighten each of them as opposed to making them seem even?

MMJ:

I find that legibility of the contrast much more interesting, also easier to control and in some ways easier to achieve. If the landscape is made to be totally even, it will degrade because it cannot maintain that evenness over time.

Q:

In terms of revisiting some of your earlier projects, have you been disappointed, saddened, or delighted by unexpected change?

MMJ:

There are always elements of both when you visit a project. Some things that you never anticipated at all—in terms of how people are using the park, plaza, or riverfront promenade—and that is always exciting and wonderful. Usually, the maturing of trees is really fun; the trees grow, the canopy becomes fuller, and the shade is delightful, and that always makes it rewarding. The biggest issue is during droughts in California when fountains get turned off, even when they are using recycled or reclaimed water. Therefore, we try not to design fountains that look empty when they are turned off—because there is always that possibility. It is disappointing to visit a space and find a fountain is not on, but we talk to people and they say, "It's just off for now, we are going to turn it back on." Typically, they get turned back on because they are beloved and a highly used feature of the place.

The Guadalupe River Park project has been in place for a long time. The site has changed a lot because it has flooded up to its banks a number of times since it was built. So trees have grown, but trees have been swept away, mostly the volunteer trees. They then replant themselves in a season when there is no flood and then they are swept away again. It's a very changeable landscape. In contrast to that, the stone terraces have not changed at all. They have weathered in a very beautiful way, hardly noticeable. This was one of these conscious moves of striking flowing lines that will not change against a landscape that changes seasonally.

Q:

What do you feel about the landscape profession's current preoccupation with the topic of weathering and durability as maintenance and maintenance alone?

MMJ:

It's a little bit of an excuse really, not facing design challenges and not thinking something through. On the one hand, you could aspire to extreme maintenance, as in the example of Versailles; secretly, all landscape architects wish they could expect that level of maintenance where everything is kept perfect for generations as a National Historic Treasure, but that is not even the case for every landscape in France. Contrast Versailles to the Mall in Washington, DC, and it looks like a "shaggy dog" in comparison. So you see a difference in attitude to landscape maintenance as well as a difference in approach to design.

We think about a design that does not show its every flaw, but instead is a big, strong enough gesture that allows minor blurring to occur and actually is made more interesting. You see an underpinning of design and then an overlay of time that together makes the landscape more interesting than a set piece that is always maintained in perfection at a certain, almost-captured moment that never changes. It is most interesting if you can acknowledge that in the way you design something, so it becomes part of your thinking in that first stage of design.

Q:
Could you describe how that has resulted physically in built form in your own work?

MMJ:
One thing we have talked about a lot is how in large parks, for instance, use and cultural attitudes of how you use a park change greatly over time. The examples of Central, Prospect, and Franklin Parks, where Olmsted's original ideas of bucolic perfection have been replaced by attitudes of recreation such as ball fields and golf courses, bears this out. To some degree, you have to acknowledge that will happen, that you can't design for a culture of the future to every degree. You try to create places that are platforms for human expression and cultural change. There are certain strong simple design moves that can support an application of overlays of different uses over time. You always have something to fall back on that is still there through the ages. It's different when you get in a scale of, say, a university quad at the University of Cincinnati that is a more tightly designed landscape, a smaller space. Half of these landforms are fountains and plazas that are carefully, tightly put together. They are more of an object landscape and they are less of a process landscape by their very scale. However, we still try to allow some process change even if it is just light, shadow, and texture. But in some projects like Bxybee Park, for instance, the landscape will change significantly over time because it's built on a landfill. (See figures 4.47–4.48.) It will subside and the landform will change and that was part of the design thinking from the outset.

Q:
It will drop?

MMJ:
It will drop and change and you have to allow for that and make that part of what you do.

Figure 4.47. Aerial photograph of Byxbee Park. (Courtesy of Hargreaves Associates.)

Figure 4.48. Bikers on path, Byxbee Park. (Courtesy of Hargreaves Associates.)

In the work we have done at the University of Cincinnati, we are dealing with time in another way by capturing past physical conditions and illustrating them in new quads. We dealt with the future by setting up the quadrangles as a place of common ground, a condition that did not previously exist on that campus, so they become campus exploration, communication, and education within a total built environment—not just buildings. The other way to deal with time is knowing that landscapes will be very used in university campuses—used in a hard way. Therefore, you have to think a lot about materials and the design of details. Library Square was one of the first projects we did at the University of Cincinnati and it is on top of a parking structure. It's granite; we insisted that the pavers be granite sets and they have held up tremendously well. The spiraling seat wall was poured-in-place concrete and it is not going to last forever and should have been stone. The custom lights on top of the parking structure are glass and neon and they are holding up well. We mocked one up and hit it with baseball bats; we hit it with hammers—there is a lot of testing involved when you are going to build something in a tough environment like a university campus. Mockups are important, and I don't think enough landscape architects do mockups and test materials and build things at full scale—first in cardboard, then out of the real materials.

Q:
If you were commissioned to do work that is temporary, would that alter the way you personally work and, if so, why?

MMJ:
Absolutely. Then you can experiment and use less durable materials, you can play with them, and you can learn from how they respond to wind or light. We used fishing poles in a garden so the poles move in the wind, but this may not be appropriate in any permanent project.

Q:
I was thinking of the project under the highway—Markings—that I recently read about.

MMJ:
There, we didn't have to worry about whether or not the paint would last, and we did not have to worry about whether or not the landform would erode. We were fine with the idea that the landform would erode.

Q:
What were the basic components—I can make out in this illustration of the project elements such as paint, graphics, lighting—is that the case?

MMJ:
No, the lighting is purely borrowed from other adjacent sources by painting the columns reflective silver.

Q:

This project has a life of how long?

MMJ:

It was only supposed to have a life of six months but CALTRANS, who permitted it, have decided to leave it up longer.

Q:

So you have a chance to see how temporary is temporary?

MMJ:

We will be able to watch just how long that temporary piece holds together.

Q:

Which starts to suggest that the terms "temporary" and "permanent" are maybe very subjective?

MMJ:

They are very relative, very subjective. After all, what is temporary?

Q:

Your response to the idea of temporary work was that it maybe gave you more freedom. As a designer, is this something you are always striving for in terms of a broader palette or a richer way of doing things in the field?

MMJ:

Yes, which is why I am interested in continuing to do small temporary projects along with the larger works.

Q:

If you look at the contemporary built works of landscape architecture, many are simply not going to make it. Therefore, they may have to live through the photographs. What does that say about the landscape profession that is one that credits itself with making built social spaces and landscapes for people and ideas of stewardship?

MJJ:

That's true. Many of the projects that most informed me as a young landscape student I have never seen, because they do not exist any longer or they are private. I pored over the images and the drawings of these projects. I do not think they are any less valid. As an example, in our work we were probably less bothered by the removal of Harlequin Plaza than were others. There was a movement in Denver to save it that came to nothing, of course. In our minds, it was important; it exists in photography; we have moved on in design terms; we have other things to think about; we are not living in the past. It's sad but, at the same time, it's part of the continuum. I don't think the change of plaza is as good as it was, but it's a different client with different desires and program.

When we were asked to interview for the redesign of Skyline Park that was carried out originally by Lawrence Halprin, the first thing we did was call Halprin's office and ask them what they thought about this, because in our minds, they should be the ones to redo it. Their response was—we are frankly too busy and we are not that interested. I believe also there were mixed emotions connected with that project. It was probably not one of his better works, partly because of the constraints that were put on him at the time. Things that he had hoped would happen around Skyline Park never happened, like roads being narrowed. The project is in terrible shape, cracked surfaces, broken fountains, but, nonetheless, it was a very important project of that era in terms of a continuum of thought about what was an urban landscape.

Q:

Can you apply the concerns of process-oriented landscapes if set within a strongly restrictive ecological or engineering context?

MMJ:

I think it would be good to talk about Guadalupe River Park, which we refer to as GRP. (See figures 4.49 and 4.50.) I worked on the project for a ten-year period so that, in itself, is a process. We were hired by the city, by the redevelopment agency of San Jose, to come up with a plan that would refute the Corps of Engineers' plan, because it was a flood-control project for a three-mile stretch of the Guadalupe River where it runs through downtown San Jose. The Corps had already developed a plan to keep the flooding of downtown from occurring again, and that plan was basically to

Figure 4.49. Aerial photograph of Confluence Point, Guadalupe River Park. (Courtesy of Hargreaves Associates.)

Figure 4.50. Pathway, Guadalupe River Park. (Courtesy of Hargreaves Associates.)

riprap and channelize with concrete various stretches of the three-mile river corridor. We had to hire our own engineers and come up with a plan that would control the 100-year flood, or at least contain the 100-year flood, but also would create places for people and habitat and reinstitute and reinterpret a natural system rather than obliterate it. So it was a process of negotiation, it was a process of politics, it went to a congressional level, and it was a complete melding of the engineering and design processes. So the design was not independent of understanding the hydraulics of how the river works. I spent several days at the Water Engineering Station (WES) that the Corps of Engineers runs in Vicksburg, Mississippi, where a portion of the river project was built at a very large scale. It was about eighty feet long. And we were able to run water down it and see how the water would behave and then change the shape of it and then run water down it and see how it would then behave. First of all, we were making sure that we were containing the river and it wasn't overflowing and then we would drop sediment and see where it collected, see where sedimentation problems might occur. Dye was used as well, so that we could watch eddies and flow versus stagnation or where things were backing up. Then we actually designed the river channel and we were able to make changes to the shape of the river design and then we'd look at it again in the model.

Q

This was in an indoor environment?

MMJ:

It's a big warehouse and highly controlled. The actual model itself was plywood and a lot of clamps and some plaster, and it looked very much like the sort of sinuous, curvilinear design that we were developing. At the same time, it was fairly rough; yet they were measuring water levels with tiny needles that were calibrating to really refined levels the exact behavior of the water. The years they spent perfecting this kind of system had told them that they could do this and make a lot of conclusions based on very finite measurements of how the water was behaving in this fairly rough physical model.

So design in this case was an expression of hydrologic flows. That doesn't mean we weren't also trying to do something very conscious as a made landscape, because we were. What we were interested in doing was inserting a series of curves that were clearly man-made.

Q:

So these forms were inserted into the model and tested?

MMJ:

Then revised and then tested and revised. So we like to think of that design as being very much an expression of the hydrologic movement in the process.

Q:

Is that the first time you used research like that?

MMJ:

Well, it's the first time we had such fabulous resources at our hand. I mean, our engineers and the Corps of Engineers both were using hydrologic computer modeling as well. That was our first time to get involved with doing computer modeling and it just takes a slice down that corridor as frequently as you like. It's a series of sections that are then compiled to form a three-dimensional model.

Q:

That was paid for by the client?

MMJ:

Actually, it was paid for as part of the Corps' work; it was what the Corps had to do to before they would take on our plan. The Corps is mandated by Congress to do flood-control projects that are locally accepted. So here were the locals saying the Corps' scheme was not acceptable; the design we had developed was their preference. Our engineers showed that it worked, our Hec 2 modeling studies showed that it worked, and they needed to embrace it. The Corps said, "Then we're going to have to work together to model it and study it with our methods before we'll claim it as our own," and that's what we did. So we worked hand in hand, and eventually they took on our design as their project and that's what largely got built. And, also, that's why it took ten years, because they then had to go back and negotiate who was paying to build it, because, even though they had to make it locally acceptable, they didn't have to completely pay for everything that made it locally acceptable. So there was a local cost share and that had to be negotiated.

Q:
Could they model the 100-year floods and how the land would change over time?

MMJ:
That's what we did—twenty-year floods, five-year floods, one-hundred-year floods—to see how each would behave and because each is quite different and each had to be accommodated.

Even though we were putting in gabion basket terraces (metal cages, if you will, filled with stones) that were very much perfect arcs, we knew that they would fill with dirt and fill with plant material and roughen over time and be more hidden. So, even at this stage, there was the recognition that this would change over time. The geometry would become blurred and obscured somewhat over time. Oftentimes, the floods clear out a lot of volunteer vegetation and then suddenly the terraces are revealed again. Then you go for a period of time without a flood and much of the volunteer vegetation comes back, and it's amazing to what degree that happens. Shrub willows grow very fast. And by the end of a growing season, the river can be full of beautiful shrub willows and looking quite vegetated and lush, and after a flood much of that is cleared out and the bones of the structure read again. And this is something we embrace; this is something we were interested in actually exploiting.

Q:
Over time, you see two processes. One is the revegetation process as the sediments build up, and then the events you described, which rip it all out and reveal the structure. Is the project to remain juvenile and arrested, never being allowed to fully mature?

MMJ:
To some degree, that's true and also not true. The big trees above the low water levels don't go away; they are permanent and growing like crazy. The

Figure 4.51. Marsh, Crissy Field. (Courtesy of Hargreaves Associates.)

trees in the terraces that we planted are growing and becoming beautiful canopy trees and making a very lush landscape. The volunteer stuff is smaller and shrubbier and it's all the grasses and the reeds and the shrub willows; those are more temporal. So it has a couple of layers. We used a combination of gabion terraces and stone and schist terraces where people sit and walk and get access to the river. The schist is beautiful native rock, which came from Southern California and looks as good as it did the day it was put in. So there is, again, this contrast of materials; we invested in really substantial stone at the points of most human interaction, knowing that the planted trees and those terraces will create a landscape that will mature but not degrade, while the gabion landscape that forms the majority of the banks is intended to change.

In the upper level park out of the river, the city has come in and added elements like carousels, which we wish we had designed in ourselves, but, at the same time, we set up the park in such a way that it formed "rooms," knowing that the city would want to come in and put stuff in these "rooms" for whatever uses over the years, and that has worked great.

Crissy Field: A Tidal Marsh Restoration
San Francisco, California

Q:

I wonder if we could now talk in more depth about the Crissy Field project. What are the cultural forces at play there?

MMJ:

In terms of cultural processes, Crissy Field is responding to cultural forces on a number of levels. First of all, it's a cultural landscape, and that's a very specific sort of title when you're working with the National Park Service [NPS]. The NPS has a department of cultural resources that dealt with addressing historic landscapes such as Crissy Field. Crissy Field itself is the term for the airfield particularly used by the biplanes flown in the 1920s. That's what gives Crissy Field its status as a historic landmark. There was a great deal of time spent considering how to express the essence of the airfield, whether to do a strict restoration of an airfield or an interpretation of an airfield, and that was a large part of the design. In fact, it is an interpretation of the airfield, rather than a strict restoration.

Q:

Were there any other cultural periods that were significant there or was it simply the airfield?

MMJ:

There were many periods that were significant, and this led to a lot of the conversation because as far as the natural resource staff was concerned within the National Park Service, the fact that it had previously been tidal marsh and occupied by Native Americans was just as important. But that's not what gives it its historic landmark status. So there are certain rules for that part of it that gives it a historic landmark status that are different than the rules for the rest of it, which were interpretation. So that's why we like to think of Crissy Field as a layering of many periods of time and many different influences on the site, all expressed through the design. There was also the recognition that Crissy Field would, in terms of the cultural context of a major urban center—San Francisco—need to take on a new life. We desired to let it become a forum for the cultural expression of the people of San Francisco and the people who would visit Crissy Field. So the airfield is a simple plane of grass, with walks across it that connect some of the historic doorways and destination points of the hangar buildings and barracks that surround it. But other than that, it's pretty simple. It strikes a datum so it responds to the grade changes around it in very subtly different ways on all its edges and so it becomes a landform object, but other than that it's fairly subtly expressed. This was the shape of a grassy airfield and the airplanes would have been in the hangars surrounding it, and they would have circled around one end of it and headed toward the Golden Gate Bridge and they had to take off through that gap. They even continued to do it somewhat after the bridge was built, which is pretty amazing to fathom.

Q:

Out of the process-oriented landscape and vis-à-vis the cultural, you have ended up with a form that is a landscape as a set piece, which is your second condition?

MMJ:

Exactly, and it actually interjects into the marsh, because both of them needed to be bigger in order to work. The airfield had to be a restoration of the shape and size that it originally was; the tidal marsh needed to be a certain size to function, to stay open, to function as a tidal marsh. (See Figure 4.51.) So they actually sort of interject into each other in order for each of them to be the right size. Therefore, the airfield forms this fabulous promontory out over the marsh and these layers of history come together. (See Figure 4.52.) It's actually one of my favorite spots of the whole project, where all of this comes together, where the airfield is most objectified as a landform and juts out over the tidal marsh, and the tidal marsh creeps up the sides of the airfield, accentuating the airfield's shape.

Figure 4.52. Aerial photograph, Crissy Field. (Courtesy of Hargreaves Associates.)

Figure 4.53. Photograph of trees, Crissy Field. (Courtesy of Hargreaves Associates.)

Figure 4.54. Sunset, Crissy Field. (Courtesy of Hargreaves Associates.)

Q:

There has been recent discussion about a built or designed landscape being a measurement of natural processes. Does this influence how you would consider weathering and change in a project?

MMJ:

At Crissy Field where water moves in and out, and the water level changes throughout the day, you can mark that change through the weathering of the airfield edge. It changes the shape of the end of the airfield as the tide moves in and out on a daily basis. So the airfield is more accentuated at high tide, and less accentuated at low tide. In the same way, I would have to refer to Candlestick Park, an earlier work of the office, where the central grass plane is surrounded by water and becomes a pier into the bay at high tide. Mudflats surround it, and at low tide we call them tidal gardens. You can walk through those mudflats so that it's not a pier at all; it's a part of a landscape. In another early project, Byxbee Park, which is, of course, built on a garbage landfill, it was of great concern to the engineers that we wanted to place this pole field on one of the points where the dump extends into the marsh on one side and the Corps of Engineers' slough on the other side. We put the field of poles on spread footings, because we couldn't, at that time, penetrate the cap, because it was the belief, at that time, that that would ruin the function of the clay cap in terms of the escape of methane gases and the breakdown of the landfill itself. So the pole field is on spread footings. The engineers were very concerned that, as the garbage settled, which garbage does, that the pole field would become very crooked. They would cease to be vertical and the poles would start to take on various tilts and orientations. We were thrilled with that idea, because we actually hoped they would and, in fact, they haven't very much.

Q:

They're actually as straight as the day they were put in.

MMJ:

We thought it would be a great way of registering that this is not terra firma and what's below here is not what you think. What's always interesting to us is to somehow mark our projects. In the temporary installation we carried out below the freeway in San Jose that I mentioned before, that's primarily the root of the name. I was marking something that is a phenomenon that is happening anyway, but it's amplifying it, making it register.

I don't think I finished the cultural process issue for Crissy Field, because I think there is one last thing. There is the expression, interpretation, and restoration of the airfield as a cultural layer in that landscape, but then there's the future. We find it really important that landscapes have a flexibility in their design, so that they can be used in a multitude of ways, some of which we haven't yet envisioned. It's important that landscapes not be designed for single users, which so many are, and then they become dated or they become unusable and they must be changed. If you can figure out a way to really create a platform, a stage, for various kinds of uses, you will set up a community forum in a much better way. (See Figures 4.53 and 4.54.)

Q:
So the more things you introduce the less flexible it is?

MMJ:
That's true, and so you look for ways of making a landscape complex that are more subtle and that are layered in more interesting ways, without tripping it up.

Q:
In the end, you've got twenty different things in the space and you can't use it.

MMJ:
Exactly, and we face that more and more, especially in large parks relative to the issue of sports fields. Soccer fields are an issue. If you put up a formal field with bleachers, etc., that's the only way it's ever used. It's much better to think about big, flat, green surfaces that can be used for organized sports but can also be used in other ways.

Q:
Finally, I was wondering, again, if you had come across anything in your academic or professional travels that talks about how landscapes change?

MMJ:
No, I think there's a great absence of understanding and exploration of this idea. I would have to go back very far to Robert Smithson and some people who did talk about it. What they were lacking was what landscape architecture can bring to that subject, which is an understanding of science, an understanding of ecology, and an understanding of a different orientation that has to do with culture rather than what the land artists were thinking about. Artists like Robert Smithson were thinking of a phenomenon and exploring that phenomenon and registering change related to phenomenological experiences.

Q:
In terms of this continuum, could you give us your definition for "weathering" and "durability" from a design point of view in landscape architecture that would be applicable to current as well as previous eras?

MMJ:
To me, the words "weathering" and "durability" do not capture the full essence of the subject. They leave out process as well as notions of change.

Weathering and change are different. Weathering is what happens to an object or place when the elements change it over time by, for example, the sun beating down on it, the wind beating it, the roots underneath moving around. Durability is how well materials stand up to that weathering. To me, that's only part of the subject. Process has to do with intentional change, recognized change, or embraced change, and that's the other fifty percent of the issue. In the end, landscapes have to be durable culturally, as well as durable physically.

<table>
<tr><td>CASE
STUDY G</td><td># AESTHETICS OF CULTURAL WEATHERING</td></tr>
</table>

Figure 4.55. Graffiti image. (Courtesy of Office of Mikyoung Kim.)

Project Information A

Project: Moylan Elementary School Playground

Location: Hartford, Connecticut

Client: Hartford Public Schools, Don Carso, Principal,
Department of Buildings and Grounds,
Hartford, Connecticut

Landscape Architect: Office of Mikyoung Kim, Brookline, Massachusetts

Project Designer: Mikyoung Kim, ASLA

Design Assistants: Frank Liggett, Robert Mercer,
and Michael Norpell

Architect: Tai Soo Kim Partners, Architects

Photography: Mikyoung Kim, Timothy Hursley, and
Melissa Cooperman

Landscape Contractor: New Field Construction, Hartford, Connecticut

Specialty Fabrications: Rubberized play mats

Design Phase: Beginning of design, 1992

Date Completed: 1995

PROJECT DESCRIPTION

The Moylan Elementary School is a public school located in an African-American community in the city of Hartford. One of the key goals of this project was to empower the students with a sense of ownership of this space. The emphasis in the design was placed on a "hide-and-seek" wall that allows for multiple interpretations of play by the children. The design of the wall incorporates visual ideas found in children's games (such as hide-and-seek and pin the tail on the donkey) that use the access or denial of vision as a key to the element of play.

The wall acts as a device that allows the students to engage with it in two ways. The first is one of visual control, which allows them to monitor who enters and exits the courtyard without being seen themselves, by viewing through the many perforations in the wall. The other way that the wall engages the students is through the openings themselves. The multiple sizes of windows and doors change the speed at which the children run, crouch, crawl, jump, sit, and walk through the "hide-and-seek" wall.

The south side of the wall is divided by "play columns" that create a third space between the more public north side and the more playful south side. This tertiary space is defined by the activity that occurs within it, so that at certain times it becomes extremely active, and at other times, it becomes a sanctuary of more quiet and secretive activity between the two more open spaces. The wall wraps around the east side of the courtyard and forms the back of the amphitheater.

The entry corridor is filled with a grove of trees that the students walk through in order to enter the classroom precinct. The grove is defined on one end by the front entry and on the other by a break in the "hide-and-seek" wall and acts as a place to reorient students from the street life they have just left behind. When the trees cross the wall to the south side of the playground, they are interspersed among the other elements and break the pattern of the paving.

The project offers a space to the children that uses vision as a way of empowering them and creates a place that asks for redefinition each time they enter the playground.

Project Information B

Project:	Courtyard and Meditation Labyrinth
Location:	Chester, Connecticut
Client:	Congregation Beth Shalom Rodfe Zedek, Donna Moran, President
	Carol and Sol LeWitt
Landscape Architect:	Office of Mikyoung Kim, Brookline, Massachusetts
	Project designer: Mikyoung Kim, ASLA
	Project architect: Raphael Justewicz
	Horticultural consultant: Jane Shoplick
Architect:	Sol LeWitt and Stephen L. Lloyd
Photography:	Mikyoung Kim
Landscape Contractor:	George Amarant
Project Manager:	Michael Fiorillo and David Burkett
Specialty Fabrications:	Benches: Gustaf and Frederic Carlson
Design Phase:	2001 (Phase I, Courtyard), 2600 square feet
	2003 (Phase II, Labyrinth), 18,700 square feet
Date Completed:	Summer 2003

Rhode Island School of Design (RISD), Providence, Rhode Island, students participated in design *charettes* and fabrication activities: Sage Van der Swaagh, David Dwight, Zachary Stevens, Victoria Su, Davit Elecson, Kelly Lee, Maria Beatrice Mestre, Andrea Fox, Vanessa Eickhoff, Michelle de Tarnowsky, Shane Zhao, Brennan McGrath, Katherine Wong, Lauren Bello, Lauren Carter, and Hue Nguyen.

PROJECT DESCRIPTION

This design is an exploration in the ways that cultural rituals intersect with the natural cycles. The design incorporates two time cycles of ritual. The first is the formalized agricultural ritual of the Jewish festival of Sukkoth in early fall. The second is the private daily engagement of meditation within the labyrinth, here made of epai wood and decomposed granite framed by steel. A mosaic of different grasses and vegetation defines the walls of the meditation labyrinth. This experience within the labyrinth changes throughout the year. In early spring, mustard grasses predominate the site. Later, in early summer, a combination of native grasses takes precedence, followed in late summer and early fall with the grasses changing to a reddish and gold autumn color.

During the Sukkoth celebration, the central area of grass is mown to create a room where the festival occurs. The ritual of the Sukkoth is marked in this construction by eleven permanent wooden totems. In their red color and in their scale, they relate to the columns of the interior sacred space. In the early fall, temporary structures (known as sukkahs) are built against these totems. Natural materials are used to create a partially protected shelter for meals and the harvest festival. The redefinition of this landscape from path to room, or clearing, and then back to path, marks the shifts in the reading of this labyrinth/sukkah.

The design allows for a direct engagement of individuals to place, for humans to carve out their spaces for rituals in both private and public ways. This engenders an understanding of the shifts in nature and a greater connection with the cycles of ecology.

Materials Utilized in the Project

Epai wood (boardwalk of labyrinth)

Decomposed granite with aluminum edging (labyrinth)

Light gray concrete, black integrally colored concrete (courtyard)

White oak timber and stainless steel solid legs (benches)

Plants

Native grasses and wildflowers

Amelanchier laevis

Christmas fern and native ferns

Clethra alnifolia

Viburnum dentatum

The same designer presents two projects here. They both demonstrate a singular approach to the subject of weathering and durability where the issues of the cultural uses of a site, the markings and wearing of built landscapes in the course of daily use or more ritualized activities, are balanced against a robust material approach to the realities of making built landscapes for the short or long term. For the young landscape architect or student, there is a longer discussion here regarding the role of maintenance as a necessary activity early on in the design process and the close relationship between the research and documentation of materials and finishes. Cultural markings, whether graffiti on a concrete slab or mowing regimes in a field of grasses, are transformed into landscape strategies for controlling the passage of time or acting as a measurement of small local human activities as well as larger social or religious traditions.

INTERVIEW WITH THE DESIGNER

Discussion with the landscape architect Mik Young Kim took place on February 22, 2001, and March 17, 2003, at the offices of Mik Young Kim, Brookline Village, Massachusetts. Interview participants are identified as Mik Young Kim (MYK) and author (Q).

Q:
If we look at the drawings on the wall here in your office, they describe a design project, they describe a spatial form, they describe materials, both living and inert, and particularly patterns and particular organizations, but, as a designer, how do you think about this project after the implementation and after the execution—as it will change or not change over time?

MYK:
I think, in the context of the life of a project, one is always thinking of the life of a project and thinking about the beginning. The beginning is always a known moment where a project opens and you do a set of drawings that prepares you for the beginning.

Q:
The beginning for you is, therefore, not the completion of the project on site, rather the start of the design process?

MYK:
When you think about the life of a project, it always has a kind of death to it, like our own lives. For me, the idea of durability is something I discuss with clients a lot. The first question is often what will this look like in three years—but that's a contrived condition that we look at through cultural lenses. Weathering is really a consideration of time and phenomena, and when a project begins is often a perception of what is acceptable socially. So often when we say, "the project begins," we would like, on the one hand, to say after the trees are twenty years old—that's the ideal—but also the tectonic architectural elements have just come from the fabricator, they are that new. So when I think about the issues of weathering once the project leaves my hands, what arises are the traces of human interaction and phenomenology that always lend a layer of poetics to a project. They are beyond your control and you don't know the patterns that these shifting conditions will place on a project. That unpredictable quality is something we are all attracted to. What I am interested in my own work is a kind of cultural weathering.

Q:

How would you define "cultural weathering" rather than, say, climatic weathering?

MYK:

As humans, we are part of the natural process, so it's about the "leanings" on a project and the range of the traces we place on the landscape. Most of my work is in highly trafficked, intensively constructed urban conditions. So I am interested in the daily passage, the recurrent rituals of people through the space. For example, minute traces of cultural weathering occur when I take my hand and place it on a surface. The residue from that hand creates a mark, an interaction. I try to create canvases that encourage the markings that we make as human beings. I am currently working on a project in Seattle where a series of laminated pieces of glass that have fiber-optic cables in them is being proposed. I was asked by the client what would happen if someone shoots a gun at it. I thought it was a valid question based on its location; it's a tough neighborhood, and it was the first time I had the clients talking about the possible beauty of that violent interaction or marking. It's an extreme example, but clients often want to deter landscape architects from acknowledging markings in their work, violent or not. I have carried out work in urban playgrounds where I create surfaces that encourage the voice of people through, for example, spray painting. I find those to be the most evocative murals you can find in urban neighborhoods rather than contrived ones that are the work of someone hired to carry them out.

Q:

Would you describe alterations or significant additions brought to your work by others who may be design professionals as cultural weathering?

MYK:

That's a natural part of the design process—it's probably more a form of conceptual weathering. When I think of weathering, I think of it as a material-based endeavor—a transfer or redistribution of materials from one place to another. The oil from your fingers or paint from a can to a landscape surface and, reciprocally, the decomposed granite that is embedded in your shoe and leaves with you, eroding the site.

Q:

Do you see that as layering as opposed to a process of entropy—a process that starts with a mass of material and eventually decays to dust or weathering as slowly accreting and accumulating?

MYK:

I think it's both. I think that's why we perceive weathering to be so poetic, because it's a visual manifestation of these incredible juxtapositions of time—one being accretions or erosions that happen over minute daily increments and the other what happens over decades—we see these two conditions at once. In fact, weathering in my work has to do with the juxtaposition of the design I control and the moment you let it go. That's where I create these places where letting go is a relatively easy way for the layering to occur. I think the notion of sedimentation or accumulation of things happens in a time frame that is shorter. The idea of erosion or eventually something dying or becoming dust happens over a much longer period of time. Weathering is also concerned with our perceptions of beauty—we accept most types of phenomenological weathering. For example, I am working on a project with the artist Sol LeWitt using Corten steel that seeps and creates stains on vertical walls and the ground plane, a kind of erosion and sedimentation, and everyone is getting very excited about that possibility. On the other hand, I have photographs of one of the urban playgrounds I worked on prior to demolition that had moments of what could be called "urban markings" that were clearly done over time. Someone placed spray paint, someone scratched on surfaces, asphalt was overlaid—a palimpsest occurred. I showed these to the clients, and they did not find it an acceptable form of weathering.

Q:

Does attention to this form of markings and change in the landscape run counter to a real understanding of the thing itself? The designer falls in love with the phenomena of weathering rather than weathering itself?

MYK:

There is an extreme position often found in the public realm that defines maintenance as a fixed condition. I was in Cambridge in the early 1980s and thinking of becoming a landscape architect at that time. I remember walking through the quad on the Harvard campus and it was in the year that they had started to renovate the front staircase of the Widener Library. The approach is to the main door, and there was an eroded area at the center of the steps that described the hundreds of thousands of students, tourists, and parents who have gone up and down these stairs, the memory of their presence. That was a kind of cultural weathering for me; it tells us where they walked, all with a relatively similar route and marking. That passage has an incredible poetics for me—it made me very sad that they had chosen to erase that passage completely (through the renovation and removal of the steps). The Italian architect Carlo Scarpa gives clues as to how to approach this kind of weathering. In the Querini Stampalia, he placed a layer of limestone above an eroded stair so you have that palimpsest—the reading of different conditions of time. I think there could be a balance if there were more discussions about the possible beauty of cultural weathering in the public realm.

Q:

If we could now address weathering and durability over the longer term. As a designer, you travel a great deal and look at certain spaces, particularly urban spaces, through the study of precedents. When you realize that the space is possibly 300 years old, there is a certain interest and love of the thing itself and a sadness because you realize that how can we, as a present culture, create something that has that longevity. In fact, there is a contemporary notion that the spaces are what they are because of that passage of time they still have to acquire. It requires a form of buffing. I wonder what you think of that in relation to looking backwards and looking now at the work that you do?

MYK:

I accept that the work that I do has its own cycles and duration, whether these are three years or a hundred years. There are lots of landscapes that I know that are gone, and I can only imagine them, but I'm not sure I wish for them to be re-created. I am not a nostalgic person; I always like to look forward as I learn from the past. A place I have spent some time in is Paris, and the aspects of that urban landscape that have become more and more interesting to me are the ways in which layers of time are integrated into the city. For example, where a curb now has to meet the concerns of handicapped accessibility. Somehow four different materials meet at a corner, which start to define it as a place in a very different way from American cities where still things are relatively new. We save landscapes, but our notion of saving them is very different; we encase them and view them from a distance. I believe that unless we start this dialogue about time there will not be any opportunity for this rich palimpsest of materials and experiences. I remember hearing a lecture by Eduard Sekler on rehabilitating or renovating buildings rather than thinking we are going to obliterate, at one extreme, or going to renovate them perfectly to some period. He was advocating a distillation of the tenor of a place.

Q:

What is the relationship between weathering and materials and materiality in your own work as it relates to the issues of presence and perhaps absence?

MYK:

My current work really focuses on the relationship between materiality and different types of human interaction and engagement with the site. I'm interested in the reciprocity between the body and the materials of a landscape. At Kent State University in the Liquid Crystal Science Center, we developed a series of aluminum plate walls, which have fiber-optic light threaded through the plates. The lights are triggered by human heat through a laser sensor. This was an analogy to the way in which liquid crystals themselves are triggered by a specific temperature. But what interests me most about this idea is that the landscape is not necessarily physically touched, but engaged at a distance—and that interaction brings color and light to the walls.

Moylan Elementary School Playground
Hartford, Connecticut

MYK:

In our playground at the Moylan Elementary School (see Figures 4.56 to 4.59), the concrete walls are intentionally built with subdued muted colors to encourage the kind of urban markings I was talking about earlier. Again, that the landscape is not prescribed, a fixed product once the last brick is in place, but that it is a fluid and evolving condition changed by the daily rituals of humans and the shifts in phenomenology. It makes for work that may not always be photogenic because it relies on that relationship of individual to the landscape to trigger the multiple readings that emerge.

Q:

Leading on from this, what people commonly think of when they hear weathering is this issue of climate in a more specific way. What is the relationship to climatic change in your design work, especially as your projects move out of this region?

MYK:

I can talk about it in terms of water and the reading of temperature shifts where there is a freeze-thaw condition. We are working on a project in New Haven, Connecticut, which focuses on both the freeze-thaw condition of water and the containment and collection of water. We are creating a series of stainless steel collection leaves that divert water into open rain columns. Right now, we are testing ways in which the pattern of water collection and the freezing process of water add a layer to the design of this project.

Q:

Materials in the designed landscape don't exist inert, whether they are steel or stone. Through climatic conditions as well as an approach to craft, they are worked in many different ways. As a designer, how does the proposed workmanship of these materials change your attitude to possible weathering?

MYK:

It has to do with the intention of the designer. My premise as a maker and an artist is that there is a level of intentionality to my work that will eventually be eroded and accreted by different kinds of weathering. There is a point during the life of the project where I am not shy to say that there is a recognizable hand. I feel very strongly that there are certain types of landscapes that need that and that's what often is the beginning point of giving character or tenor to the space. Sometimes it has to do with surface—

Figure 4.56. "Hide-and-seek" wall. Moylan Elementary School, Hartford, Connecticut. (Courtesy of Office of Mikyoung Kim.)

Figure 4.57. "Hide-and-seek" wall. Moylan Elementary School, Hartford, Connecticut. (Courtesy of Office of Mikyoung Kim.)

Figure 4.58. Peeking high at "hide-and-seek" wall. Moylan Elementary School, Hartford, Connecticut. (Courtesy of Office of Mikyoung Kim.)

Figure 4.59. View of playground. Moylan Elementary School, Hartford, Connecticut. (Courtesy of Office of Mikyoung Kim.)

although I have noticed that there is often a tendency towards a surface of nostalgia.

Q:

"Surface of nostalgia" for you, then, is a processed industrial weathering?

MYK:

A contrived weathering, to be more precise. It has to do with intentionally creating a false reading of time in the materials and their surfacing. It is a veneer that often hides something. I guess I am distrustful of these types of surfaces because they intentionally mislead the participants in their understanding of a project. When was it built? How was it built? As a maker of landscapes, I walk around the city and look at built works like an archeologist trying to understand the manner of construction through the clues that remain on this veneer. It's wonderful when a project moves beyond the surface . . . or that the surface is informed by a material integrity, the core of the project. I think this connects to weathering—as the project erodes or accepts the impact of sedimentation, it eventually reveals anything that you are trying to hide. Better to make landscapes that embrace or acknowledge this process.

Q:

Have there been any designers or artists who have influenced you in thinking about this particular issue?

MYK:

I don't know a designer off the top of my head. However, I think part of it is a reaction to the glossy pictures in magazines, in the desire to fix a place and find that ideal position of it. There was a film that I saw many years ago, done by the British artist Tom Philips, where he started on a piece of paper with charcoal and then photographed it at increments, until he felt the drawing was completed; it was a process of accretion on the page. Then he continued to film as he removed it completely so it came back to the white piece of paper.

Q:

Was that by erasing or painting on top?

MYK:

Completely by erasure and so it was a complete circle. It began and ended with a white piece of paper.

Q:

So the product was the film?

MYK:

The product was the film and the process. What I found interesting were the photographs, the stills of the film. What he was saying or the message he was giving out was—I'm not showing the actual drawing because the drawing was finished at ten different moments. And that really informed me about a new way of thinking about drawing and also a new way of thinking and watching landscape evolve. I lived in San Francisco for three years, and there the changes are much more subtle. I think it's just being in different geographic locations and understanding the different types of change and durations of those changes. I think a lot of times when we talk about ecology we talk about it as we are separated from the processes of nature and we're going to renovate a landscape to some ideal position. How we choose that, or the discussion of what native and what nonnative is—I always wish that those discussions were more nuanced and more about the middle ground than between black and white.

Q:

How does that sit, then, with your role as a practicing landscape architect and seeking clients who possibly don't embrace that idea or maybe have no concept of what they should embrace?

MYK:

It's often finding opportunities. In the beginning, I worked on projects which had limitations, either budgetary or they were projects that maybe other people didn't think were sexy projects. I had to find a way of getting a certain constituent to embrace the landscape and steward it and participate in it. That probably has contributed to the way in which I work now; we have the luxury of finding clients or clients find us because they want something different or something special. When I start off by talking to them about their part in this design, it's different from the community process of design when people say that you're part of this; we don't ever relinquish our hand in design. We make it very clear that we are the makers, that's the first step, and that's why we're brought in, but that they are also part of that vision. We haven't yet stumbled upon somebody who's not interested in that. I think people, whether it's public or private, their eyes light up when we offer them that possibility. I have found that they are much more amenable to doing something that's visually innovative... something they haven't necessarily seen before because they feel like they are embarking on a new relationship, so they're willing to actually try new ideas. I know there's a lot of project work that's clearly designed, that's clearly contemporary, and that's done behind closed doors, then in ten years gets removed. It doesn't get taken care of because people don't understand it. You work on something for many years with a client, and if I felt that they didn't understand what we were doing, I would feel that I hadn't done my job.

Q:

The notion of the materials themselves is very important to you. I thought we might talk in more detail about a project or specific projects where this is brought out more fully.

MYK:

One of the things that's becoming more important in my work is the idea of weathering at the most simplistic level through a maintenance plan. The issue of engagement, of how human beings actually change or transform the landscape, might not just be through the way they rub against something or other forms of inadvertent interaction. What's becoming more clear in my work is an interest in becoming more aggressive about that interaction, offering our clients the opportunity to take control of the project. For example, we're working on a Jewish community center and synagogue again with the artist Sol LeWitt.

Q:

Where is it located?

Courtyard and Meditation Labyrinth
Chester, Connecticut

MYK:

It's in Chester, Connecticut, on a wetlands site. Sol designed the building with the architect Stephen Lloyd. (See Figures 4.60 to 4.63.) They initially commissioned us to design a meditation labyrinth funded by a grant from a number of their congregation members. We then studied how they would use the space and found that they had actually saved an area for a ritual of Sukkoth building. It's a temporary structure related to a fall agricultural ritual. It has to be a structure that's made purely out of natural materials. It also has to be temporary, so the individuals in the synagogue build this structure, they eat in it, they do different rituals, and then they take it down.

In order to expand the scope and the budget of the design, we merged the meditation labyrinth with the sukkah structure—two different types of rituals, two different time components and durations of rituals. One is everyday, maybe five times a day and less controlled—the meditation labyrinth—and the other, the Sukkoth, which is once a year in the fall.

Q:

Which is the temporary building or structure?

MYK:

Yes, the sukkah building. In this project, native grasses were planted to create a choreography of different kinds of colors that merged with the native vegetation. In the fall, there's a path, a pedestrian circuit, that is framed by high grasses that will eventually reach six feet in height—that's the

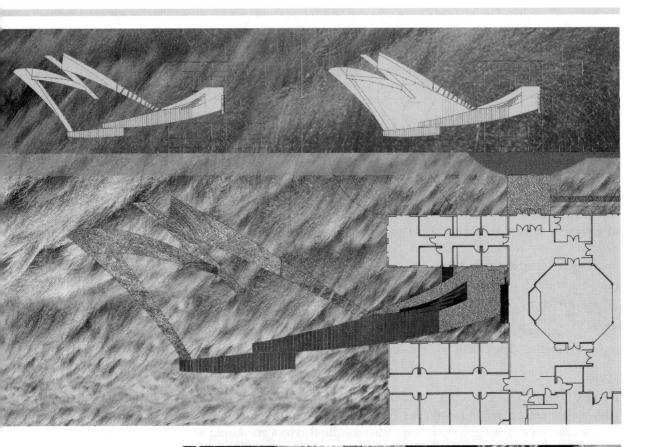

Figure 4.60. Design plans. Courtyard and Meditation Labyrinth, Chester, Connecticut. (Courtesy of Office of Mikyoung Kim.)

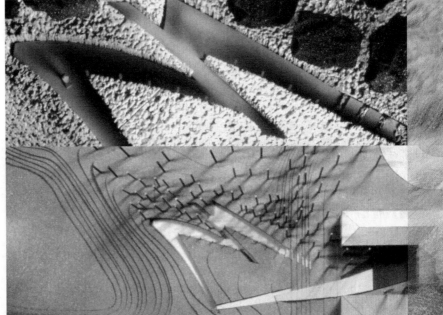

Figure 4.61. Design models. Courtyard and Meditation Labyrinth, Chester, Connecticut. (Courtesy of Office of Mikyoung Kim.)

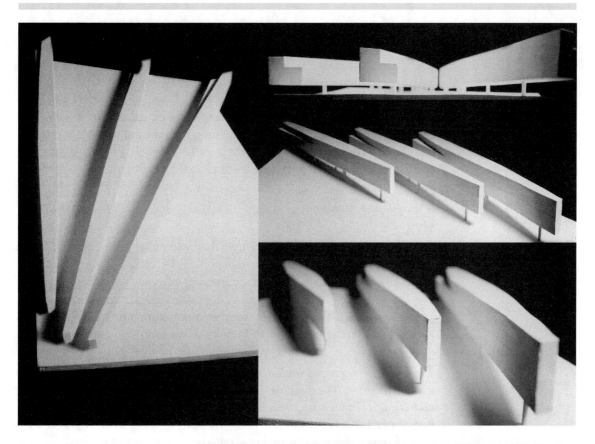

Figure 4.62. Bench studies. Courtyard and Meditation Labyrinth, Chester, Connecticut. (Courtesy of Office of Mikyoung Kim.)

Figure 4.63. Bench models, Courtyard and Meditation Labyrinth, Chester, Connecticut. (Courtesy of Office of Mikyoung Kim.)

labyrinth and clearly an individual experience. Once a year, the grasses that are located in the central space are cut or mowed in a pattern and we have offered a maintenance plan for these first two years. The grasses from the mowing are then used for the thatching of the temporary structure of the sukkah. So it's a much more aggressive way of saying here's how you actually change the understanding of weathering and durability of the site. Not only in terms of the cycles of nature, but it's a message that we wanted to send to the congregation, which they really embraced, which is you (the congregation) are part of the cycles of change.

Q:
Is the mowing ritualistic?

MYK:
Well, that's up to them. I believe that they will make it that. So the design in the end is basically the maintenance plan. We laid down a path that is made out of epai wood and decomposed granite and Corten steel. But if they chose to, the whole thing may become a wild patterning of mowing. We've laid down the bones or the basic structure of the labyrinth and within that our clients define and redefine this evolving landscape.

Q:
There are two ways you could look at that. One is positive and one, let's say, is a little negative. The positive is that you've actually discovered a way of addressing what for a long time has been this misnomer called maintenance. It's been the excuse for everything; it's been the thing that one scolds a project on — the lack of maintenance, the wrong maintenance, or no maintenance at all. And you aggressively take it on as a part of the design process, a design element in itself. The more negative way might be that you are extending the designer's control of the project further, but that may be a more cynical way of looking at it.

MYK:
I think it's a little bit of both to be honest. I think it comes from an ethic of how I view my work. I don't believe that landscapes are a fixed ideal condition and, as a designer, I embrace the evolving nature of landscapes. That's why it's difficult to give lectures about my work because projects built ten years ago look different now and it's hard to explain the experience of being in that space. I think embracing that evolving aspect of landscape, and of any design that's put into place, is both relinquishing a level of control and taking a bit of control. We would only do this with the clients that we have an unbelievably trustful and reciprocal relationship and, fortunately, we have many clients that we can have that dialogue with. They understand what our sensitivities are and we share the same sensitivities, so that we make them the stewards of the vision that we offer them. In all likelihood, we come to the table with similar visions of what landscape is, that it's not

a kind of perfectly manicured condition, and we embrace both cultural and natural changes.

I think as I've worked through this idea in the last year, it's become clear to me that the more rich and the more layered aspect of this kind of engagement of process actually happens with materials that change and grow in a maybe shorter duration or time frame that you can, especially here in New England, see from season to season what will happen.

Q:

It's a very specific practice that is probably also related to the scale that you work at. I don't know if it's the scale of the office, but the scales of the projects and that you've kept your office deliberately small.

MYK:

That is one thing that we have deliberately done. Also, it's not a way of thinking about landscape design that necessarily is relegated to say a thirty-foot-by-thirty-foot courtyard. We're currently working on a Food and Drug Administration master plan, with a large team of designers and engineers and local constituents. The master plan is about embracing process amongst this large group of people and the overlap between the engineer and the artist, the landscape architect and the architect. That has become a requirement of the master plan to say you must find an overlap; you must embrace not only the process of change within the design process, but also the process of change of this landscape that covers 700 acres.

Q:

It doesn't, therefore, preclude this larger working process?

MYK:

It maybe makes more sense because it says that there are twenty people on this project, so how can you have just one vision of the project? The vision may be that the landscape actually structures everything—the way in which the landscape works. I can argue that if it works with an incredibly complex network as the federal government, it could work with anything. If we can get the federal government to embrace something like this, then why not anybody else? So weathering and durability comes from my interest in bringing these rituals back to our life, that we have lost, for better or worse, as a democratic society. I think it might be a way of bringing some kind of engagement back to our culture, through the changing landscape.

CASE STUDY H	URBAN LEGACIES

Figure 4.64. Foundation stones reused from the site contrast with the ashlar-finished water channel. Steve Hennessy. Cook + Phillip Park, Sydney, Australia. (Courtesy of Elizabeth Mossop, Spackman + Mossop. © Grahame Edwards.)

Project Information

Project: Cook + Phillip Park

Location: College and Williams Streets, Sydney, Australia

Client: Sydney City Council

Landscape Architect: Elizabeth Mossop, Spackman + Mossop

Artists: Anita Glesta, Steve Hennessy, Phillippa Playford, Wendy Sharpe

Architect: Lawrence Nield & Partners (now Bligh Volter Nield)

General Contractor: Boulderstone Hornibrook

Landscape Contractor: Simpsons Landscapes + Arborcraft

Specialty Fabrications: Sydney Fountains Waterforms

Design Phase: 1996–1999

Date Completed: 2000

Project Cost: $35 million

PROJECT DESCRIPTION

Cook + Phillip Park responds to the increased demand by city of Sydney residents and workers for passive and active recreation facilities. The project resulted from the consolidation of Cook and Phillip Parks, located adjacent to the high-density residential area of East Sydney, Australia. Cook + Phillip Park is also surrounded by the major cultural institutions of Sydney and represents one of the city's most ambitious open space and building projects. The consolidation of the site through the removal of Haig Avenue and Boomerang Street and the alteration to the surrounding road network created a new parkway link. The extensive use of water on the site links to the swimming pools nearby, and the open space serves as both direct urban pathways and meandering urban walks. The objectives of the project were to improve the open space offered by both parks by merging them and removing major roads, to create active recreation facilities, to create passive recreation areas, such as the cathedral forecourt, water features, grassed terraces, open lawn, seating areas, café, and underground parking. The parts of the scheme are as follows.

COLLEGE STREET TERRACE

The project incorporated College Square and the cathedral forecourt, creating a formal and a ceremonial edge to College Street and establishing a forecourt to the cathedral and museum. The terrace becomes a highly visible platform that now serves as an outdoor sculpture gallery at this ceremonial city edge. The terrace is linked to the rest of the park by the Fig Ramp and a grand stairway and is echoed in the terraces that continue across the park.

THE PARK TERRACES

The grass terraces are the major structuring devices of the central green space. Over four levels, each level grass terrace is connected to the next by a gentle grassed bank, creating a formal, open space. At the perimeter of the park, these grass banks terminate to retaining walls as an integrating element to the urban streetscape. Strong tree planting at the perimeter coincides with the change in the form of the terraces. This gives the park a strong vegetated edge when viewed from outside, while creating a sense of separation and "oasis" for park users. The interaction of the Fig Ramp further subdivides the space, so that the terrace consists of a range of spaces, providing opportunity for quiet contemplative areas, sunny areas for passive use, and open informal active recreation.

THE TERRACED RECREATION AND POOL CENTER

The Center provides for the recreation needs of the contemporary urban residential population and city workers and integrates a variety of swimming pools, recreation and community complex.

WATER GARDEN

The Yurong Water Garden is an environmental artwork by the landscape architect and artist Wendy Sharpe inspired by retracing the path of the Yurong Creek that once ran from the area. Roughly hewn boulders of sandstone and original pavers and rocks from the former park have been arranged to form a course for the creek that flows down three terraces of gardens. The use of sandstone reflects the cultural and natural landscape of the surrounding area. The source fountain on the upper terrace is created from water seeping out of small holes in the sandstone boulders. The water runs through the middle terrace and down to the lower garden where it culminates in a calm reflection pool.

The project displays a range of weathering and durability concerns that the landscape architect was required to address through the normal course of the design process and beyond. These included the evolution of a material language that reflected both the concerns of place, robustness, and the traditions of available workmanship. Again, the issues of maintenance, or lack thereof, were raised in this most urban and public of projects. Concerns were raised regarding the changes brought after the implementation phase was completed. Finally, this project stands as typical of the interdisciplinary issues arising from complex city work. These include, in addition to budget and economic concerns, the desire on the part of the landscape architect for durability at the expense of more exploratory landscape forms and elements initially. However, young landscape architects and students should note the resulting elements capture the essence of a regional landscape tradition that is evolving in time and in formal expression.

INTERVIEW WITH THE DESIGNER

Discussion with the landscape architect Elizabeth Mossop took place on June 4, 2002, and October 21, 2002, in Cambridge, Massachusetts. Interview participants are identified as Elizabeth Mossop (EM) and author (Q).

Q:

How in your practice do you approach the idea of materials and material use?

EM:

We are more project driven in that the particular design and an approach to materials comes from a specific problem on a case-by-case basis. One of the key things is there is a consistency in our approach, but the solutions that would come out are very much driven by issues to do with the site and issues specific to that project. It is important that the materials design is consistent with the conceptual ideas informing the project. We also try to be faithful to the nature of the material in the way it is used and we often work with very ordinary and cheap materials.

Q:

What about specifics of place in terms of climate?

EM:

Most of the time, the issues we are dealing with are a lot kinder than a climate where there is a lot of snow. The particular things we deal with are exposure to sunlight, limited availability of water, in addition to cost factors. Sun is probably the harshest thing we deal with.

Q:

Have you, in your practice, gone back into the tradition that exists in Australia of building or making landscapes, or, putting the question another way, is there a tradition that you can go back to?

EM:

The tradition that we come out of most clearly is the beginnings of modernism, which only really took hold in Australia in the 1970s. That is very much the tradition of working with natural, indigenous, and raw materials, for example, unfinished timber, the use of sandstone in the Sydney region, and the discovery of native plants. My design partner Michael Spackman and I were trained in the 1970s by the people who really developed that kind of work regionally and were a strong influence on us, although we do not work with it in the same way. Much of their work was focused on bushland parks and gardens; although we do work occasionally in natural areas, much of our work is very urban. The projects have more intense use and require collaboration with engineers that create very different technological requirements.

Q:

What are some of these technological requirements?

EM:

In the Australian context coming out of this bushland tradition, the design industry is still relatively new. There has always been an issue for us in terms of quality of construction, particularly trying to achieve more highly finished projects working with nontraditional landscape materials like concrete. It was relatively easy in the past to find people who would work very beautifully and extensively with natural stone. Even now, for us to achieve very highly finished concrete work is very difficult. We work with concrete a great deal for a variety of reasons—durability as well as aesthetic. In some instances where we have been forced to work with builders who are not particularly skilled, it has been a huge issue and tends to influence to some extent the way in which we detail things.

Q:

Could you give an example of a piece of built work that is not your own where you were first aware of the relationship between the conceptual ideas and the way a project would evolve and weather, say, in the material selection?

EM:

The first instance where I became very conscious of material use was initially in some of the best examples of bushland work—where there was first seen a designed version of an Australian landscape. I am thinking particularly of the Klaura Reserve by Bruce McKenzie at Balmain in Sydney. What you see there is very powerful use of sandstone, both in the existing natural rock and then reused on site in pavement and wall elements. The indigenous plant material here has a very short life span and the built components of the project clearly were going to be much more successful in time. It was obvious that the planting was always going to change dramatically, while the bones of the project in the stonework would stay. Other projects that were very influential, in terms of material use, were those I saw when I worked in Japan relatively soon after graduation. There was an incredible commitment, on the one hand, to the quality of construction, and on the other, a commitment to amazingly long-lived materials like stainless steel fixings and members in pergola construction that I had never seen before. The amount of money they were prepared to spend on durable materials was incredible. They had also an ability to use more ephemeral materials such as bamboo, string, and woven materials with the full knowledge that they were going to be replaced on a regular basis.

Q:

Why do you think that type of temporary and ephemeral material use is absent from most North American and European landscape practice?

EM:

There is this idea that the landscape can be finished and perfect and everybody has a dream of somehow finding the "no-maintenance" landscape, whereas the Japanese are less concerned with this and more committed to an ongoing interaction. Built into the landscape is the idea that you are going to come back and shape the trees or retie elements of the fencing.

Q:

Taking this a step further, people talk about weathering and durability from a very practical point of view, which may be perfectly appropriate. On a broader level, however, should landscapes last and how does that influence how both designers work but also how the body of built work is looked at?

EM:

We are often striving for durability in our work to withstand use or stand up to difficult environmental conditions. I must say that the more projects that we build, the more I realize how fleeting the work is without any ongoing commitment to maintaining the project. Far more of our work is destroyed by client neglect than by overuse or what could be termed natural weathering. It is much more likely that something goes wrong politically in a project and it is forgotten about. In addition, what we think of as completely inappropriate changes are made to the project or parts of it are destroyed and not replaced. These are more common events in my experience than the project living out what we tend to think of as a "natural life" or time span.

Q:

You can accept quite readily the weathering of materials specifically with the use of raw materials and the use of landscape space?

EM:

You can design landscape elements to deal with certain urban uses. However, beyond a certain point, legitimate social and cultural uses that are not generally accepted programs (for example, skateboarding) bring variety and life to these projects. We do landscape design work where vandalism is also a concern. It has been a particular issue in the Western Sydney Regional Park where landscape materials and elements have to stand up to long-term neglect but should also be immune to short-term vandalism. That drove us to a palette of industrial materials and a very particular type of detailing.

Q:

Would you accept or encourage graffiti as part of the project as some designers do?

EM:

That seems to me to be completely missing the point. In a way, you are bringing graffiti into the project and sanitizing it. The point of graffiti is transgressing, so I don't think you want to civilize it. Depending on the level of maintenance, either it stays and that's that, or someone has a contract to clean it off within twenty-four hours. It seems to me very difficult to build interaction and change by users into the sort of public project that we do, given the liability constraints on the one hand and the requirements of public clients on the other.

Q:

There is clear indication in contemporary landscape work and in design schools that change has become a central part of the design, particularly embracing natural processes such as stormwater and water detention. How might that affect the designer's spatial ideas as well as ideas of duration?

EM:

I think we don't really know that much about what we are dealing with, in that there is a relatively small number of projects that have been implemented that embrace that form of development and change over time. I don't think it is a passing fad, because it addresses so many environmental concerns and how we provide these public landscapes and resolve their development over time. The marriage of ecological concerns with crude economic issues is a powerful thing. The projects where we have implemented this approach have involved setting up a strategy for vegetation where management over time allows the harnessing of successional processes as a way of developing the structure of a landscape. This is most evident in our broader scale park projects where we use strategic moves to encourage natural processes to develop—that's a long-term strategy.

Q:

Why do you think there has been so little interest, in practice, on landscape change at the project scale?

EM:

It has been dealt with in a preservation context in the past. We have the research on what do we do with all these historic gardens. Pull out the trees, let them fall down, replant, redo, but all within that specialized context. In an Australian context, it makes perfect sense because the profession is relatively new. Projects particularly done since the Second World War have now reached the stage where they are falling apart and don't satisfy the changing needs and uses of the client. In those landscapes, we are only just beginning to deal with the issues of preservation and not very successfully. There is endless controversy about landscape architects being invited to revamp other designer's projects. It seems to me the issues to do with materials and performance until now have been regarded as in the realm of the technical as separate from design.

Q:

With art perceived as a higher purpose?

EM:

No, where the technical and the art have always come together as equal is with the "design and construction" tradition in Australia. This is where landscape architecture started in the Australian context, and there was a very different kind of relationship between those who designed and those who built than there is now. It came out of a strong artisan tradition. There was, for example, very little conventional documentation carried out, there existed a tremendous local knowledge and skill with materials brought to the design development process, and, finally, often a lot of design work was actually done in the field with designer and builder. There is also little in the way of a tradition in revising the results of this process.

Q:

If you had to do a temporary installation for a season or a year, how would that affect the way you conceived of the project in office?

EM:

The thing about a temporary installation is the liberating nature of it in terms of what you can do in design as well as in construction terms; it is always a fantastic opportunity to experiment. It allows you to use materials that you cannot use in a permanent project because they will not last. It also permits you to use all the strange new materials that are available (in theory)—plastics, fabrics, and resins. These all become a possibility, but, again, the problem and the place drive any design decision.

Q:

Does that suggest that durability is a restrictive aspect of practice?

EM:

I think projects can last, and the important things in the structure of the project do withstand the effects of time in such a way as to continue to be usable. I think that is tremendously important and I think, particularly with the public projects that we do, this is often a very basic requirement of our work. The materials research and the detailing and its ability to last more than five years is often very important.

Q:

What do you normally use as a timescale—is five years really enough or should it be the lifetime of a designer or a client?

EM:

You do see projects with the fabulous photographs of them brand new, and we see them three years later and they have fallen apart. That's very important for us to outlast that kind of a time frame. Some of our projects will last for twenty, thirty years easily. I think that the projects that we do in urban environments tend to have a shorter life span than the ones we do in less built up areas. We do quite a bit of work in suburban and rural settings, and there is simply less money to come back and redo things. It is a concern, but materials have a limited life in many projects that we do, often related to the resources available for implementation.

Q:

Why is so little research being done on the subject and, more significantly, why is there really no writing on the subject of weathering?

EM:

I think that it relates in part to the way that landscape architects are educated. I think that certainly until relatively recently materials and their relation to construction and weathering has been relegated specifically to construction and technology streams within landscape architecture courses. That's the way that it's framed—as a technical issue that needs to be solved, rather than being an intrinsic part of design and design development. A few designers learn that as they practice, but I think for most designers they have to unlearn that it's a technical problem and relearn it as something to do with design. Also, I think a lot of landscape architects, even though they may know quite a lot about landscape construction on paper, really don't know that much about the materials that they work with in a real tactile or visceral way. Landscape architects who do know about plants tend to be a rarity and so that people who do know about plants are described as being "a great plants person," and this is seen as something very special, rather than being something normal. I think the same thing applies to materials and weathering. You really learn about materials by repetitively using them, and you also learn about what happens after the project is finished. When I did my professional landscape degree, we had a requirement that we had to have construction experience, and we also carried out some building projects within the program.

Q:

Do you carry out research on materials now?

EM:

There is barely the time to really research or prototype or experiment with materials unless it's a very unusual situation. Almost the only time we ever have the opportunity to do that is when working with an artist or when you call something art rather than landscape design. You do become cleverer about understanding how that works and perhaps giving yourself a little bit more room or a little bit more money or a little bit more time to develop something. This gives you the leeway perhaps to make a prototype for something like a water feature.

Q:

We talked at some length about the insistence for durability in built work, particularly in harsh places or, let's say, a climate that really acts on the work on a day-to-day basis. Could you give some examples from your own work where it has informed daily design practice?

EM:

Devil's Back Ridge is a small park within a very large park, Western Sydney Regional Park. This is a fairly isolated area at the moment and subject to incredible amounts of vandalism, as well as not very much maintenance and exposure to the elements. The strategy and the design of the individual pieces had to be very robust, in that it had to be something that was going to last during the development of the park and later as the park changed over time. It still had to work when the park around it was completely different and it also had to be just incredibly physically durable. It had to withstand these conditions and the fact that it really wasn't going to get looked after. Also, the budget wasn't fantastic. (See Figures 4.65 to 4.68.)

Q:

How did all that affect your design thinking? Did it restrict you or did it suggest straightaway we're going to work in this palette and this way?

EM:

It drove us to a very limited palette of materials, and we decided to invest in the built elements and spend money where we had to, to make those durable. In terms of the planting, the only thing that we knew that would survive would be the tree canopy. It was going to succeed if that was done using regeneration techniques and also broad-scale replanting of locally collected species. So that was done with a very low per unit cost over a fairly significant area. The materials we used were concrete for all of the stairs and platforms, and we built the walls using gabions, which, as well as being cheap and strong, also allowed us to do some things formally with the walls that were very big. The shade structures were all steel, and where there was furniture and barbecues, they were all made from precast concrete and steel.

Figure 4.65. Gabions, concrete, and stabilized gravel form the path system. Devil's Back Ridge, Western Sydney Regional Park, Sydney, Australia. (Courtesy of Elizabeth Mossop, Spackman + Mossop. © Grahame Edwards.)

Figure 4.66. Gabion-defined path leads to hilltop climb. Devil's Back Ridge, Western Sydney Regional Park, Sydney, Australia. (Courtesy of Elizabeth Mossop, Spackman + Mossop. © Grahame Edwards.)

Figure 4.68. Simple steel and concrete stairs allow access from the ridge platforms down a planting-stabilized embankment. Devil's Back Ridge, Western Sydney Regional Park, Sydney, Australia. (Courtesy of Elizabeth Mossop, Spackman + Mossop. © Grahame Edwards.)

Figure 4.67. Robust steel pergola provides shade and frames views from the platform. Devil's Back Ridge, Western Sydney Regional Park, Sydney, Australia. (Courtesy of Elizabeth Mossop, Spackman + Mossop. © Grahame Edwards.)

Q:

So, in a sense, it influenced, at the general level, how you worked your palette of materials, and, second, at the detail level, how they were tectonically put together. The images will show that that aesthetic actually fits in very well with that particular context, that place, which has a harshness to it.

EM:

It meant that the actual pieces themselves had a certain presence because they were big and strong. Also, we were specifically trying to avoid creating a picturesque landscape of the traditional nineteenth-century park that you would normally see in this Australian context. So this related more to an agricultural/industrial aesthetic.

Q:

Can you continue with another example from your own work where you had restrictions but in a more urban environment?

Cook + Phillip Park
Sydney, Australia

EM:

Cook + Phillip is a new urban park and terrace created by taking a couple of streets away and joining together fragmented parklands. It was finished in 2000 in the lead-up to the Olympics as part of the big urban renewal project in central Sydney. It's on the eastern edge of the central business district, and the parkland had to include a significant amount of underground parking and a major sport and recreation center, which includes an Olympic swimming pool, a leisure pool, basketball courts, a gymnasium, community center, cafés, and restaurants. All in such a way that the parkland dominated the built facilities. (See Figures 4.69 to 4.72.)

Q:

What was on the site before? You said it was two streets...

EM:

It's a whole urban block about four hectares. It was basically sort of an X, with two streets and then four little triangles of parkland, one of which was given over to a bowling club. They were quite steep, they were not very well used, and they were fairly small, so that, although it has historically been parkland, the joining it together increased its size dramatically and basically remade it.

Q:

When did the design work start?

EM:

We started working on the project in 1996. And it had a very, very long process of public consultation because it was a very controversial project.

Figure 4.69. Water, mist, and light effects transform the cathedral terrace at night. Cook + Phillip Park, Sydney, Australia. (Courtesy of Elizabeth Mossop, Spackman + Mossop. © Grahame Edwards.)

Figure 4.70. Stone blocks directly from the quarry frame the upper terrace of the water garden. Cook + Phillip Park, Sydney, Australia. (Courtesy of Elizabeth Mossop, Spackman + Mossop. © Grahame Edwards.)

Figure 4.71. The water garden terminates with a reflection pool and ashlar sandstone finishes. Cook + Phillip Park, Sydney, Australia. (Courtesy of Elizabeth Mossop, Spackman + Mossop. © Grahame Edwards.)

Figure 4.72. The Boomerang Ramp combines concrete and stainless steel custom lights by artist. Cook + Phillip Park, Sydney, Australia. (Courtesy of Elizabeth Mossop, Spackman + Mossop. © Grahame Edwards.)

Then it had a very short process of design development and construction because of the fixed deadline at the other end—the Olympics.

Q:

Was it a temporary project or was it a project where it had a first life and then afterwards would be reworked or changed?

EM:

It was always a project for the long term. The strategy that the city took for the Olympics was always about the legacy of the project. It was a facility for the games, but then would have a life after. The city-side boundary of the project is on College Street, which is part of the main historic spine that goes from the opera house to Parliament House. This project falls between the major Catholic cathedral and the major science museum, which is called the Australian Museum. It's part of a chain of very significant sandstone historic public buildings. The project is a huge urban terrace that connects the cathedral to the museum. Our desire was to make it a part of that spine, to finally give the cathedral a setting and an address that it hadn't had and to connect it through the use of materials. It was also very limited by technical constraints, all built on a slab, on the one side, over an underground car park, and on the other, the swimming pool. The other element that was a big part of this project was the inclusion of water. I had always wanted a lot of water in the project because Sydney has a warm climate and the park was always going to be different from the surrounding city in having shade and water. The great urban terrace always had a lot of water, fountains that were going to lead people down into the project, and we also used great big sheets of water on top of the project to reduce the structural load and stop the roofs being trafficked. Sandstone was, of course, the obvious material, but Sydney sandstone is very soft and, therefore, not durable.

Q:

Is it very porous?

EM:

Yes, we couldn't use it for steps or the pavement, so that, whenever we had any vertical surfaces, they were sandstone. The forecourt pavement was all detailed in granite, which was then later changed for cost reasons to bluestone, which is much thinner and cheaper.

Q:

But it does flake?

EM:

Not as durable. It would have been much more desirable to maintain the granite.

Q:

So, in other words, this is not unlike projects when there's a desire to use the most durable material, granite, but one has to eventually use bluestone.

EM:

We have granite steps and some granite details at key points and then the rest of it is bluestone.

Q:

I didn't think Sydney had bluestone.

EM:

The bluestone comes from Victoria. Melbourne is bluestone. Sydney is sandstone. The same process happens throughout the park in that much of the surfaces, the paved areas in the park, were originally bluestone and then became concrete. We knew that cost constraints would never permit us to detail it in the way that we did the urban terrace.

Q:

Did you conceive of it as a municipal park that would have a variety of uses and that, over time, the maintenance and programs would change?

EM:

It had to cater to a really diverse range of users. It was always going to be very heavily used. We didn't know how it was going to be used in even ten years or twenty years. While there were specific things that were designed in, much of the rest of it was flexible. The park has a big central open area, which is a series of grassed terraces. On the edges of the park, one is a buffer to a very busy street, and down the northern side of the park is a series of water gardens that step down the hill and provide a much more intimate and intricate experience. The materials of the park were always going to be softer than the terraces; for example, where possible we used compacted gravel surfaces. The water garden was designed in collaboration with the artist, Anita Glesta, one of four artists we worked with on the project. The water garden runs along the original drainage line and connects into the water on the urban terrace. It's about making a series of gardens where the water and stone take on different forms.

Q:

What are the material qualities of the park?

EM:

The sandstone is the bedrock geology and so the water source for the gardens is from some giant pieces of sandstone, which are stacked up in the blocks as they came out of the quarry. In the first garden, some pieces are made with the sandstone footings that were demolished from the original walls that were on this site. Then it moves down through a water stair to another garden where the sandstone is made into benches, which are the positive form of the water troughs, and then the water moves across the line of travel and then into the bottom garden that is a beautiful crisp retaining and reflection pool.

Q:

The maintenance here is really not so much about stopping and starting, cleaning and filling; it's about the wearing, it's about erosion, and, therefore, the need to obviously watch as various pieces are scoured and have to be replaced and cleaned.

EM:

We were very conscious of the issues of management and maintenance from the beginning of the project. Like many other municipalities, the city council had moved into a contract management arrangement for their urban parks, which, although tremendously cost effective, was in some ways leading to the gradual deterioration of things like the mature tree canopy in the city, because there was nobody who really cared what happened from one year to the next. We did a lot of work with the client to get them to do a nonstandard maintenance contract for the park that would be better than their usual contract that they used. It would have different performance indicators in it because of its location and the amount of use it got. Unfortunately, they didn't use our advice about the maintenance contract for the landscape and how that ought to run, particularly having so many water features in a project. They rolled it into the management contract for the sport facilities and what you've got is a pool manager looking after the fountains. It hasn't worked particularly well, and the standard of maintenance is not good enough.

Q:

What hasn't worked quite well?

EM:

If there were problems with plant selection or with the wearing of a particular area, the maintenance crews have gone back and replaced it with whatever plants they thought were nice. They've built a little log retaining wall in one piece of the park. As part of the water elements on the big terrace, there is a big tank that runs along the side of the reflection pool that has water plants in it, mostly water lilies. When the project was opened, the water lilies were not looking spectacular enough, so they stuck a whole bunch of extra plants in there. Now you've got what looks like a whole bunch of dead reeds. Some of the site problems are related to the construction and the enormous pressure to get this project finished on time. The quality of construction in many areas was not adequate and the landscape work really suffered there. The unseen things like drainage and planting preparation were often unsatisfactory and unimportant to the project managers. So that has given them a legacy of built-in problems, for example, problems with drainage and the successful growth of key plantings. There may, some time in the future, have to be a second phase, post 2000, which addresses where the park is going to go for the next ten years. I write them a letter every six months, detailing what the problems are. They have actually done quite a bit of remedial work on the interior of the built works, but they're less concerned about many of these exterior things that we perceive as problems.

Q:

So how do you think it will play out over time?

EM:

The structure is there and the canopy is there. If I were to redo it now, I would carry out the planting design quite differently. I would make it much more robust. We were trying to make a lot of effects with particular kinds of planting, which I think is appropriate to a park in a city that people use all year and the same people come back again and again. I wanted that richness to it. The city council swore that they were going to give it the necessary maintenance and I certainly wouldn't believe them again. But, you know, the big things are largely in place.

Q:

So the lessons learned were to do with being even more robust than you could ever imagine and accepting that not all the maintenance, even though it's in writing, would take place.

EM:

I think it's increasingly the case with public authorities that they are not prepared to put the resources into the long-term management. It's sad, because it means that you move away from using plants and towards using built structures to achieve separation, spatial effects, and level changes. If you can afford to do it, it's going to be there in ten years, whereas the plants will not necessarily be there.

CASE STUDY | EVOLVING ECONOMIES

Figure 4.73. Sunset pool. Casa Cabo, Cabo San Lucas, Mexico. (Margie Ruddick Landscape.)

Project Information

Project: Casa Cabo

Location: Cabo San Lucas, Baja California, Mexico

Client: Claire and George Weiss

Landscape Designer:	Margie Ruddick
Architect:	Steven Harris Architects
General Contractor:	Alejandro Trevino
Date Completed:	2001
Project Cost:	Landscape, $250,000

PROJECT DESCRIPTION

In one of the few places in the world where the desert meets the sea, this built landscape blurs the lines between the built and natural environment, bringing the desert landscape into the interior spaces of the compound. Forms and materials were created and selected to weather with the harsh environmental conditions.

A quite different approach is presented here to the issues of weathering and durability with regard to the careful understanding of the larger social, ecological, and cultural changes that are brought to a project. The mention of the "blurring" of landscape forms and elements is balanced against the need to understand not just the physical context in which a designer works but the human context along with the concerns of wildlife and communities. The Casa Cabo case study, while representing a more commonly understood type of landscape, applies similar site strategies to the scale of a garden and residence.

INTERVIEW WITH THE DESIGNER

Discussion with the landscape architect Margie Ruddick took place on December 21, 2001, and January 30, 2003, by telephone. Interview participants are identified as Margie Ruddick (MR) and author (Q).

Q:

How did you come to the subject of durability—through the work of another designer or some other media?

MR:

I think when I was in graduate school there was a number of books more than projects that really changed me. I thought about landscape not just in terms of durability but the interaction of people and landscapes and how that is the key to landscape form. Two books were really instrumental. One was *Staying Alive* by Vandana Shiva, which described the hidden economies of many cultures that are integrated into forest systems. The extent to which people are interacting or intervening in the landscape is very subtle and it can't be quantified necessarily. There is a strong interrelationship between the activities of humans and the sustainability of a forest. People from aid organizations will often go in and want to do projects that are going to improve the economy or help this particular area, town, or region. They will think in terms of successive projects, things that are very visible to the eye such as dams and roads. In the book, it is described how these often undermine the very subtle economies and ecologies of an area.

Q:

They are thinking of, frankly, Western capital projects as a discrete activity, whereas the author is describing more subtle and complex interaction between culture and place.

MR:

Plants, animals, and everything.

Q:

How would one practically address that notion in your design work?

MR:

A project that we are working on in India is a resort in the Western Ghats, in Maharashtra. It's a 2,500-acre parcel in an undeveloped area with some scattered villages. It is going to be developed within the next number of decades, perhaps with holiday bungalows. The first instinct of the owners was to put a fence around the 2,500 acres and claim it. However, the existence of the landscape in its present form really depends on the people and animals that still move through this site. There are wildlife corridors that run through it, and people who have grazed animals and collected wood for fuel historically and who have farmed the rice fields. It goes from a high ridge to rain forest to savanna and then down to rice fields at the bottom, so it has a huge diversity of landscape types. Most of these landscapes have been maintained in their current state by having people derive some need within them—the savanna is kept open because of cutting for fuel and grazing and the rice fields have been farmed. So the designer cannot just come in and do a design—you actually have to understand the social, cultural, and ecological networks that are interrelated: Build as part of your design a program that actually involves the people who are there now; understand the types of jobs that people will have; some new uses will maintain the actual uses that are there now, keeping the landscape the way it is. Therefore, how do you shift some of these into uses that will keep pace with the changing economies as it turns into a resort area from a subsistence area? (See Figures 4.74 and 4.75.)

Figure 4.74. Site location. Shillim Eco Resort, Shillim, Maharashtra, India. (Margie Ruddick Landscape.)

Figure 4.75. Plan, scale 1.500. Shillim Eco Resort, Shillim, Maharashtra, India. (Margie Ruddick Landscape.)

Q:

So, it's really a very subtle understanding of the evolution over time of this place not just in terms of the physical design but an economic and social construct?

MR:

The economies of a site are part of their ecology. When people talk about sustainability, they often are talking about water, sun, and energy, but the economic sustainability of a project is the backbone that holds together all of the others. If you do not have a way of the place being self-sustaining economically, the other systems are going to fall out. This is having an impact on almost every project that we do.

Q:

You mentioned one other source in your graduate education, another book?

MR:

The other book was *Woman and Nature* by Susan Griffith. That was a huge revelation to me about the culture of science, and how the culture that I came from so valued measuring and ordering things and was pretty horrified by the things that could look like a mess or chaos. In terms of weathering and how things actually evolve over time, many of the projects that we work on have to do with the mess of a place also being very rich, with the unruly edges being the location where things happen. For instance, in the project in India, the edges and the forests are places that a conventional resort developer might think looks like a mess—that need to be sanitized or repackaged. However, the best habitat and the most sacred places in the area are to be found there. *Woman and Nature* questioned the formalizing of the world in a way that can be measured and organized easily according to a rational system.

Q:

What I am trying to reach towards is a much broader understanding by what we mean by weathering and durability. Conventional practices within landscape practice tie it to ideas of maintenance and materials possibly. Do you think your fairly broad approach results from or comes out of the specific place where you are working now?

MR:

The projects that I have worked on in other countries, for example, in China were key in helping me understand real shifts in perception of place, how sites actually work, and not to import preconceptions. The project in India has influenced projects that I work on at home in the United States. For example, I was at an arboretum yesterday in Philadelphia looking at their master plan that was done over ten years ago. It's an arboretum that does not have walls, surrounded by a very rough neighborhood. It has community gardens, an organic farm that is used by a food co-op. The idea of a cordoned-off "museum-like" landscape is not really that maintainable or durable an idea here. Other arboretums in Philadelphia can do it, for example, the Morris Arboretum in Chestnut Hill, because the University of Pennsylvania funds it through a huge commercial campaign. What actually maintains that landscape in its present done-up form is a model train that runs through a part of the garden—it's the number-one draw and brings in a lot of money.

Q:

I remember it as also a very bounded arboretum.

MR:

Yes, and it's marketed as a destination. In a much poorer neighborhood with many fewer resources, the idea of the arboretum as a destination that is going to bring money in is not applicable. The arboretum here is a collector of all sorts of community resources and programs that will actually give enough back to the community. They take a proprietary interest in the landscape; for instance, there is no graffiti in the arboretum—why is that? There are many people in this community who think of this as their garden. So the idea of the durability of this place depends on involving all of the smaller networks of community needs that will support this place over many years. This is an underfunded neighborhood, so what kind of resources are these community groups going to have? They actually have the ability to keep this place from being vandalized; they have many sets of eyes on the street to keep it from being a dangerous place to walk. So you look at the long-term maintenance of this place in terms of how do you foster a sense of proprietary interest with the people who live across the boundary. This requires eliminating the contract limit line that landscape architects have traditionally accepted and thinking of your design contract as extending way beyond the bounds of your project to involve communities that are surrounding it.

Q:

The premise, though, in the work you have talked about is it is necessary for those projects to endure; there is an underlying belief in the enduring qualities of landscape. Can landscape works that are temporary represent those same qualities?

MR:

I don't think they are exclusive; they are just different frameworks for thinking. For instance, I think it is very important for this arboretum to endure. I don't think it's important for the actual landscape form to endure.

Q:

You see the arboretum as a cultural idea but that may have geographical shifts?

MR:

Geographical shifts as well as design and other formal shifts. There is a huge area that has been let go and completely overtaken with vines. We were talking about that area and how our training as landscape architects tells us that it's actually a mess and needs to be cleaned up. You need to have forest regeneration, get rid of the vines, and save the trees. In fact, there are many places where that landscape is a very rich habitat and serves an ecological function. Maybe that could be a place where installations come and go to make people understand that landscape in a different way. Help people experience that landscape not as before and after—that's let go and that's not—rather as a living landscape that can have, for example, a series of tree houses in it. They are built and they then degrade; it's a landscape that allows things to be made and then fall apart.

Q:

As a designer, then, you view the idea of the temporary in a more holistic way. Those elements that change and degrade and those that will endure, are they the same?

MR:

They exist in the same projects. For example, if you look at plants in residential projects, they will not live for that long or will not grow the way you imagine necessarily. You are installing them side by side with a structure that is going to live for a long time. In fifty years, the stone is still going to be there, but the surrounding landscape is going to look totally different. That's a pretty modest version of the idea that when you choose materials you are conscious of which are going to change very quickly and which are going to last for a long time. The same is true for a master plan: What is going to be carried through forcefully over a number of generations and what are the things that will come and go? In the project in India, for instance, the rice fields will be kept in rice for now because that's the way the landscape looks; it's the character of the landscape. As soon as the surrounding area is no longer farmed for rice, that's going to be an inappropriate use. Then you plant things that will change how the valley looks and functions. So you have to understand that some components of the landscape are going to be totally transformed by the decisions that you will be making. The decisions, however, are going to be made at different levels and on different parts of the project.

Q:

What are the other sources that are central to your work as starting points or pulses?

MR:

It's funny because I think the tendency is to fix on one source, and you get attached to it. The others are just waiting in line. The India project has, for example, cycles of water that are so violent in many ways. That really does underlie the thinking from the larger planning issues down to the detail because of the varied cultural associations with the different characteristics of the water cycles that exist. There is monsoon to also completely dry, almost desert-like climate, and the tendency from my northeastern United States training and upbringing is to assume that one will be favored. The planners would say, "You don't want to put that there because nobody is going to be there during the monsoon period." In fact, people flock to these places in the monsoon because they are so tired of being so hot and dry. In the monsoon, you will find people walking, riding horses, people outside just being in the rain; that's the destination and that really changes the way you think when you are involved in such a project.

Q:

Similar to the custom here of going to the sea edge during a storm just to experience the dangerous conditions.

MR:

In design, you tend to want to favor one way of behavior because of an attachment to it.

Q:

There may be different modes of change for a designer, but we fixate on one to maybe the detriment of others. Changing subjects for a moment, if you look at the built work of the landscape field, many of the projects live on only in photographs. What does that say about the field?

MR:

I also find that photographs rarely represent the projects that are the most incredible and progressive. My practice has veered away from the published image in public sources, because I am very involved with the people that I work with. If you have a long-term relationship with clients and communities you are working with, the idea of the project is complete when photographed is outmoded. You are actually working over a long period of time and there is no point when a still photograph is ever appropriate. So I feel as if that is the way my practice has evolved. There are many projects where there is not a single photograph that would show up in a magazine. I feel that design schools do not support this idea because there is so much emphasis on the big slide shows. It's an approach to design practice that when people encounter it they say, "This is why I got involved with landscape architecture; to do projects like this. I didn't know people did work like this." In design schools, it is often focused on the magazine cover shot. For the project I did in China, I did take photographs that were not magazine-like in quality but mainly as a result of a lack of direct sunlight.

Q:

Although I have seen these photographs in a magazine.

MR:

Though that was a pretty marginal magazine. *Landscape Architecture* magazine said this place looks very dingy in the photographs. Well, the city could be thought of as dingy, the site was gray, and there was pollution in the air that blocked out the brilliance of the sun. I think that the ethos that favors the desired image of a sun-washed landscape cuts out a huge percentage of the landscapes in the world. It says a lot about the field and what is pretty atrocious in our field.

Q:

Can you illustrate where you have taken quite a different stance from other landscape architects who focus much more on normative ways of thinking about the durability of their work?

> Casa Cabo
> Cabo San Lucas, Mexico

MR:

The Casa Cabo project in Mexico is a good example. (See Figures 4.76 to 4.81.) It's very much a glamorous project, but a lot of the things that we have covered in this discussion are actually at work there—it is a project in another culture and it's a project that really was built to evolve over time.

Figure 4.76.
Courtyard. Casa Cabo, Cabo San Lucas, Mexico. (Margie Ruddick Landscape.)

Figure 4.77.
Intersection. Casa
Cabo, Cabo San
Lucas, Mexico.
(Margie Ruddick
Landscape.)

Figure 4.78.
Emerging rock. Casa
Cabo, Cabo San
Lucas, Mexico.
(Margie Ruddick
Landscape.)

Figure 4.79. Wall shadow. Casa Cabo, Cabo San Lucas, Mexico. (Margie Ruddick Landscape.)

Figure 4.80. Stone. Casa Cabo, Cabo San Lucas, Mexico. (Margie Ruddick Landscape.)

Figure 4.81. Yellow courtyard. Casa Cabo, Cabo San Lucas, Mexico. (Margie Ruddick Landscape.)

Q:
How would it be described? What type of project is it?

MR:
It's a resort compound hanging on a cliff over the Pacific. We carried out a different approach from what is generally done around there. It reflects some of the durability and weathering concerns as they really are borne out in a landscape, although there is only a marginal economic sustainability component there as opposed to my other project work.

Q:
How large is it?

MR:
It's less than an acre. There were a lot of things that we were testing or challenging in the approaches that are traditionally found on these high-end residential projects. I guess the first thing to note is it's a desert and it's not a place that people are traditionally going to go to as resort visitors. It's not a

tropical paradise; you go to this place in order to empty out, rather than to fill up on visual and sensual experiences and moods. It retains a southwestern expansiveness and is one of the only seven (I think) places in the world where the desert meets the sea. The norm has been to take sites in this locale and build them out in the middle, then make a courtyard in the pile of architecture or have some courtyards that are tropical oases. What Steven Harris, the architect, and I did, was to make a void in the middle of the site, so the building actually comes out of the landscape and creates the spaces that are the place. Then all of the landscape is actually a desert landscape, but reshuffled to relate to the architecture and to relate to the fact that this is a domestic landscape and not the desert. I think that one of the things that it does is to reject the idea of the duality of natural environment and the built landscape.

Q:
Who was the client?

MR:

It was a couple that really want to push things a little to the edge and do things that were a little different. This is the second compound that we've done for them. It seems a little funny to be talking about such a high-end project, but it was really fantastic to be able to do things that were testing ideas that now we're using on either larger projects or more public projects.

When you have the zone that's inside, one question is "How do you deal with the relationship between inside and outside?" Also, in this case, it's a desert that goes right down to the sea. We, therefore, took that whole landscape, all the ground covers and the plants that erupt in the desert, and used that as the design palette. We took the mess of the desert and brought it into the domestic zone. We used many more species than we would use normally, for example, eight different species in three square meters— that's what happens in the desert. It was just taking the chaos of the desert that's very fertile and trying to use it to reestablish a structure once construction was over. It's to make a landscape that you just let go, not something that's highly maintained and highly irrigated. It is clearly a constructed landscape, and the paving and the layout and the way that we organized these things is actually quite structured. It's not trying to look like nature or trying to look like the desert. It's clearly a domestic zone, but the language is relating it back to the desert. I laid paving made up of strips of concrete so that there wasn't a particular geometry. There are no right angles between all the different arms of the buildings and the strips of concrete come and go. Given the incredible rainfall that you get there and the incredible winds and drying action, it's a kind of a configuration that, given all of that action, will not look like something that got messed up, because it's already starting off a little bit messed up. The premise is that it's a landscape that is constructed so that it will fit into all of the various forces that are already at play on the site. It will turn into something new, but it won't be fighting against those climatic forces; it actually accommodates them and receives them in a way that's part of the design.

Q:

How do you see it evolving over time?

MR:

One of the things that will happen is the continuous wind and the water action from the very fast, torrential rains in the wet season. The paving is already started out in an eroded layout. So as it gets more weathered, it's just going to look more eroded. In this landscape, built elements get bleached out and the hard edges get softened. The site when we got there was very overgrown with prickly, creepy vegetation, so we've made areas where it's fine just to let it go and it's intended to look overgrown and gnarly and pretty chaotic. So that'll just keep happening, and it's already started. The construction and the plantings, I think, are just going to end up looking more like each other and are going to blur a little bit. It seems to me one of the big lessons of landscape design and watching built projects over time is that anything you think of as highly distinct takes a huge amount of energy to keep distinct—the natural trajectory is the first thing to blur, for things to become more alike and more interconnected.

Q:

By "blur," you're referring not just to visual blurring, but also textural, material blurring?

MR:

Yes, material blurring from different parts of the water and planted systems. All of the different components start to knit together in a way where things start to become a little more indistinguishable from each other.

Q:

This is quite counter to many people who see landscape as requiring differentiation.

MR:

The task is how do you create a system that allows for differentiation but also allows for all the blurring that's going to happen. In the Cabo project, there are some areas that are highly constructed, and over time they're still going to read because nothing can grow there. Then there are other areas where things can't blur and mass together and it's not going to actually compromise the basic design layout.

I was up at a design review recently, and one student had made a system that worked so well and it was so highly readable and all the critics were very troubled by it. We all realized that she needed to go in and loosen it up. Sometimes, you work so hard to make things all work and be legible and be rational, but, in fact, it's single-minded and what you need is to go back in and make it a little more complicated and a little more loosened up. This is a large theme in the work that I do and in the books I like to read. Also, ecologically, it's such a key concept, that the minute you start cleaning things up you're reducing the richness, the possibility of somebody or something making a place there.

I think one of the fallouts from Ian McHarg's work is that for a long time people would just go cordon an area off and say, "Don't build there." It helped you to know where not to build and where to build. You'd cordon off the ecologically valuable areas and just build on flat sites, but it didn't actually tell you, if you were building on a sloped site, how you can do it for minimal impact. We're building on eroded slopes in India and responsible for setting the format for this activity by building everything off site and bringing it in. Everything is on timber pilings, so they're stilt buildings, and they're actually going to enhance the woodland on these slopes. So it's a little more of a nuanced approach than simply seeing the places that you're going to do the least damage and then building there. That ends up with a very homogeneous building program; it also doesn't deal with the middle ground where you might want to do some enhancement and you might want to build there. But build very carefully. All these conventional ideas of cordoning this area off because it's in great shape and build over here, I think are pretty outdated like the notion of never building within 100 feet of wetland. Well, if you're making the wetland, you can build on it because you're making it and you're making it all at once and you can do it responsibly. I'm using methods from other cultures where our training would say clean it all up; it's not healthy.

Figure 4.82. Paving detail, 1999. Advantica Plaza and Park, Spartanburg, South Carolina. (Photography by Tim Buchman. Courtesy of Peter L. Schaudt.)

Project Information

Project:	Advantica Plaza and Park (formerly Spartan Food Systems Plaza)
Location:	Spartanburg, South Carolina
Client:	Spartan Food Systems (former owner of Advantica Plaza)
Landscape Architect:	Peter Lindsay Schaudt (while employed with Clark, Tribble, Harris & Li of Charlotte, North Carolina)
Architect:	Clark, Tribble, Harris & Li Architects, Charlotte, North Carolina
General Contractor:	Fluor Daniel, Inc.
Landscape Contractor:	Gene Merritt–Merritt Brothers, Easley, South Carolina

Specialty Fabrications: Cast Bronze Water Spouts

Design Phase: 1987–1988

Date Completed: 1990

Project Cost: $18,000,000

Total Landscape Cost: $2,000,000

PROJECT DESCRIPTION

The Advantica Plaza and Park, formerly Spartan Food Systems Plaza, represents a gesture by Spartan Food Systems' founder to a small city in decline for the role it played in the company's success. Instead of opting for a large suburban headquarters site, the architects, Clark, Tribble, Harris & Li of Charlotte, North Carolina, working with the landscape architect, integrated the building into the city. The design for the plaza and park, with a strong central lawn panel offset by fountains, seating, and planted areas, achieved an urban presence and maturity. The project also includes a small, intimate informal triangular public park that contrasts the formality of the plaza with material similarities.

For young landscape architects and students, the case study demonstrates the rigorous formal approach to the structuring of a site to enable change to take place. A careful approach to the selection of plant material is coupled with a traditional and durable sense of materials and their application in a public place.

INTERVIEW WITH THE DESIGNER

Discussion with the landscape architect Peter Lindsay Schaudt took place on December 17, 2001, and August 15, 2002, by telephone. Interview participants are identified as Peter Lindsay Schaudt (PS) and author (Q).

Q:
Can you recall a designer or a writer in your training whose work demonstrates as a central part of the proposal how a built project or environment will change and evolve over time?

PS:
Dan Kiley, to me, is that designer. The fact that he has lived this long life, he has gone through several generations or decades of work, and the fact that I can physically go and see his work here in Chicago is quite a plus for me. It started when I was a student. My architectural background was very much influenced by the architect Louis Kahn and his essays about ruins, and how

he designed his buildings to last centuries, as well as my love of Rome and having spent a year there (at the American Academy). J. B. Jackson's book *The Necessity of Ruins* is another great source for me. It is not necessarily a nostalgic trip—it is a sense of what you are giving to culture and it is an ephemeral thing that just lasts one lifetime (which is not bad) or it might endure. One thing that struck me about Kahn's work was the beauty of form and surface. When you see the Roman ruins, there is this beautiful layering of geometry, technology, and construction that has a clarity to it. (See Figure 4.83.) My first influence was architecture and then I became aware of Dan Kiley's work through my architectural education in Chicago, going to see the acclaimed projects in Columbus, Indiana. I saw Irwin Bank, the outside of the Miller Garden, and, in particular, the Indiana Bell structure covered in ivy. I had seen pictures of it when it was built and that it was now very different. Time had evolved. The most memorable physical design example for me, however, is the McCormick Court at the Chicago Art Institute by Dan Kiley, where I have been able to see it evolve over my lifetime. The fact that it is a completely artificial landscape with just two and one-half feet of soil over a roof deck is mind-boggling.

Q:

So, from your early student days you were drawn to a wide range of design work and expressions where the notion of durability was uppermost?

PS:

Yes, for example, I know a lot of people use Robert Smithson's work as an inspiration, maybe more than it deserves. I went to an exhibition in the late 1970s at the Museum of Contemporary Art in Chicago on his work on entropy and "site/nonsite" projects when I was a student. The notion then of bringing "nature" into the gallery and having his photographs of landscape change was also very influential. I think that maybe that exhibition impacted me more than Olmsted's work or the work of Dan Kiley did at first. I did not know about Olmsted until later.

I must also reinforce this by noting that when I was a student there was less understanding or collaboration between design fields. I submitted a design proposal carried out as an independent project in school for the Vietnam War Memorial Competition in Washington and won a merit award. However, I had to take an art class where I moved from the architecture studio into a sculpture classroom in order to get academic credit for this independent work because it dealt with landscape. Working with a sculptor, therefore, was my first transition into landscape architecture. Architecture is a very fixed object-oriented art form and this fourth dimension was a real interest to me. At this point in architecture school, "passive solar energy" was becoming part of the curriculum.

Q:

It was tied to an environmental ethic, then?

PS:

That was not so important to me as making form through art, sculpture, and landscape rather than the environment at that point.

Q:

At what point did you make a connection between the ideas of form and durability that drew you to those projects and working on a project yourself?

PS:

I would argue that, as a student, issues of longevity and durability are rarely heard as issues. To me, it's more a maturing phenomenon, and you need to go through several cycles of site landscape construction and let a project weather ten years. As a young landscape professional, it was not all that important to me, because you tend to be totally fearless. You haven't screwed a project up yet. It was not really important until I traveled and saw ancient Rome and Egypt and realized how young America really is. At a point in your career, you ask the question: What am I going to leave behind? And right now I am doing that. Having won an award from the ASLA for Advantica Plaza after ten years, the project was finally photographed and it really looked beautiful. However, up until that time, I was confident that it would turn out well, but I just had to wait with the help of outstanding maintenance, too. That's one of the frustrating things about our profession. It's not something you can just push a button and make the project mature.

Figure 4.83. Pompeii, 1991. Masonry detail. (Photography by Peter L. Schaudt. Courtesy of Peter L. Schaudt.)

I think we are all designing for future generations, and I know that sounds utopian, but I truly believe that now. We are all able to enjoy the fruits of the work of Daniel Burnham in Chicago, Jens Jensen, and Alfred Caldwell. What I would like to see now in my work is a seriousness with which a culture will embrace it, protect it, and value it.

Q:
Even if that means changing certain things?

PS:
Especially working with plant material. At a certain point, for example, on Biltmore Estate (by Olmsted), you are going to have to replant the tulip poplar allée and will have to either cut them all down and start over or you are going to have to insert new trees between the old ones.

Q:
Which is something that the French in the Parisian streets have no problem with—to cut down their chestnut trees and replant them.

PS:
I think in our culture we look at landscapes, particularly historic landscapes, in such a romantic way while satisfying the urge for instant gratification and not looking towards the future in design terms.

Q:
How do you convey that notion in your own practice in design terms?

PS:
Here, in Chicago, the winters cause havoc to our landscape. I think the fact that we live and work in a very extreme climate means I try to focus on the durability of construction detail, on material selection, and working with the structural engineer when soil borings are being obtained. Also, really understanding the right way to construct. In my opinion, it is just as expensive to do bad construction as good construction. I think that I am really concerned, having studied ancient gardens and seen the longevity of beautiful, simple, and straightforward details, to want to replicate that, too. How I inspire and motivate my office is a sense of responsibility that we have to focus on the issue of timelessness, which I know can be thought of as a somewhat nostalgic notion, but it has a certain validity—lasting as it does through differing styles and periods of design fashion.

Q:
What do you mean by "timelessness" in this context?

PS:
I think it means simplicity, elegance, and restraint. I know some designers who would totally disagree with that, but I think it has to do with craft, how

Figure 4.84. Ericsson Stadium, 1995. "Before" Live Oak Walk. (Watercolor by Dick Sneary. Courtesy of Peter L. Schaudt.)

Figure 4.85. Ericsson Stadium, 1995. "After"—25 years in future—Live Oak Walk. (Watercolor by Dick Sneary. Courtesy of Peter Lindsey Schaudt.)

good you communicate it to a contractor. I also like minimalist architecture and landscapes and, therefore, do believe in the notion of not doing one thing more than you have to do, for example, in how you design a stair, a railing, and paving. It is also about making a decision that you are not everything to everybody. Planting beds and flowers are ephemeral and open to stylistic gardening moods—miscanthis is in this year; next year, it's feather-reed. The structure of a landscape is trees. I would, therefore, consider the architecture created by trees as representing this idea of what "timelessness" might mean. I think architects are very envious of trees as a material and the structure brought about by trees because of their power and beauty. What makes a landscape timeless is that we have the continued use of primal living materials and a palette that has been effectively used over the centuries: trees, soil, stone, and water. (See Figures 4.84 to 4.85.)

Q:
If you were commissioned to do a temporary built landscape and it was understood that it was temporary, would that alter the way you worked and, if so, how?

PS:
I think I would be stubborn and still approach it from the ways I described. I think I might design something that would just evaporate or just go away.

Q:
Would that give you more freedom or a broader palette?

PS:
It would be a career-changing experience to look at things differently—that's for sure. I think that I am too stubborn in my work and focused.

Q:
When you go back and look at your own built work, are you interested in looking broadly for that which has persevered, the maintaining of the idea—that it is as you designed it and executed it—or are you looking for surprises? Little delights of weathering that maybe you didn't expect—and is that disappointing to you?

PS:
It's the opposite. I think that design is a constant struggle, and I never really consider the project over—what makes it over is reality. Surprises or delights of weathering, as you call it, give life to my work. What gives me most delight or surprise is to see a project long after it's been finished. I have always looked at my projects as children—they are constantly changing and I still love them as much as if they are young or old. I have not had the luxury or the time to look again at my early work or if I will ever see much of it. The biggest surprise is really growth; the trees grow, but sometimes they don't. I have been fortunate enough to be influenced by Jim Urban's work

Figure 4.86. Curved wall, 1990. Advantica Plaza and Park. (Photography by Steven Brooke. Courtesy of Peter L. Schaudt.)

for some time and, to this day, I have not specified a Bradford pear or tree grate in seventeen years of practice. To see growth is the biggest experience. The other is how people use the space; it has nothing to do with technology, but has to do with use. That corner that I thought would be a perfect place for them to have lunch. The social aspects of designing urban space are fascinating and I don't think you can be prescriptive at all. The biggest compliment I have ever received for my design work is to discover that a public space I designed is where people now get married—because of the beauty of the space, not necessarily the use. There are a couple of gardens I designed with no intention of that happening, and it becomes a local icon where you have to be photographed—it's corny, I know, but it implies there is some intrinsic beauty that is conveyed to laypeople—and that's okay.

Q:
Related to this, do you think there is something, then, called cultural weathering?

PS:
Yes, it has to do with use. One of the biggest examples just now is skateboarding and how space is being used in ways the designer never intended.

Where people drive their cars, drop people off, where people cut through your park, the diagonal "cow path" or unaccounted route—it's the other dimension of human intervention, where they go at night, during the winter. I think it's an extra layer that has nothing to do with whether the weather is cold or warm. I think it's a valid concern and it's okay that spaces change over time. When you look at all the famous piazzas in Europe, they were not built in one generation or through one commission. In the U.S., there is a concern with getting it right the first time, of course, but what's wrong with tinkering with something and changing it and making it better? Like Copley Square in Boston, for example, it seems we keep redoing it because it's not quite right and I do not have a problem with that.

Q:

When discussing the issues of weathering and durability, the subject of materials and materiality inevitably comes up as well as how materials are selected and worked. You said you like to build in a durable way. What does that mean?

PS:

It has to do with connections, about fragile parts, and how you put units of a material together. Wood, for example, can be durable, but how do you connect it, pin it, the direction of the grain, etc., with honesty about the life span of the material? If you design a project where every twenty years the wood gets changed on a deck—I would consider a durable, but not necessarily sustainable, material application. When it's well crafted and thought through, then in twenty years you can say, "Well, I'm just going to redo the two-by-fours and leave the underlying structure." Durability has to do with the knowledge of strength of materials such as wood and, as I learned in several architecture school classes, concrete and steel. What I try to do is listen to people who know more about the material than I do. I try to distill information and I have high respect for manufacturers and really good builders. In the back of my mind, I am always trying to keep the design concept. I have learned over time that earlier in my career I was stubborn and ignorant about certain things. So I would stand firm with the idea, but it would not be the right technical solution. Now I am getting to the point where I can accept losing some battles in order to get the war won. And a lot of it has to do with durability. In my mind, a good practitioner is one that can build something that can last. This might be an old-fashioned notion now. There is a responsibility, especially if you are doing a public job, to understand this from a professional point of view. I think ethics has a lot to do with it. Toru Mitani, the Japanese landscape architect, stated that he wanted his work to last generations. If there was an earthquake or a bomb—a huge disaster of some type—and if they later uncovered and resurrected his project that it would be worth saving by its pure form. Almost a Kahn-like thought. It struck a chord with me not only in terms of its poetics but his ethic as a designer. If there were an award 300 years from now for a design project, would there be enough substance or form to judge? For example, the foundations of the garden or the concrete wall in the land that is clearly the work of human hands and all overlaid with the phenomenology of natural processes over time.

Q:

Continuing on from that point, if you look at the contemporary body of landscape architecture within our time and how much of it is actually very ethereal that future generations will only be able to experience much of it from photographs, is it possible the field has accepted lack of durability as part of landscape architecture? And how do you feel the needs of future designers should be met in this regard?

PS:

I have no problem with a landscape architect agreeing with that statement. I do not think you can fight natural processes. Maybe the notion of cultural history will become more important as an offshoot of what we do. We archive things, and I am not that nostalgic or sentimental but maybe, as a profession, with an ephemeral fourth dimension, it is incumbent on us to train a future generation where part of the phenomenology of what we do is also photographed for future use. Wouldn't we be so lucky to make photography like A. E. Bye of all our built environments for the Smithsonian Museum?

Q:

What does that say about the field?

PS:

I think you have to preserve the living organism. I remember how Dan Kiley had problems with historic preservation of landscapes. I have heard him vehemently deny that he cares about the preservation of his own work; it's all about growth and change. Alan Ward's photograph of the Miller Garden in the 1980s, in my opinion, was an important contribution to the profession to fully appreciate Dan's seminal work. One of the joys of working in landscape is that you can't preserve it really. There is a certain phenomenon of what we do — of the moment, of the time — and then you just can't rebuild the building using the same brick. I think we have to let go and be optimistic for the future and not try to hold on to this idea of keeping all the elm trees in the allée. So I think we have to enjoy things of the moment and what they were built for and consider change to be part of what we do and not fight it. If a garden or a public space gets changed with a different tree over time and, let's say, there is a Japanese beetle or something and you use a different tree, it's a change of the designer's intent. Do you just rip the garden out completely or just change the tree? I personally think you can just change the tree. I am not black and white on this issue. We are just so fanatic about saving everything, but there is a certain hierarchy of projects that has to be acknowledged. Take the Miller Garden, for instance. That needs to be preserved the way it is—the honey locusts need to remain honey locusts, the arborvitae needs to remain arborvitae. However, the redbuds, unfortunately, were changed.

Q:
Though our experience of landscapes is usually with the everyday, the quotidian, rather than the canonical works of landscape architecture—isn't it?

PS:
Yes, the normal is really our everyday experience. I, for one, have never seen the Miller Garden in person, just the photographs.

Q:
You have, therefore, an absolute fundamental concern for durability in your work and also a very sensitive understanding of how work changes—and it does change—through looking at history—past and contemporary. A very clear association with materials and material choice and how they are put together and that you're working within a very clear and defined way of looking at how your landscapes change, and you expect them to change primarily through cultural weathering. The notion is also clear that people will interact with the spaces and, by doing so, change them. Is that a fair assessment?

PS:
Most all of my new work, when I show it to clients, I show the project twenty-five years in the future. I subscribe to the before/after model, say, of the *Red Books* by Repton, very much. We need to do that, and do it all the time, and people laugh when you tell them that. If we don't design for things to be better over time, I don't understand why we do it unless it's an installation, or pure art for art's sake. I really believe in the responsibility and welcome change and do not fight it.

Q:
As you get older, do you start to have a longer view of your work?

PS:
Yes, I agree. I think that you get a sense of value of the evolution of your project. I think when you don't have the experience . . . when you don't have ten years' experience, when you don't have twenty years' experience, and you're just fresh out of school, you're fearless and everything is new and bold and exciting and there's no sense, in my opinion, of longevity and kind of the language of what you're doing because you're young.

Q:
What would your advice be, then, for younger designers?

PS:
My advice for young designers is to talk to older landscape architects. I think the value of being a young student and having worked for Dan Kiley was

that there was an extensive amount of photographs and cataloged information of his early work. I was able to see it twenty years down the road and also talk to him about things. I think that planning requires a sense of value in how things are actually put together. We need to look at those people in their sixties and their early seventies and we should start to outreach to them, if they're not included. If they're not involved in academia, let's bring them in. Travel, see things, and talk to the people who actually conceived of the idea—and I think it goes back to talking to the author of the work. I think that we could all guess and suppose and make value judgments, but I think it's more of a learning process when you actually talk to the person doing them.

Q:
What was the professional background you found yourself in as you approached the Advantica project? (See Figures 4.86 to 4.90.)

Advantica Plaza and Park
Spartanburg, South Carolina

PS:
The project is the corporate headquarters for a food franchising chain. I think the third largest behind McDonald's and Burger King. They own

Figure 4.87. Wall detail, 1999. Advantica Plaza and Park, Spartanburg, South Carolina. (Photography by Peter L. Schaudt. Courtesy of Peter L. Schaudt.)

Figure 4.88. Pergola under construction, 1990. Advantica Plaza and Park, Spartanburg, South Carolina. (Photography by Peter L. Schaudt. Courtesy of Peter L. Schaudt.)

Figure 4.89. Aerial of pergola, 1999. Advantica Plaza and Park, Spartanburg, South Carolina. (Photography by Peter L. Schaudt. Courtesy of Peter L. Schaudt.)

Denny's and Hardee's, and it's the headquarters for this company. The CEO grew up in the area, and the original headquarters was in the suburbs along the highway on an interchange, and we influenced him to come back to the downtown area, which, at the time, was pretty much depleted of life and retail activity, not unlike many cities in the country.

Dan Kiley's work had a high level of design quality but they took forever to do, and local landscape associates were making a lot of the detail

Figure 4.90. "Spring Fling," 2000. Advantica Plaza and Park, Spartanburg, South Carolina. (Photography by Peter L. Schaudt. Courtesy of Peter L. Schaudt.)

decisions, which was frustrating. I was very eager to get into the construction documentation and actually execute projects for myself. This led me to join a practice in the Southeast where there was a different culture, a different plant zone, and also the construction schedules in the mid-1980s were just as fast as lightning. I needed volume, exposure, and things happening. The Advantica project came up when it was a perfect opportunity to collaborate from the beginning with in-house architects, engineers, and the client. I was given tremendous responsibility off the coattails of working in Kiley's office. There was a great pollination of thought where I was able to influence the lobby plan; there was a see-through lobby on access through a garden, where I had an impact on getting the elevator cores pushed on the extreme outside of a very thin rectangular plan to leave the center open, so the garden view can penetrate through the building. The architects, conversely, also had a lot of say in the garden and I think it was a great collaboration and I think it's going to stand the test of time. It's a very simple, beautiful space that transcends style.

The client took a huge risk and he wanted a legacy piece that would stand the test of time. So it was a vertical tower, eighteen stories in a city predominantly four stories. We sold the idea that, you know, this is definitely going to be out of scale with the community and it's going to be a vertical monument and this tower must be integrated with a beautiful pedestrian environment. The grounds need to be pleasant spaces as well as a corporate symbol. The CEO donated money for a public park across the street from the corporate plaza and they were designed together with the same materials. It's truly a public space; the corporate plaza is public/private space and has security. It's open, people can use it, and it's also used for a lot of public activities.

Q:

In the design stage, what were some of the durability issues you were dealing with as part of the team?

PS:

We wanted it to be very strong and bold, and there was a part of the garden that was actually a footprint for the future building. We proposed a peach grove, a whole peach grove landscape all around this area. We literally mirrored the tower on the other side of the block and made a garden out of it. I even designed a retaining wall/bench in the shape of the new tower that was supposed to have been built—it's just a grid of trees with a fountain. It was never meant to be permanent; however, the inside of the garden was. So the garden was bracketed with two bookend buildings. Well, the CEO and the community liked it so much that when they did expand, they did it off site. The flowering trees were never meant to last forever; the proposed second building would have replaced it on the site. We've had to change the peach trees to more of a traditional type of crab apple, because they did not survive. We wanted to tie in the brick paver materials in the surrounding community to the project and also integrate that with a precast grid so that the paving was a hybrid between the new and the old. We decided to do a herringbone brick pattern inside of the grid that produced a million brick cuts. I would not do that again, although it looks quite beautiful and was a perfect execution.

Q:

What was the specific problem with the pavers?

PS:

The building was, unfortunately, the origin of the grid and it didn't quite match up with a four-inch module. We had to make special precast pavers to offset that. I think we might have studied more of an orthogonal brick infill, but it didn't work and so we went with forty-five degrees, but you just don't want to have little triangular slivers of brick in the pavement surface. I now consider them to be bad things you just want to rip out.

Q:

What about the planting?

PS:

The planting was meant to be a southern tradition of crape myrtle, azaleas, dogwoods, and, as I mentioned before, I made the mistake, really, of over-planting. As a young designer, I was a little nervous about the CEO saying, "You know, I want this thing looking good right away." Kiley's rule was always to overplant in the design phase, so that when you have to reduce cost, you still have a pretty solid planting plan.

Q:

You'd come back and take every second plant out?

PS:

Correct, but the owner was pleased with the initial effect in terms of get-ting leases and getting people to go there. So I think it worked for him, even though the longevity there was really never considered. The planting, as I mentioned, was really overdone in terms of spacing and growth, and, hav-ing come from Chicago to practice in the Carolinas, I was overwhelmed with the extra two to three months of growth, the irrigation, and heat. The growing season was much longer, and that was a huge lesson that I learned. The wisteria, I never thought I'd see them grow that fast in my lifetime. The detailing of the trellis was done with tongue and groove, a beautiful kind of cabinetry detailing, with slotted stainless steel angles that clipped onto the precast columns. That would be a detail I would reconsider because the wisteria is probably going to just torque that thing apart because of its pat-tern of fast growth in that climate.

Q:

Is it going to pull it down?

PS:

It will have to be replaced, probably in the next ten years. They'll probably have to take it down completely. It was much too delicate, much too archi-tectural for a wisteria. It looked beautiful, but had I known more about the growth cycle, I probably would have rethought it.

Q:

More generally, what are the important practices that you have developed or would like to develop in relation to the durability of your work?

PS:

As landscape architects, we have a responsibility to the stewardship of our projects. We need to educate the clients and the community, the public, of how things will grow and change. It's most obvious with plant material, but I also think it relates to materials and materiality. In the same vein, we need to describe to the community how things deteriorate, and I know it might not be a popular item that people want to hear. What makes a garden beautiful is age and the idea that things aren't perfect, that there is nature and man. And, to me, the marriage of those two is what makes our profession an art form. I like to show before and after images that were inspired by the work of landscape architect Laurie Olin and his influential gift of drawing and communicating. I make a point of always having these vignettes of, "Here's what it's going to look like when we finish and here's what it's going to look like twenty-five years from now." It's a very effective and powerful tool. It communicates that we're an optimistic profession where we say what this project is going to be like for our grandchildren. We know what it's going to look like next year or two years, but I think we have this responsibility especially in public work. In our planting plans, we always show the future. People always laugh, saying, "You know, this is fifty years from now." And I always say, "Of course, this is what we are designing for."

I actually believe that our work should be legitimate, whether it's new or when it's decaying or falling apart. People then should say—this is worth redoing, or this is worth replanting. I think things should change, and there's some things that shouldn't, that have a collective memory forever.

PERPETUAL MATERIALS

Figure 4.91. General view. Aluminum Garden, New York, New York. (Courtesy of Ken Smith, Landscape Architects.)

Project Information

Project: Aluminum Garden

Location: New York, New York

Client: Withheld

Landscape Architect: Ken Smith, Landscape Architect, New York, New York
Project designer: Ken Smith
Project team: Elizabeth Asawa and Yoon Chul Cho

Architect: Margaret Helfand
(townhouse restoration)

General Contractor: Ian Banks, Inc.

Landscape Contractor: Richard Heller
Mornhurst Gardens
(timber construction and plants)

Specialty Fabrications: Dragoslav
(fountain runnels, aluminum screens, and light
column fabrication and installation)

Design Phase: Fall–Winter 1998 (duration of project, one year)

Date Completed: Summer 1999

Project Cost: $75,000

PROJECT DESCRIPTION

This simple urban garden rejects metaphor and narrative content in favor of using contemporary materials and plantings as the landscape medium. The direct and beautiful expression of materials creates a garden of perceptual qualities: lightness and darkness, reflectivity, transparency, depth, movement and growth.

The L-shaped 585-square-foot rear courtyard space is structured around an existing mature maple tree. The garden area steps back in a series of shallow terraces held by heavy timbers, which are stained aluminum. The timber structure supports panels of industrial grating, which are placed over common traprock crushed-stone fill. As viewed from the townhouse, the garden has a forced perspective quality, which is emphasized by the "tilting up" effect of the terraces and the skewing of the garden's edge, increasing its apparent size. Running along the skewed edge is a water runnel that is made of marine aluminum channel, which cascades down the terraces. Two sides of the garden are defined by a bamboo grove, and an expanded aluminum screen defines the third side. Aluminum commercial-supply kitchen pots provide for plantings of flowering vines. A 115-square-foot private terrace on the third floor overlooks the garden. A painted aluminum floor, planter with grasses, and expanded aluminum screen give structure and frame views from this elevated position. Two illuminated acrylic columns provide an ambient glow for the garden spaces. Detailed landscape elements are as follows:

TERRACE CONSTRUCTION

The terraces are constructed as a series of stacked industrial-grade eight-inch-by-eight-inch pressure-treated pine timbers, which are pinned together with lag bolts. Five terraces, each with seven-inch risers and a slope of one percent, create a total grade change of thirty-two inches from the existing townhouse doors to the back of the garden. The void areas created by the terraces are filled with one-inch crushed-stone traprock, a type that is commonly used in road construction. The timber construction was stained with a custom-formulated aluminum-based exterior wood stain.

TERRACE GRATING

Gray industrial fiberglass grating is used to create the terrace floor surface. Seven-foot panels span the openings created by the timber terrace structure. The crushed-stone subgrade is visible through the grating openings. The light-weight grating panels are factory fabricated to fit the terrace configurations.

BAMBOO GROVE

Forty yellow grove bamboo plants, *phylostachys areosulcatta*, are planted eighteen to twenty-four inches on center. Installed at a height of twelve feet, they will grow to eighteen to twenty-five feet in height. The planting soil consisted of a mix of seventy-five percent topsoil and twenty-five percent organic compost. The bamboo plants are contained within an eighty-millimeter polyethylene root barrier to a depth of three inches. The bamboo grove is illuminated with metal halide up-lights.

ALUMINUM WATER RUNNEL

Industrial marine-grade 60-61 structural aluminum U-channel is used to create a set of five water runnels that spill from one to the other as they step down the terraced grade changes. A three-inch-diameter U-shaped aluminum spout rises from the ground in the bamboo grove and spills into the top runnel.

ALUMINUM SCREENS

Privacy screens are fabricated with square tubular aluminum frames that are infilled with expanded aluminum panels.

ALUMINUM POTS

The aluminum planter pots are commercial-grade mixing bowls purchased from a restaurant supply wholesaler. They are drilled with a weep hole and planted with clematis vine.

GLOWING LIGHT COLUMN

Custom-designed light columns are fabricated out of six-foot-long acrylic tubes eight inches in diameter, sanded to create a translucent effect. Aluminum mounting brackets hold the column away from the wall to create a floating effect. Metal halide uplights are mounted in the paving surface and illuminate the columns from below.

For young landscape architects and students, the desire to work with a single material and within its manufacturing constraints may appear to be limiting aesthetically as well as formally. However, as the designer in this case study discusses, the performance of aluminum over time can be tested and evaluated *in situ* so that each project builds progressively one after another. In terms of the durability of the material application, the designer learns what is possible and what to avoid, the resolution of the design in terms of the material finishes, and forms are matched against new and traditional landscape elements, here from the residential garden. This case study demonstrates the result of a careful study of historical precedents in built landscape work in the twentieth century, allied with a precise modernist approach to the manufactured and natural materials of the built landscape.

INTERVIEW WITH THE DESIGNER

A discussion with the landscape architect, Ken Smith, took place on May 11, 2000, in Cambridge, Massachusetts, and on May 6, 2003, by telephone. The interview participants are identified as Ken Smith (KS) and author (Q).

Q:
What do the terms "weathering" and "durability" mean to you in terms of the way you work in landscape design?

KS:
Every project is different, and my office is a little odd in that we do temporary installations, where we deal with things that are quite ephemeral in terms of their durability and construction. The glowing topiary garden was constructed to exist for six weeks and it only had to be durable for that period of time. On that project, we used a material palette that fitted that purpose. In other projects like public works, things have to be very durable because of the project life cycle. Public projects often don't get maintained or rebuilt other than on a thirty- to fifty-year cycle, so you have to work with very durable, proven materials and construction methods.

Q:

Durability becomes almost an end in itself?

KS:

Yes, durability has the goal of overcoming the lack of maintenance, which the system is incapable of providing. The commitment to soil and things underground becomes very important because you can't replace these items very easily. The durability and performance of the soil as a planting medium becomes in many ways more important than selecting the plants. The plants actually can be changed and altered and have less of a requirement for durability than the soil medium and drainage underneath. So you start thinking about how to put the project together in these terms. The residential projects lie in between—they are not totally ephemeral or they may have only aspects of that, and they don't have to last for a century, although most clients feel they want something that will last their own lifetime.

Q:

These are the same residential clients, however, who are used to changing other parts of their lives over time—cars, clothes, houses, work.

KS:

Although they seem to be less interested in changing their landscapes!

Q:

One thing that is common, then, to the whole discussion of durability is time and the notion of the variance of time in your own projects, which you very clearly pointed out—temporary work, public permanent work, and private permanent work. Is this your way of starting to think about how weathering and durability may start to affect a project in terms of material and finish choice and method of construction?

KS:

It's a question of performance, I think! Another thing is the notion of standards, and by these I mean what is good and what is bad, rather than a definition concerned with codes and regulations. Sometimes, so-called "bad" methods, for example, how a joint is made, how concrete is poured, or how a paver is made, have lasted longer than "good" methods. A problem then arises about what is "good" and that the designer should always be seeking the "best" methods or the "best" methods of manufacture or choice of materials. An example of this is exposed aggregate concrete. It's a perfect choice, but it's actually bad practice, preaging the concrete so it wears out faster. In the end, it's an aesthetic decision; designers make that choice based on the fact that it can be replaced and repaired and is just part of the life cycle of the project.

Q:

Can you say, therefore, that for you weathering and durability concerns in the end are aesthetic?

KS:

Or budget sometimes!

Q:

What projects have you looked at for precedents that have qualities that address change over time and issues of durability?

KS:

When I travel, the gardens I like most are often simply constructed. Gardens that have gravel floors—they really work, they feel like the landscape, they drain; I look for the way that gravel floors and grade changes are put together. The other specific inspiration for this garden was the work of the modernists, particularly Garrett Eckbo, who did an aluminum garden of his own, which I thought was very beautiful. Eckbo does not get as much respect as he should as a designer. I was not trying to copy his garden here, but I really found his use of unconventional material to be very provocative and interesting.

Q:

You also have an interest in the very visible works of modern landscape architecture in our cities and the nature of how they are changed over time. Recent articles have focused on your efforts to draw attention to destructive maintenance and inappropriate changes to landmark landscape projects. What are the current issues related to the body of landscape project work, particularly carried out in the 1960s to 1970s, and their possible absence in the future for scholars, practitioners, and students?

KS:

The subject of urban landscape projects from the 1960s and 1970s is being read as a stylistic issue, and this body of work will, therefore, be vulnerable to change. They are, in fact, quite good gardens in the way they were put together, spatially, and in their materials and construction. There were wonderful projects, for example, Paley Park on East 53rd Street in New York (landscape architect, Zion & Breen, 1965–1968). This urban landscape space, which will survive because of its patron, is fundamentally a result of medium and method. The garden is beautiful because it works so well; the soil, the drainage, and the trees all work together; the landscape is a whole construction and an exposition of the methods of making landscapes. This it also shares with the Lincoln Center for the Performing Arts Plaza, also in New York (landscape architect, Dan Kiley, 1960).

Q:

I was wondering if you'd now reflect a little bit more on Lincoln Plaza as it is right now and what you see the future of that and other contemporary spaces that we admire.

KS:

The Lincoln Center project employed a method of making a landscape on structure—all things that are present now in contemporary discussions about making landscapes.

Q:

Isn't it true to say at that time there was not a lot of knowledge about building on structural decks and their drainage and insulation and the issues of structural soil?

KS:

Kiley really knew what he was doing. The installation of street trees in city landscapes were things that were pioneered by Kiley as well as Bob Zion in those early projects, and they had developed enough experience in building landscapes that they had really good intuition. I think Lincoln Center will probably be lost—it looks that way. Looking at those projects was important in terms of sort of understanding the medium of landscape in a contemporary or modern way. I always thought that Lincoln Center was quite remarkable because of the way that Dan Kiley invented those roof planters sitting on top of a garage structure. He was able to create a forest-like canopy in planters that had only thirty inches depth of soil. He did it with shared soil volumes that now, of course, have been discovered as the way you should grow urban trees. At the time Kiley was doing it, he was really operating instinctually. I just find that, looking at those projects, they've always informed me in terms of the use of materials and thinking about durability.

Q:

How, in terms of your own practice, do you start to address the issue of weathering and durability? How does that directly translate into material choice or construction language?

KS:

We are just finishing a project in the Hamptons on Long Island, where I have built a really quite beautiful arbor out of aluminum. (See Figures 4.92 to 4.96.) It's a telescoping structure that sits on a major axis that runs through the site, and the entire structure is made out of really quite hefty aluminum angles. They are five-inch-by-three-inch angles with a thickness of three-eighths inch. So it's actually quite substantial aluminum structural pieces. On this project, I was using aluminum because we're within a quarter mile

Figure 4.92.
Aluminum arbor, private residence, Hamptons, Long Island, New York. (Courtesy of Ken Smith, Landscape Architects.)

Figure 4.93.
Aluminum arbor, private residence, Hamptons, Long Island, New York. (Courtesy of Ken Smith, Landscape Architects.)

of the ocean and so any kind of ferrous metals are going to be problematic in terms of rust, with the salt water. So we could have used either aluminum or stainless steel. I think aluminum is more interesting because of the way it weathers. It's also lighter in weight and has a substantial thickness that I like.

Q:

Why did it have to be metal?

KS:

I'm interested in metal. I've been doing a number of structures in recent years out of metal, and arbors, in particular, interest me because they're an interesting structure for landscape architects to design. I imagine they're similar to an architect rethinking the interior stair, which is a functional feature that you do over and over again, but yet it has expressive qualities. The arbor is something like that in landscape, though it actually has less functional aspects; it's more purely expressive. I'm working through a number of arbor ideas using aluminum elements as a structural system. By using these L angles, it actually sets it up as a structural system. So it's not a decorative arbor in sort of the normal sense of, you know, columns and beams. I mean it has columns and beams, but they're all structural in nature. It's very modernist in that sense.

Figure 4.94. Aluminum arbor, private residence, Hamptons, Long Island, New York. (Courtesy of Ken Smith, Landscape Architects.)

Figure 4.95. Aluminum arbor, private residence, Hamptons, Long Island, New York. (Courtesy of Ken Smith, Landscape Architects.)

Figure 4.96. Aluminum arbor, private residence, Hamptons, Long Island, New York. (Courtesy of Ken Smith, Landscape Architects.)

Q:

Had you had a wealth of knowledge in the office already, having studied the material, that you could call on or that you could relate to?

KS:

I had been playing around with these L shapes from other projects, and so I was interested in them. I have used the U channel, which is a standard structural piece, and so the Ls are just part of that structural family of materials. On this project, I didn't leave the aluminum natural. I had wanted to, but the aluminum that came from the factory had some scratches and things in it and so the fabricator I was working with suggested powder coating it. We went through a number of powder coat studies, and actually the clear powder coating was quite interesting and shifted the finish only slightly, maintaining a reading of the material underneath. Even though the aluminum stands up pretty well to the salt in the air, the client wanted a more refined and protected finish and the powder coat allowed us to do that.

Q:

How did you go about thinking about how it's joined?

KS:

We built little cardboard models in the office, and we actually did a number of studies, figuring out how to construct them, how they would bolt together, what would bolt to what, and how that would connect to something else. After it was basically all designed, I consulted with a structural engineer who reviewed the documents and made sure that my footings were adequate and also reviewed all my bolt connections just to make sure that they were all working. We pretty much had it right and, in some cases, I had actually overdesigned things, so we were able to lighten up some of the material.

Q:

You see this arbor as a single material element?

KS:

No, I don't think so. In the canopy of the arbor, there's a series of Ls that are designed to hold another finlike member. Originally, I had thought the fins were going to be wood, but the client and I could never agree on what color the wood would be stained. And, in the end, we just did a mockup this past week on site, where I was looking at using half-inch acrylic fins that are sanded so they are translucent. So we're putting these fins of acrylic into these slots of the aluminum. And it's actually really quite interesting because the aluminum, the arbor, is quite reflective in terms of its surface. The acrylic is quite interesting in that it captures the light and it has a kind of really soft glow, which is quite nice. I'm also using aluminum Ls throughout the site. There's a gate that I've designed also out of aluminum that is part of the swimming pool enclosure. Then I designed a whole series of custom light fixtures, a line of lights that go across the lawn, and these lights are also fabricated out of aluminum and acrylic. The acrylic on the light fixtures catches the light and glows. So bringing the acrylic into the arbor was a natural idea.

Q:
What you have is a collection of different pieces on the project?

KS:
The aluminum becomes a kind of material that threads its way through the site.

Q:
What eventual planting do you see as part of the arbor—is it a vine or a wisteria?

KS:
We're going to plant wisteria on it. Although the arbor is actually so striking, a number of people have said that we shouldn't plant anything on it, but I think we will plant it.

Q:
Where did these material explorations into metal and the continued ideas of weathering and durability start?

Aluminum Garden
New York, New York

KS:
The Aluminum Garden project is a contemporary garden placed into a nineteenth-century brownstone setting. (See Figures 4.97 to 4.99.) There was an existing tree in this small yard, and it was sitting in an elliptical-shaped raised planter, and the planter filled the entire site—the space was basically unusable. It was an awkward position in that the space inside the ellipse was not really usable, while the space outside was marginal. I realized that I had to make a new floor—so it became a question of how I could lift up the garden to float over this tree. The big design move was to skew the entire floor so that it created a wedge around two sides and that became the planting zone, which we then filled with soil for the bamboo. The rest of it was a construction of wood timbers that could span the width of the space and then, suspended between those, are the fiberglass decking panels. The client had suggested suburban wood decking, but that requires a fairly thick section to get in joists, decking, and other supporting members. It would have meant that we would have had to lift up the garden much higher or cut into the tree roots, which was unacceptable to me. The fiberglass decking required only a one-and-a-half-inch section, which allowed everything to work with minimal depth in order to not disturb the tree roots.

Figure 4.97. View from above, Aluminum Garden, New York, New York. (Courtesy of Ken Smith, Landscape Architects.)

Figure 4.98. Fountain runnel detail, Aluminum Garden, New York, New York. (Courtesy of Ken Smith, Landscape Architects.)

Figure 4.99. View from town-house, Aluminum Garden, New York, New York. (Courtesy of Ken Smith, Landscape Architects.)

Q:
The crushed rock was placed to fill in the space between the timber joists?

KS:
The wooden structure and the set of terraces were established in seven-foot increments, which was the maximum span that the manufacturer could provide the fiberglass decking material. At the maximum span of this material, it deflected, so I filled the entire void underneath with coarse gravel. I did not want an awkward space under there, and the gravel was a way of giving the panel something solid to sit on that took the deflection out of the middle.

It's a very small garden, and the spatial considerations of each of the terraces and screens sets up a whole set of layers. The terraces step back, making the space appear deeper; the runnel reregisters that stepping; the bamboo and the screen also introduce a transparency.

Q:
Was the selection of materials very deliberate in terms of using manufactured elements and taking very precise machined and regulated objects from one design field to another?

KS:
It's all transgressive. The aluminum panel that became the runnel is actually a structural aluminum beam that is used in the construction of waterfront piers. It worked here because it is a marine alloy so it does not corrode like most other aluminum, and because it was structural, it had an internal strength that did not need to be augmented.

Q:
In terms of why you chose these materials beyond the issue of cost, is there an understanding of how these materials are going to change or not, over time, in terms of their accuracy?

KS:
The marine aluminum will change less quickly than the aluminum screens. The screens are made of expanded metal panels, which are cut and stretched, and this creates weaknesses—it actually tortures the metal, and the aluminum screens will, therefore, deteriorate faster.

Q:
Could you not, then, replace the screen panels?

KS:
The panels could be replaced, but if they get an efflorescent bloom on them, it actually can be quite interesting. The frame around the screens will also weather slower than the screen itself. The one thing we kept in the garden from before was the cedar picket fence, which, when I first saw the garden, I hated it.

Q:
This is the fence just seen behind the new aluminum fence?

KS:
Yes, and I wanted to get rid of it. The client was absolutely not going to spend money on it, and so we kept it. It's very old and rotted, but in the end becomes a counterpoint between the different ages and qualities of things; it gives the garden a lot of its character. The structural part of the landscape will devolve, but the organic part will actually evolve with time. Gardens are

not complete when they finish construction, only after maintenance, care, and growth.

Q:

Why did you not choose to go a more conventional route in the runnel material, say, stone or brick, one that would change over time, build up a patina with the washing of water?

KS:

I wanted this element to have the capacity to keep its clean edge through time. The material is thick enough that it can be maintained with seasonal cleaning with steel wool. However, the property was sold and the new person never moved in and they sold the property again. So there's actually someone now, who owns the property, who didn't commission the work, and I've had very little involvement with the project since then.

Q:

At the present moment, you've no idea if the original design intentions have been honored or even understood?

KS:

I did speak with the new owner, and at the time I'd met with her, the aluminum bowls, the planter bowls, had somehow disappeared. She didn't know what had happened to them. They weren't there when she moved in. At that time, she wasn't operating this fountain because she didn't know how to operate it. There was never really any follow-up after that to continue working on it or to make any revisions or to get it operational. So I've really lost track of it at this point.

Q:

Will you continue to return to this material repetitively over time and develop it and change it in different ways?

KS:

We're starting a new project for a condominium on the Upper East Side in Manhattan. On that project, I'm designing a topiary wall, a kind of folded scrim structure that will have vines growing on it. And it's going to be made out of stainless steel. And we're using expanded steel as the scrim material that the vines will grow on. One of the things I learned at the Aluminum Garden was that the expanded aluminum was actually quite weak. When they fabricate the steel, they cut it and stretch it, and the stretching process really weakens the material. In carbon steel, it causes the metal to actually rust faster than it would normally and, with aluminum, it weakens it. So, on this project, we're using stainless steel that I think will be a little more durable than either of the other two materials.

Q:

And less economic?

KS:

I always get in trouble because I never let the budget strictly rule the project. I always have a problem with that—but it is a reality. I do keep it at the back of my mind. If I have a tight budget, I know I am looking for efficient or economical solutions. A lot of times, the client does not want that. The client will go for a more conventional solution, even if they understand some other method or material is actually more interesting and cheaper but it does not have the normative look that many people want.

COMPRESSED

Figure 4.100. Wire mesh screen in winter. "Compressed": Landscape Installation, Stone Quarry Art Park, Cazenovia, New York. (Courtesy of Office of H. Keith Wagner.)

Project Information

Project: "Compressed": A Temporary Landscape Installation

Location: Cazenovia, New York

Client: Stone Quarry Art Park

Landscape Architect: Office of H. Keith Wagner

Principal Artist: H. Keith Wagner, ASLA;
Associate: Karin Klinefelter

General Contractor: H. Keith Wagner

Landscape Contractor: H. Keith Wagner, Karin Klinefelter

Design Phase: Two weeks in May of 1999

Date Completed: June, 1999

Project Cost: $2000

PROJECT DESCRIPTION

Integrated into the very pattern it intends to interpret, "Compressed" abstracts the hedgerow and its presence in the landscape. Metal mesh, as a metaphor of human intervention and order "woven" across the landscape, compresses the materials found within the hedgerow just as humans compress the landscape into the remnant hedgerow.

(H. Keith Wagner)

The designer is a landscape architect and metal artist, who was inspired by a childhood agrarian landscape and his father's passion for design and fabrication. In beginning a professional career, there was a single focus solely on traditional practice in landscape architecture, but it has now evolved into an amalgam of art and landscape and reflects a lifelong love of minimalism, a curiosity with industrial forms and details, and a fascination with texture and materials. The artistic work began as a release from dissatisfaction with the conventions of design practice. A turning point transpired when three-dimensional assemblages with metal were explored as part of the design process for specific projects. Here, art functions as a hands-on testing ground for an interest in the sculptural expression of materials such as honed stone, crushed limestone, and rusted metal. Artistic experiments in textures and subtle variations in hue are furrowed back into practice. Aesthetic inspiration is drawn from the pure abstraction of the visual world into the repetition of objects, order of grids, and tactile qualities and patterns of materials. The layering and composition of these elements are expressed in assemblages, sculpture, and landscape design. Art has continued to inform the built landscapes, emphasizing the richness of textures, and materials help to define a space. The tactile qualities of materials, their history, evolution, and inherent nature become a vital part in evoking memory of place.

The lessons from this case study are primarily focused on the interaction of the activities of art and design and the mutual explorations of material qualities in time. The design processes in landscape architecture are informed by the hands-on research into material performance and the tactile qualities of weathered surfaces, patinas, and stains. The short-term installations in the landscape, as shown in the case study, allow for the testing of design ideas and strategies that may find their way into more longer lasting works.

INTERVIEW WITH THE DESIGNER

Discussion with the landscape architect H. Keith Wagner took place on August 29, 2000, in Burlington, Vermont, and January 28, 2003, by phone. Interview participants are identified as Keith Wagner (KW) and author (Q).

Q:

What is your understanding of the term "durability" in terms of a built landscape?

KW:

To me, there is a dual issue in the question of durability: the inherent nature or composition of a particular material and its longevity in time. I also think of durability as it informs the design—does the material transcend time? The Miller Garden by Kiley is an example. Obviously, the material properties have held up as it is maintained, but also, the design is fortified by being crafted of noble materials, which affords the original design intent.

Q:

I think we may have an understanding of how a material holds up—that stone that has been worked is still physically intact or metals, even though they may have gone through certain surface processes, are still intact—but, for you, how does a design hold up?

KW:

By that I mean, does design hold up in terms of the original maneuvers—do they still hold true—classic principles such as axial relationships or terminus or creating a movement or sequence through the landscape? With the Miller Garden, there was a rigorous organization and geometry and, to me, it is still as beautiful now as it was when it was originally built.

Q:

Although the irony of the Miller Garden is that the materials are themselves changing (or growing) and, by definition, altering—the medium or materials are not static. Do the forms have a resonance, then?

KW:

This is the reason that I pursued landscape architecture rather than architecture; there is a dynamic quality to the maturation of a living plant. Once a building is completed, it is not going to change other than by acquiring a material patina or to start weathering. Plant material can change over time—the sense of scale changes as a tree starts to exceed the height of a building or a hedge gets broader and denser in order to create a screen or possibly frame a view.

Q:

What other precedents do you go to in your own work and the work of the office?

KW:

My work is sculptural—I am influenced by the work of Donald Judd and Richard Serra. In the design process, I try to break it down in terms of some very simple gestures. My design work wants to be a series of pure movements. I tend to conceive and integrate materials in an elegant, simple way.

Q:

There is an implication there that you want your projects to last?

KW:

I want the gestures to be poetic—to be relevant now and in the future. The choices we make as designers become what materials we are selecting. The other thing you can't control is the maintenance of the projects. We have had some really wonderful projects built, and either the owner sells the property and the next owner does not share the same passion for that landscape space, and the landscape starts to erode to a point that it undermines the original design intent and aesthetic. All you are left with, then, are the photographs when it was as near perfect as you could desire.

Q:

What about the notion of a landscape that, as part of its initial design concept, is bound to change over time? I am thinking here particularly of urban-scale projects—streets, plazas, squares—that are being rebuilt fairly frequently, twenty–twenty-five years, sometimes less.

KW:

Maybe that's all right if you look at these public projects as temporal or evolving—similar to installations or to public art. Over time, an installation can be dismantled and a new installation comes in by a new artist.

As an artist, I work both within temporal artworks and more objective frameworks. Some of my art, like my installation "Compressed" or my beach pieces, which are constructed of found materials on the shore of Lake Champlain, are only intended to last a brief time. My metal sculptures are intended to last much longer as objects placed within a landscape. There is a freedom within art that is not always available to landscape architects. (See Figures 4.101 and 4.102.)

Figure 4.101. Keith Wagner in sculpture workshop. (Courtesy of Office of H. Keith Wagner.)

Figure 4.102. Metal box by H. Keith Wagner. (Courtesy of Office of H. Keith Wagner.)

Q:

On the subject of weathering and durability, the notions of weathering and maintenance tend to be thought of in the same sentence. For example, in the technology manuals, reference to the term "durability" in a built project is cast by the word "maintenance." A quotation from David Pye states, "durability is an end in itself, a thing is not made properly unless it is made to last." Can durability be one of the driving forces of a project?

KW:

I think there are constraints that are layered on top of my design process, such as budget. You may want to select a material that you know is going to last for thirty–forty–fifty years, but the client just cannot afford it. So I think as an ideal most designers want their work to last. A client will pull the rug out from under you—because you cannot buy that most perfect or durable material. There is a point between durability and maintenance—to me, the durability and aging of a material, those are the things that I find beautiful. My sculpture work is all in rusted metal. The process of decay of a material is as beautiful to me as the creation or maturation of something—like the patina of copper—we do a lot of copper planters just for that reason—their softness; they become tactile and increase their texture and depth. Our designs tend to be a play on these subtle changes in hue and textures. (See Figures 4.103 and 4.104.) The hard materials we choose we want them to

Figure 4.103. Copper screen detail, private residence. (Courtesy of Office of H. Keith Wagner.)

Figure 4.104. Copper planters , private residence. (Courtesy of Office of H. Keith Wagner.)

have a patina and modeling. If you can get moss to grow on them, that just adds to that layer of age. With reference to maintenance, if your grout joints split on a bluestone terrace—is bluestone not a durable material? It is, but if care is not taken to recaulk that, then water will get in there and the bluestone will spall. What it takes is a little bit of what I would call general maintenance. So there is a balance. Bluestone is a wonderful material when used properly; maintained properly, it can last a very long time.

Q:

You used the term in relation to the use of copper planters as wanting to increase or densify the tactility. What do you mean by that?

KW:

As I mentioned, I believe the materials and their textures add to the memory one takes away from a space. When materials have a patina to them, I want to touch them, because they are so tactile. As soon as I touch them, I have a connection with them that is different than purely a visual connection. My hope is that, whether it is a stone wall or a well-crafted bench or a planter, I want people to be drawn to touch them and activate more of one's senses. The tactile quality of the physical forms is what's intriguing to me, as well as their spatial relationships in defining a landscape.

Q:

In your work, there is a great emphasis on craft. Not just your craft—the work of the designer—but in the way it's actually made. We see a lot of stone walls, hand-formed elements, one-off landscape forms built in your shop here or in a factory, that is quite deliberate. The previous comments on humanness and this are tied together because you're clearly exploring an expression of a material through the handling, which, in itself, comes with a set of rules about how it will change. Do you believe that is true, and if it is true, where did that come from— did it evolve over time or did it come from your sculpture work?

KW:

I think it is true that it did come from my design process over time— sketching or painting. However, I do a lot of exploring with my sculpture. The act of me fabricating pieces, I think, adds a layer of craft to the work— it is this connection to material that I try to employ in the spaces we design.

Q:

Does that restrict you in any way?

KW:

No, my design philosophy to landscape is about integration and layering of materials.

Q:

By "restriction," I was meaning the ability to use a lot of industrialized products or products that necessarily do not have the longevity. These are less present in your work than, let's say, natural stone materials. Another thing I have noticed about your work, it is less about placing designed objects in the landscape and more about building into the landscape or layering on the land or integrating or bedding or intermeshing existing elements as opposed to dropping pieces here and there. Is that true?

KW:

Yes, an example, at Bicentennial Hall–Science Building project, at Middlebury College in Vermont, I deliberately did not want to buy benches as a way of providing seating, because that just becomes visual clutter. I wanted to make simple gestures in the landscape, the introduction of stone walls amongst a grove of birch trees as seating for the students. So there is a deliberate reason on my part in projects to reduce that "clutter"—working on integrating materials to engage users.

Q:

When a project comes into your office, at what stages and in what ways do you start to think about this project completed over time and the issues it has to address—snow, ice, rain? Clearly, you do not sit down and say—today is the day we deal with weathering. Is it embedded in particular phases of the work or is it something you feel throughout the whole design process?

KW:

That process starts from the onset—I begin to think of the materials while we are on the initial site, which already possesses inherent clues and related materials. I have a fascination with textures and subtle variations in hue and their role in making a memory of place. Perhaps the most successful landscapes are assemblages of my initial site perceptions and inspirations, which are then further developed in my sketches.

Q:

How do you, then, direct or teach your office to have those concerns?

KW:

My process is in some ways design inspiration...others within the studio are nurtured from my insight. The process will begin when I walk the site and I begin to do concept sketches, usually in my sketchbook, then develop them to plan scale and give those to other staff designers to develop and engage. At that time, we will start talking about my concerns regarding design intent and durability because textures and materials are integral to my work. So they absorb or are exposed to my philosophy and predilections over the course of many projects—not just one. Our influences regarding materials include how they appear, the geographic region of the project, and the corresponding materials that are being used in the architecture.

Q:

Durability is not taught as a subject in design schools. Also, in school you are more removed from that topic than any other, because your work is paper based. It is based on the conceptual design/schematic design phase of work and apart from an odd site visit or two, you don't come into contact with the subject until your first job. Things you thought that you could do, you can't do.

KW:

I firmly believe that my initial interests in materials and their durability is a product of my father's inherent experimentation and fabrication of materials for industry. He is a retired engineer who once worked as an architect and possesses a mind for problem solving. Though you are correct that durability is not taught as a subject in design school—I feel the exposure to this topic at ESF, Syracuse, was valuable.

Q:

You do temporary work that is sometimes seen as part of group or individual installations. I'm thinking of the work at Shelburne Farms. Is that work for you thought of as something separate? For a project that only has a life of a few days or weeks, do you think about it differently?

KW:

Yes, it is different. They are an installation and they don't have to live a long time. But they are also experimentations in part of my bigger design process—so they are equally as valuable to me, even though I know they are not going to be up forever. In the Shelburne Farms installation, I took a meadow and mowed a fifty-foot grid in the tall grasses, basically mowed a checkerboard. In the center of each mowed panel, I placed a suburban lawn ornament—a blue gazing ball. It was referring to Vermont's meadows as its lawns and formed part of the Hay Art Festival. I liked the idea of articulating space by simply mowing grass. The following spring, someone who flew over the site told me that the faint outline of the checkerboard was still present as the grass started to grow back in and it looked great.

Q:

Which would suggest it would have been interesting to follow it up as the grid breaks down?

KW:

I wish I had had that opportunity. I think that the ghost of the grid still intrigues me—to think that there's the trace of man still on the landscape as the land is converting back to its natural state.

Q:

I am aware that work of that type (either temporary or permanent) is less done by landscape architects and more by site artists who have taken it upon themselves to study and address landscape ephemerality and durability as themes in their work. I continue to discuss with landscape architects how they resolve this question in their own professional work, and one issue that comes up again and again is the issue of unpredictability—that is, materials not working in the way you expected them to do. Have you encountered this in your built work or the work of others?

KW:

I think you see it in old metal, copper, or bronze pieces that have a patina that is quite subdued and beautiful—I love that. On one project, I wanted to have concrete walls, but I wanted them to be cast with metal in them so that they would have a patina of rust over time. In fact, in my basement workshop, I cast spheres out of concrete and applied metal shavings that I collected from my sculpture studio for that reason, just to see what it would do.

Q:

So this was a test of the idea?

KW:

One of my little experiments solely to convince a client, especially if you talk to a client about building a stone wall and building a copper planter on top of it. The beauty of how that planter would acquire a patina and turn the stone green—a lot of them react, "I've just paid a lot of money for this beautiful wall and I don't want it stained." But you can show them through historic images that it can be quite beautiful if you just let it be, and while some accept it, some do not want anything to do with it. So I think there is a fear that designers have to overcome—the fear brought by the client. To let them know that weathering is a process and it adds to the project and is beautiful.

Q:

The subject of weathering in other design fields, but especially architecture, is not only fairly well studied but well accepted. Books range from the extremely technical studies of maintenance of materials all the way to the poetics of weathering, which attempts to see weathering as architecture plus time. I was wondering why the subject engages a number of landscape architects in intense poetics but has not had any serious study within the landscape field?

KW:

I just wonder if the issue has not been noticed in the landscape field because it is focused on the outdoors. If you think of a building, a great part of the design work is concerned with protecting and making the building weathertight, and you can speak of the weathering of its external skin. As designers, we think of the landscape as ever-changing and that the phenomena of change and weathering are happening all the time.

Q:

You could also argue that about a building elevation. This industrial building structure we are in just now is being baked and tonight it will be cooled and some weak acidic rain may wash it. Is it because it is just so complex, what is going on out there, and it's difficult enough just to build something and trust that it will endure? Weathering and durability for many designers is concerned with issues of erosion using soft landscape materials such as water and earth. Issues of stream bank collapse, runoff, pond swales—predicting and controlling based on analytical concerns, formulas, to prevent weathering or your work sliding off the hill. Is weathering, therefore, seen in different theaters of work?

KW:

In my particular case because the work tends to be architectural and I draw geometry into the landscape from the architecture, I etch these lines in the landscape through hard materials. If you look at our design work, we tend to use simple, bold gestures. But they're expressed or our concern is in what materials they're expressed in. We may be minimalist but we're not stark.

Q:
What, for you, is meant by the term "minimalist"?

KW:
I mean simple, bold gestures, movements, and economy. To equate it to something, in writing, it would be a haiku poem. How do you pare it down to these simple movements that still convey the meaning? In the Middlebury College project, I deliberately did not want to buy benches as a way of providing seating.

I wanted to make simple, bold gestures in the landscape, where I could introduce a New England typology, native stone walls, which could function as seating for the students. It is something you feel throughout the whole design process and it's embedded in the whole design process.

Q:
What, for you, are the issues related to the preservation of a landscape?

KW:
We don't do a lot of preservation work, but we did work on an estate here in Burlington that was originally designed by Olmsted's office, the original grounds for Henry Holt's summer home built in 1896. Our role was to look at the historic landscape context and try to replicate some of the site elements that over time had disintegrated, including a driveway allée of twenty-five maple trees. The challenge was to adapt the current design and user who had their own goals and objectives, which included a family and who wanted to entertain. The first set of criteria for its evaluation was—is it still serving a purpose? I mean, is it still doing everything that it was originally intended to do? Does it satisfy all those requirements for its modern context?

Q:
What is the relationship between your sculpture and your landscape architecture work? Is the landscape the test for the sculpture or vice versa?

KW:
I think the interesting thing about my sculpture work is it started as a way for me to express my creativity at a time when our firm wasn't satisfying my desires for creative landscape projects. In time, it has become a vehicle to explore the dynamics between textures, color, and materials that are brought not directly into our landscapes, but more indirectly, intuitively, and maybe even more subconsciously. There is a direct correlation between my creative sculptural work and how it influences my landscape work.

Q:

Is everybody in the office involved in this work or is it just you?

KW:

No one else in the office is doing sculpture. My sculpture studio is now about fifty yards from the office here in downtown Burlington. I bring the work into the office here to show people or they'll come over and want to see what I'm working on. So they're exposed to it and then we have a few people seeking some artist pursuits such as photography. So they have studio art interests, but it's not sculpture, and, interestingly enough, not three-dimensional.

There are times when I just have to leave the office and I go over there and I close the door. My sculpture is about material textures and layers.

Figure 4.105. Sod mesh screen in summer. "Compressed": Landscape Installation, Stone Quarry Art Park, Cazenovia, New York. (Courtesy of Office of H. Keith Wagner.)

Figure 4.106. Sod mesh screen in winter. "Compressed": Landscape Installation, Stone Quarry Art Park, Cazenovia, New York. (Courtesy of Office of H. Keith Wagner.)

Now I've also done a lot of bad paintings, but there's a couple that I really like because they capture interesting layers that I then weave into how I look at landscapes. I think I become something different (from a landscape architect) in my sculpture studio. I don't have a client, I don't have a specific site, I don't have specific requirements, and there's a freedom that I think is healthy for me. In time, I bring that freedom back to the office for a specific project. So, in a way, my sculpture is almost cathartic or therapeutic along with my studio explorations in terms of material combinations. (See Figures 4.105 to 4.108.)

"Compressed": A Temporary Landscape Installation Cazenovia, New York

Figure 4.107. Stone mesh screen in summer. "Compressed": Landscape Installation, Stone Quarry Art Park, Cazenovia, New York. (Courtesy of Office of H. Keith Wagner.)

Figure 4.108. Stone mesh screen in winter. "Compressed": Landscape Installation, Stone Quarry Art Park, Cazenovia, New York. (Courtesy of Office of H. Keith Wagner.)

Q:

What was the context to this project?

KW:

Cazenovia is a small hamlet, a delightful little town south of Syracuse. In Cazenovia is the Stone Quarry Art Park, and I was invited as one of a series of artists to work on what they call the narrative landscape that was specific to that site. I visited the site, and what really jumped out at me was the beautiful setting of the art park. The park was surrounded by housing developments that were encroaching on the park. The perimeter landscape around the site had been reduced to hedgerows.

Q:

To screen the housing?

KW:

No, they had been left from earlier agricultural practices along property lines. So that became the whole premise for this installation—fascination with remnants left or encapsulated within the hedgerows. I did a series of seven vertical metal panels, three feet by ten feet. I went into the existing hedgerow that bordered the art park and pulled out artifacts trapped there. In my panels, I used two sheets of metal mesh, and I compressed the found artifacts between the metal mesh. The landscape around here was being compressed into these hedgerows that became an allegory for what was happening in this area of the Finger Lakes region of New York. One panel was all stones, one was all barbed wire, another was red twig dogwood that was growing at the edge of the hedgerow, etc., and I composed it within these metal mesh panels. The series of panels was organized as an implied line that marched across the old meadow at the art park.

Q:

How long was it up for?

KW:

It was up for about a year and a half.

Q:

Now, clearly being outside, the actions of weather would change them?

KW:

Oh, absolutely, artifacts fell out. In one panel, I'd collected all these little pieces of branches, and I put them through the grid, perpendicular, so that the points were on either side. They were basically piercing and filling the entire mesh. By the end of the installation, a lot of those had been knocked out or fallen out and suddenly there was a beautiful array of transparency.

Q:

And it's now gone?

KW:

The installation is now gone — a number of the panels were purchased by an art collector in Syracuse, and I still have a couple in my basement. I went back a number of times and tried photographing them at various times of the year. The vertical supports for these metal mesh panels were wooden fence posts. They got soft over a year and a half and some of them started to lean back. As you looked at the installation, they were no longer these upright soldiers marching across the meadow, but rather, like the hedgerows that they attempted to honor, were now tattered remnants of something larger.

PART THREE

Afterword

A final section returns to the main concepts and principles of Part One and reviews the design achievements and failures of the landscape architects in addressing the opportunities and problems of weathering, time, and durability in their work as illustrated in Part Two. Commentary is also offered on the design challenges resulting from built work and future research studies that need to be carried out in the landscape field on this topic.

Achievements and Challenges

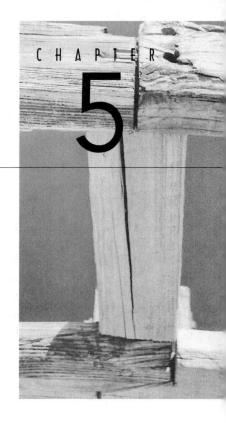

1. ACHIEVEMENTS

2. LESSONS FROM THE CASE STUDIES

3. CLOSING REMARKS

NOTES

This chapter returns to the key design approaches and topics of Part One and reviews the achievements of contemporary landscape architects in addressing the challenges of weathering, time, and durability as discussed and elaborated on in the case studies in Part Two. Commentary is also offered on the challenges posed by emerging areas of practice in built work.

1. ACHIEVEMENTS

> Everything with a beginning must have an end, otherwise there is no beginning.
>
> *(Dekkers, 2000)*

To return to the fundamental idea in this book, landscapes endure through weathering. Making a built landscape occurs in sequence and is derived from site and context, as shown by the case studies in Part Two. In addition, for a built landscape to gain significance, it must be durable. A landscape architectural project is a work in progress and concerned with durability in all phases of design work. Durability in landscape design is, therefore, concerned with the soundness, constancy, and permanence of design elements and constructed landscape forms during these periods of time and beyond.

Lessons Learned

Although as seen in the case studies contemporary built landscapes have clear beginnings, there is in most cases less of an understanding of when and how the project ends—much is given to chance, hoping for enlightened clients, landscape connoisseurs, or habitual and creative maintenance to take place. In addition, the means at the designer's disposal to research and study the evolution of built landscapes over time continues to be limited. Still, the durability of a built landscape within the design process warrants the landscape architect's complete attention and focus if for no other reason than the longevity of the design ideas in the public realm and a portfolio of existing built work.

Questions arising from this condition in Parts One and Two have included the following: Who determines the longevity of a particular built landscape—is it the original designer and clients themselves or various agencies and users during subsequent periods of ownership and alteration? In addition, how do designers ensure permanence within the continuity of their built landscapes or, if not, are they sensitive to the temporary nature of their undertaking?

Since the late nineteenth century, the techniques of handling as well as manufacturing or producing materials has paved the way for the steady expansion in the variety and form of available types. This expansion still continues today in the diversity of material and multiplicity of textures, colors, and finishes. A short glimpse at the back of landscape architecture magazines reveals a staggering amount of research, development, and investment in landscape materials by the industry, ranging from the novel to the absurd. In addition, technological developments have been coupled in recent years with new modes of thinking about the role of materials and their uses in landscape architecture, as shown in Part Two by Julie Bargmann (Case Study A) for materials of cleansing, Michael Blier (Case Study D) for materials of sensory experience, and Mikyoung Kim (Case Study G) for cultural materials.

These modes of thinking emphasize a layering of both traditional and nontraditional design elements and the resulting projects have exhibited a mixture of conflicting forms and materials. This period of material experimentation has been rich and engaging but has not been without its share of disappointments and oversights. Recently, there has been an increasing concern with the quality of the environment itself that the built landscape is located in and a range of conditions that directly contribute to the durability of a project—whether these are airborne pollution, the persistence of toxic soils on the site, or the quality of the water passing onto and across the site.

The Introduction and Chapter 1 described the design application and treatment of the large metal plates that gave the space its particular name. For the landscape architect Peter Latz, the large corroded and pitted slabs in Piazza Metallica are a symbol of the renewable and adaptive nature of the landscape medium within the built environment. Here weathering as an external design force and as a broad series of actions of climate and use is acknowledged and encouraged as the next stage in the evolution of the site and the landscape design. The fear by landscape architects of change and destruction of their built work has given way in this project to a calm and practical acceptance of the existing site conditions. Here weathered steel and concrete, air pollution, toxic soils, and landscape processes have set the parameters for future design proposals. Alternative ways of proceeding could have swept away everything to start from a clean slate or used landscape design as a point of departure for criticism of the site's derelict state prior to regeneration. Instead of making the site and the surrounding context vibrant again, the material built elements of the landscape are constructed and renewed. The corroded steel, metal plate, watercourses, slag heaps, and railway lines at Duisburg Nord are the basis of a new built landscape vocabulary of materials and forms.

The challenge of built landscapes such as this requires new ways of addressing weathering and durability in landscape design that accept their existing physical qualities, as well as the delay or acceleration of the processes of weathering as a positive and legible design activity. With that, let us return to the case studies from Part Two.

2. LESSONS FROM THE CASE STUDIES

> The decline of landscape materials over time, especially such modern materials as concrete, plastics and metals, makes these designed landscapes vulnerable to alteration, and destruction at the very moment that the generational cycle of style or fashion holds the work at its lowest esteem.
>
> *(Smith, 1999)*

Viewpoints from the Designers

The case studies in Part Two are a collection of separate and distinctive viewpoints about weathering and durability in landscape architecture and in particular how practice addresses these viewpoints within contemporary landscape design. They demonstrate many of the approaches and themes introduced in Chapter 2, Aspects of Permanence, and a number of the design approaches reviewed in Chapter 3 were also present and discussed. It is necessary to return to two points that were not directly mentioned but that have an important bearing on the subject of weathering and durability for students and young practitioners. These include, first, the individual nature of the case studies and, second, the relationship between landscape design and change in the built landscape. We return again to the question raised in the Introduction regarding the performance desired over time for landscape work, and how it can be achieved.

Character of the Case Studies

The case studies did not include the entire nature of the design process and the scope of work of the design projects in question. The conditions surrounding the site of the project prior to the project were, with the exception of the case studies of Julie Bargmann, Michael Blier, Elizabeth Mossop, and Margie Ruddick, rarely discussed, the amount of maintenance carried out by the client in many cases was absent, as was that of other groups who would be involved in using the built project whether as a casual visitor or a habitual user. In addition, those who constructed the project were heard only through the words of the named designer. Although it is important to recognize that the designer's voice has been the dominant force throughout the case studies, there are others who add an important dimension to the entire effort. It should be noted that Eric Fulford did furnish a full list of craftsmen and specialist contractors to contact and interview that will be taken up at a later date.

From the case studies, we have heard from twelve well-known and accomplished landscape architects of their own understanding and ways of working with weathering and durability in design. No designer addresses the processes of durability and change in built work in exactly the same way or follows the approaches that have been identified and described in earlier chapters. Some, for example, rely on different strategies to produce built elements and forms, using research into precedents of design durability (Elizabeth Mossop and Peter L. Schaudt) or draw upon the nature of plants and the altered qualities of landscape materials (Eric Fulford, Ed

Blake, and Keith Wagner). Others focus on the performance of landscape materials and elements (Ken Smith, Cheryl Barton, and Mikyoung Kim), weighing short-term effects against the need for interim or temporary design forms, or extending the duration of more fleeting phenomena such as captured rainwater to allow more direct contact with water (Michael Blier). As a result of the nature of landscape work, in time there also exists the interchange of natural processes and site "flows" at each stage of a project, as demonstrated by Margie Ruddick. Here a continuum is introduced across a range of forces and at different times (Julie Bargmann and Mary Margaret Jones). Finally, there are examples where the design process and any notion of permanence are presented as totally disconnected, the concern for durability appearing to follow at a much later time in the process. For young landscape designers, it is important to recognize that these are not necessarily singular models to follow in your own design work, but that they reflect how these individual designers in their respective practices have been able to address professional opportunities afforded by this aspect of design, within their own design experience, backgrounds, training and influences.

3. CLOSING REMARKS

> To design is human; to follow up divine.
>
> *(Kayden, 2003)*

The case studies of built landscape work demonstrate for landscape architectural students and young design practitioners the enormous capacity for change over time in completed design projects. In addition, the way in which weathering and change is addressed by each designer is quite distinct and reflects individual methods of designing and working, from exchanges of temporary and stable site elements to the selection and placement of materials and landscape elements. This is instructive for those whose education is solely focused on the earlier stages of the landscape design process and the development of conceptual ideas. There are no sets of guidelines or methods presented here that will automatically result in the development of durable built projects. There are, however, clearly ways of designing that reflect an attitude to change in built work that is optimistic and accepting of "accidental alterations" and unplanned transformations. The case studies have illustrated a number of exchanges between landscape design and materials brought about by the patterns of human use over time, cultural practices, and the actions and processes of climate. As shown here, these exchanges can be modest, ranging from material alterations to a handrail by daily wear to temporary but drastic site transformations.

Weathering and durability in the landscape architectural work of the case studies is concerned with the permanence, or otherwise, of built elements in the designed landscape. The landscape architects have explored and continue to examine and illustrate the nature of change in landscape materials, forms, and elements in their projects as they evolve, alter, or degrade over time. Durability as illustrated in their work is concerned in a broad way with the soundness, constancy, and permanence of design elements and constructed landscapes over periods of time, which are to some extent predetermined.

Even in the most ordinary or modestly built landscapes and in great works of landscape architectural design, there is usually a clear pattern of a coherant conceptual idea, though perhaps modified by time. Changes to a built landscape or new uses can, by adaptation and compromise, be made to fit in, or by further analysis and thought be made to form a new framework or structure against which the original framework can be contrasted or complimented. Such landscape design opportunities need not be judged as separate from entirely new built work. On the contrary, success in one area of landscape architecture should invigorate thought in another field of landscape design. The common denominator of landscape architecture and the landscape architect's special skills lies in the organization of space over time and the manipulation of landscape form toward a coherent entity.

The magic of these designed landscapes emanates from what appears to be a contradiction. A belief by the landscape architect in the permanence of the built work exists alongside the avoidance of a slavish devotion to durability. What unites these contradictory positions is the many faces of beauty and artistic design expression that result in the act of making familiar and well used places as well as temporary or fleeting landscape installations. The resulting landscape design projects through their design elements, forms, and materials acknowledge and celebrate growth, change, and the shortfalls in permanence. In return, opportunities to design built landscapes that are more easily adaptive to change will increase as built work and the inevitable changes brought about by use, climate, and wear are better understood in landscape architecture. Weathering and durability will see to that.

NOTES

Dekkers, Midas (2000). *The Way of all Flesh: The Romance of Ruins.* New York: Farrar, Straus and Giroux.

Smith, K. (1999)."The Challenge of Preserving Lincoln Center for the Performing Arts." *Preserving Modern Landscape Architecture. Papers from the Wave Hill–National Park Service Conference.* Cambridge, MA: Spacemaker Press.

Kayden, Jerold S. "Public Defender." *Landscape Architecture,* Vol. 93, No. 3.

Bibliography and Further Reading

PART ONE:
Weathering and Durability in Landscape Architectural Practice

Arnold, Henry (1994). "Preserve the Present: It's Not Too Early to Protect Modern Landscapes." *Landscape Architecture*. Vol. 84, No. 4, pp. 50–51.

Blanc, Alan (1996). *Landscape Construction and Detailing*. New York: McGraw-Hill.

Birbaum, Charles A. (ed) (1999). *Preserving Modern Landscape Architecture, Papers from the Wave Hill-National Park Service Conference*. Cambridge, MA: Spacemaker.

Carpenter, Jot D. (ed) (1976). *Handbook of Landscape Architectural Construction*. McLean, VA: Landscape Architecture Foundation.

Cantor, Stephen (1996). *Innovative Design Solutions in Landscape Architecture*. New York: Van Nostrand Reinhold.

Dines, Nicholas T., Charles W. Harris, and Kyle D. Brown (assistant editor) (1997). *Time Saver Standards for Landscape Architecture*, 2nd ed. New York: McGraw-Hill.

Dines, Nicholas T., and Charles W. Harris (1997). *Time Saver Standards Landscape Construction Details CD-ROM*. New York: McGraw-Hill.

Hansen, Richard (1992). "Limestone and Granite: Texture and Finish." *Landscape Architecture*, October, pp. 114–117.

Juracek, Judy A. (1996). *Visual Research for Artists, Architects, and Designers*. New York: Norton.

Kirkwood, Niall (1999). *The Art of Landscape Detail, Fundamentals, Practices and Case Studies*. New York: John Wiley & Sons.

Kirkwood, Niall (1996). "Holding Our Ground." *Landscape Architecture*, Vol. 86, No. 2.

Landphair, Harlowe, and Fred Klatt (1979). *Landscape Architecture Construction*, 2nd edition. New York: Elsevier.

Munson, Albe (1974). *Construction Design for Landscape Architects*. New York, McGraw-Hill.

Nelischer, Maurice (ed) (1985). *Handbook of Landscape Architectural Construction*, 2nd ed. Washington, DC: Landscape Architecture Foundation.

Pinder, Angi and Alan Pinder (1990). *Beazley's Design and Detail of the Space between Buildings*. London: E. & F. N. Spon.

Robinette, Gary O. (1976). *Landscape Architectural Site Construction Details*. Reston, VA: Environmental Design.

Walker, Theodore D. (1992) *Site Design and Construction Detailing*, 3rd ed. New York: Van Nostrand Reinhold.

Weinberg, Scott and Gregg A. Coyle (eds) (1992). *Materials for Landscape Construction*, Vol. 4, *Handbook of Landscape Architectural Construction*. McLean, VA: Landscape Architecture Foundation Series.

PART TWO
References on Weathering and Durability in Other Design Practices

Brand, Stewart (1994). *How Buildings Learn What Happens after They're Built*. New York: Penguin.

Canadian Mortgage and Housing Corporation (CMHC). *Landscape Architectural Design and Maintenance*. Ottawa, Canada: Development Evaluation and Advisory Services Division.

Dekkers, Midas (2000). *The Way of All Flesh: The Romance of Ruins*. New York: Farrar, Straus and Giroux.

Goldsworthy, Andy (2000). *Time*. New York: Harry N. Abrams.

Loss, John and Earle W. Kennett (1991). *Performance Failures in Buildings and Civil Works*. Bethesda, MD: University of Maryland.

Lynch, Kevin and Gary Hack (1986). *Site Planning*, 3rd ed. Cambridge, MA: MIT Press.

McKaig, Thomas (1962). *Building Failures, Case Studies in Construction and Design*. New York: McGraw-Hill.

Mostafavi, Moshen and David Leatherbarrow (1993). *On Weathering: The Life of Buildings in Time*. Cambridge, MA: MIT Press.

Olgay, Victor (1963). *Design with Climate: Bioclimatic Approach to Architectural Regionalism*. Princeton: Princeton University Press.

Patterson, Terry L. (1990). *Construction Materials for Architects and Designers*. Englewood Cliffs, NJ: Prentice Hall.

Petroski, Henry (1985). *To Engineer Is Human, The Role of Failure in Successsful Design*. New York: St. Martin's Press.

Petroski, Henry (1994). *Design Paradigms: Case Studies of Error and Judgment in Engineering*. New York: Cambridge University Press.

Pye, David (1972). *The Nature and Art of Workmanship.* New York: Van Nostrand Reinhold.

Ramsey, Charles G. and Harold R. Sleeper (1970). In James Ambrose (ed). *Architectural Graphic Standards,* 6th ed. New York, John Wiley & Sons.

Richardson, Barry A. (1991). *Defects and Deterioration in Buildings.* London: E. & F. N. Spon.

Rogers, Elizabeth R. (1987). *Rebuilding Central Park, A Management and Restoration Plan.* Cambridge, MA: MIT Press.

Sternfield, Joel (2001). "The High Line Landscape." *Places,* Vol. 14, No. 2.

Templer, John (1992). *The Staircase, Studies of Hazards, Falls, and Safer Design.* Cambridge, MA: MIT Press.

Index